Teaching Ethnic Studies

Concepts and Strategies

Contributors

James A. Banks	Carlos E. Cortés
Mildred Dickeman	Jack D. Forbes
Geneva Gay	Francesco Cordasco
David Ballesteros	Diego Castellanos
Barbara A. Sizemore	Mark M. Krug
Larry Cuban	Janice Law Trecker
Lowell K. Y. Chun-Hoon	Elizabeth O. Pearson

Teaching Ethnic Studies
Concepts and Strategies

JAMES A. BANKS, *Editor*

43rd Yearbook • 1973

**NATIONAL
COUNCIL
FOR THE
SOCIAL
STUDIES**

A National Affiliate of the
National Education Association
1201 Sixteenth Street, N. W.
Washington, D. C. 20036

Paperbound, $6.00; Clothbound, $7.50

NATIONAL COUNCIL FOR THE SOCIAL STUDIES

Officers for 1973

The National Council for the Social Studies is a National Affiliate of the National Education Association of the United States. It is the professional organization of educators at all levels—elementary, secondary, college, and university—who are interested in the teaching of social studies. Membership in the National Council for the Social Studies includes a subscription to the Council's official journal, *Social Education,* and a copy of the Yearbook. In addition, the Council publishes bulletins, curriculum studies, pamphlets, and other materials of practical use for teachers of the social studies. Membership dues are $15.00 a year. Applications for membership and orders for the purchase of publications should be sent to the Executive Secretary, 1201 Sixteenth Street, N.W., Washington, D.C. 20036.

Dedicated

to

JOHN JAROLIMEK AND JEAN FAIR

Two distinguished NCSS Presidents
who struggled to eliminate racism and social injustice

Foreword

We are all immigrants, yet one of the great blots on the record of American democracy is the manner in which the fate of the first inhabitants, later arrivals, and minority groups in general has been entrusted to the Anglo-Saxon majority. Native Americans were exterminated, cheated, relegated to less desirable lands, and deprived of justice. Black Americans were brought here against their will, enslaved, treated as inferiors, and omitted from the mainstream of American society. Spanish-speaking Americans have been dealt with as aliens rather than citizens and have likewise been exploited and discriminated against. Oriental Americans have been regarded as different, inscrutable, mysterious persons, and have experienced loss of civil rights and other privileges of citizenship. Many European ethnic groups have fought their way up from the bottom of the economic ladder only to find themselves on the cutting edge of our great urban problems. Unfortunately, those groups along with the urban poor and other minority groups do not realize the extent to which they are pitted against each other to the advantage of the power structure. American Jews have been the victims of anti-Semitism and often stereotyped, with the diversity that exists among them overlooked. Women have been subordinated in our history and treated as second-class citizens in the economic arena, as well as in day-to-day personal and social relationships.

Textbooks and school curricula too often have sustained the status quo, helped entrench the stereotypes, and narrated the myth and the folklore. In some instances gestures were made to indicate that various individuals had contributed to American culture but, in general, Mark Twain's "great lie of silence" prevailed.

The demands of minority groups for an equal opportunity to sit at the American table of abundance and for an equal chance at the starting block became a major part of the great social upheavals of the 1960's. There were many who believed that the conscience of America was speaking and that we were in turmoil because we took our ideals seriously and, in spite of everything, have guilt feelings over our shortcomings. Some have said that the self-criticism in which we have engaged and the tolerance granted the protestors indicate that as a society the United States is receptive to change and that many share in part, at least, the belief that things could be better. It has even been suggested that our complacency has been shaken while there is still time to set things right. There have been indications that many are ready to recognize the pluralism of American society and even to value the differences among us more than to insist on conformity.

On the other hand, there are some indications that the revolution of the last decade has lost much of its strength. The forces that are opposed to change are firmly entrenched, the affluent majority has lapsed into indifference, and many Americans are tired and frustrated.

This Yearbook is evidence that the National Council for the Social Studies has not lessened in its concern or given up in its attempt to make the social studies meaningful and useful in aiding teachers and students to understand and to contribute toward the solution of the desperate problems of our time. It is further fitting that this should be a hard-hitting and courageous work, for while there has been some improvement in the treatment of minorities in textbooks it has not been enough. The membership has a right to expect that NCSS publications will deal more forthrightly with social issues than might be expected of commercial publishers. It is a hopeful sign that in recent years the National Council for the Social Studies has actively been dealing with the real issues that are of prime importance. The programs, the work of its committees, its publications, and other actions indicate that the Council is "getting it together." This Yearbook is further testimony to the direction we have set for ourselves.

The editor and the various authors have made a significant contribution in increasing our knowledge, sensitivity, and awareness of many things that teachers need to know about in this critical area. The contributors are not only distinguished scholars, but experts, who have dedicated their lives and their professional careers in teaching and working with the minority groups of whom they write. Teachers will not only gain insight into a sensitive educational issue, but will learn teaching strategies ranging from problems of bilingualism to the cultural differences between groups that require a variety of approaches and understandings. Any teacher will profit from learning more about the covert cues to teaching about various ethnic cultures.

The National Council for the Social Studies is very much indebted to the authors of this Yearbook. Their contribution is further evidence of their commitment to the profession and to humanity.

HARRIS L. DANTE, *President*
National Council for the Social Studies

Introduction

For any reader, this book will be a profound experience. It will evoke a wide range of emotions, including pain, anger, compassion, disillusionment, despair, admiration, and *hope*. It is a hard-hitting book written by a group of fighters who have an unrelenting commitment to social justice. Their words are sometimes bitter and incisive, but their restraint is a tribute to their wisdom and scholarship.

This is not a book written by a group of irrational radicals who use these pages for a counterproductive catharsis. Rather, it is a book penned by a distinguished group of scholars—social scientists and educators—who have spent the bulk of their lives fighting for human rights. Although they have experienced many frustrations in their perennial struggles—which their writings reflect—they have not despaired. They believe that change is possible and that what teachers do in the classroom, or don't do, can make a difference. This is probably the greatest significance of this book. It is bound to help every teacher who reads it to sense the urgency of the racial crisis in our nation, and to develop a commitment to *act* to resolve it.

The reader who wants a rosy picture of ethnic relations in America and a veneration of American democracy should avoid this book. However, the teacher who wants to help make this a more just and open society will find this book very helpful and edifying. The authors describe some concrete things which the teacher can do.

From the time that I was very young, I have had a keen interest in the problems and frustrations of Black Americans. Because of this interest, I have spent much of my career researching and writing in Black Studies. To some extent, I became so encapsulated with the plight of my people that I was blinded to the problems of other oppressed groups. I was unable to fully see the oppression of Blacks as an integral part of a larger problem shared by all exploited groups in America. I have learned a great deal from the authors of this book, most of whom I know personally and highly respect. They have helped me to broaden my perspective and to intensify my commitment to help make this a humane society. While I must still focus much of my energy on the problems of Black Americans for personal reasons, I now realize that Blacks will not be free until institutionalized oppression and racism—in all of their ugly and destructive forms—have been eradicated and power relationships in this nation have been radically modified.

I am deeply honored that I convinced the people from whom I have learned so much in recent years to share their rich experiences and wisdom with you in these pages. Jack D. Forbes, while we were fighting to eliminate racism in the California state-adopted textbooks, taught me about the sins and genocide which have been committed against Native Americans and to appreciate the beauty and stamina of his people. Before I knew Jack and his seminal works, most of what I knew about Native Americans had been learned from antiseptic textbooks and Saturday afternoon TV Westerns. During the same time, Lowell Chun-Hoon helped me to see the poignant plight of Asian-Americans, and Carlos Cortés deepened my knowledge and concern for the Chicano struggle. I learned from Barbara A. Sizemore that excluded groups need power to become liberated and the stages that they may have to experience to achieve inclusion into the American social order, and yet preserve their distinctive ethnic characteristics. If you read their chapters carefully and take them seriously, I believe that you can learn as much from Jack, Lowell, Carlos and Barbara, and the other writers, as I have learned, and that this knowledge will strengthen and help you to develop a strong commitment to eliminating injustice in this nation. It is imperative that we act now to humanize this society. Racial and ethnic polarization threatens to destroy it.

The chapters in this book include a gold mine of information which should be very valuable to teachers. The authors present new conceptual frameworks for studying about ethnic groups and for analyzing American society. They also describe promising strategies and materials. Elizabeth O. Pearson wrote strategy exercises which are appended to several chapters. Mildred Dickeman, Geneva Gay, David Ballesteros and Barbara A. Sizemore provide perceptive and terse analyses of institutional racism, social justice and power relationships in America. They suggest ways in which the teacher can deal with both individual and institutional racism. Larry Cuban describes how ethnic content can be used to spearhead instructional reform.

Five of the chapters focus on the problems of specific American ethnic minority groups. In these chapters, members of the various ethnic groups speak for themselves. I feel very strongly, and the NCSS Publications Board shares this view, that we have reached a point in our history in which we must hear from the victims of racism since for too long most books have been written by writers who were members of powerful and ruling groups. This does not mean that sincere white scholars should not write about the problems of Blacks, Chicanos, Native Americans, Asian-Americans and Puerto Rican-Americans. However, we desperately need to view events from the perspectives of those who have been victimized if we are to fully understand the American drama and formulate effective change strategies.

These chapters deal with the historical and sociological problems of ethnic minority groups, and describe ways in which the teacher can incorporate their experiences into the social studies curriculum. Each author approaches his topic in a unique way. The approaches range from Chun-Hoon's largely historical and poignant description of Asian-Americans to Forbes' plea that we incorporate Native American values into the curriculum so that America may be redeemed. The reader will be moved by the powerful Native American poetry in Forbes' chapter. Cortés presents a historical overview of the Chicano experience and a useful conceptual frame of reference which can be used to teach about any culture. Banks uses elements from the Black experience to illustrate ways in which to establish a multiethnic social studies program. Cordasco and Castellanos stress the need for bilingual education for Spanish-speaking students.

The final part of this book explores the problems of two groups which have also been victimized by stereotypes and cultural assaults—white ethnics and women. While their problems differ in many significant ways from those of racial minorities, the teacher who wishes to make his social studies program truly liberating must help students to view these groups with new lenses. Mark M. Krug speaks directly to the problems of white ethnics and reveals that life for them, to quote the gifted poet Langston Hughes, has not been a "crystal stair." Janice Law Trecker argues that we will not have an open society until women are treated as *human* beings.

I am exceedingly grateful to the distinguished and gifted scholars who took the time from demanding schedules and important activities to contribute to this Yearbook. I am especially indebted to Geneva Gay and David Ballesteros for their willingness to condense projected NCSS publications into chapters for the Yearbook. Their contributions add important perspectives to the book. I also wish to thank Anna Ochoa, former Chairman of the NCSS Publications Board, who convinced me— against strong resistance—to edit this Yearbook, and who paid a high price for its completion. Without Anna, this Yearbook would not have come to fruition. I am also indebted to John Jarolimek who gave birth to this project while he was President of NCSS because he was convinced that racism must be massively attacked on every front. The NCSS Racism and Social Justice Committee played a pivotal role in the development of the Yearbook, and former NCSS President Jean Fair strongly supported the Committee. Daniel Roselle and James Cass, former Education Editor of *Saturday Review,* helped me to identify contributors for the Yearbook; and Willadene Price handled the production aspects of the manuscript. As with each of my books, my wife Cherry shared the joys and pains of getting this one done. To her, I am eternally grateful.

JAMES A. BANKS

Contents

How can "the social studies teacher help to make America a nation in which cultural pluralism is valued and social justice is a reality"?

Part One

RACISM, CULTURAL PLURALISM, AND SOCIAL JUSTICE

Institutional racism is pervasive in America. It adversely affects both its perpetuators and victims. Racism causes majority groups to develop a sense of false superiority and confused identities and ethnic minority groups to inculcate feelings of inferiority and deflated self-concepts. In a racist society, all groups are unable to develop positive attitudes toward self and others. Racism is a dehumanizing and destructive social phenomenon which must be critically analyzed in the classroom if we are to develop a more just society.

Part One of the book explores the nature of racism and some of the myths and power relationships which have emerged to justify and sustain it. The authors not only discuss problems but describe ways in which the social studies teacher can help to make America a nation in which cultural pluralism is valued and social justice is a reality. Particular attention is given to the need for teachers and students to confront their own racial feelings and perceptions before undertaking a study of ethnic content. Without such confrontations, the integrity of ethnic content will be seriously violated and its impact considerably reduced.

In the opening chapter, Dickeman critically examines the American educational system and concludes that it is racist by design. This conclusion is confirmed by her scholarly examination of the school's curriculum, its goals, and its role in forcing students to reject their ethnic cultures. Dickeman contends that the concept of individual opportunity in America, which states that we all have equal access to the riches of America, is a myth. Her mode of analysis is anthropological, her tone is

1

hard hitting, and the result is a profound chapter that will evoke serious reflection.

In the next chapter, Gay provides a candid and insightful analysis of racism in our society. She argues that racism not only harms minorities, but whites as well, and that its eradication will improve the mental health of all Americans. The author presents a useful definition of racism, and a perceptive discussion of individual, cultural and institutional racism. Gay provides a vivid picture of racism in all of its destructive forms. The reader will find her candid examples of subtle racism, which she regards as the most dangerous form, revealing and perhaps personally discomforting. She ends her chapter with some useful strategies for studying racism in the classroom.

Drawing heavily upon the cultures of Chicanos to substantiate his arguments, Ballesteros, in the next chapter, documents the gap between the ideals about social justice in America and the injustices experienced by minority groups in all of our social institutions. Particular attention is given to the devastating effects which our educational, judicial and welfare systems have on minorities. Ballesteros contends that the "Anglo-Point-of-View Problem" is largely responsible for the destructive myths about ethnic groups that have served to justify the discrimination which minorities experience in social institutions. He issues a plea for the school to play a major role in the reduction of stereotypes and fear of minorities and to help develop an appreciation and understanding of their rich cultural and linguistic diversity. Ballesteros provides the teacher with sample questions that can be used to teach about social justice in social studies classes.

The melting pot theory was created and sustained because it was necessary to legitimize and maintain capitalism, argues Sizemore in the next chapter. The author contends that many American institutions, such as the church and the school, have perpetuated the melting pot theory, which she regards as a functional myth for those in power, and detrimental for powerless and minority groups because it forces them to abandon their unique cultures. It is psychologically harmful, she believes, for a group to give up its culture. The author presents a model which delineates the steps that excluded groups can take to obtain power and inclusion within the larger society while maintaining their cultural identities. Sizemore argues that we must involve a larger range of people in educational decision-making to improve the school. She presents a model for broader participation and a sample unit that reflects her ideas about the kind of open and participatory school which she envisions.

In the final chapter of Part One, Cuban describes the value of ethnic content but expresses a fear that ethnic studies will be doomed unless substantial educational reform occurs. Without both new instructional goals and methods, ethnic studies programs are little more than traditional history with different characters. Cuban contends that the most important variable in ethnic studies programs is the teacher. Unless classroom teachers change their attitudes, behavior and strategies, ethnic studies will have little impact. Focusing attention on curriculum reform, he argues, is evading the real problems.

Mildred Dickeman

MILDRED DICKEMAN *is Professor and former Chairman of the Department of Anthropology at Sonoma State College. She is a graduate of the University of Michigan (Phi Beta Kappa) and received her Ph.D. in Anthropology at the University of California, Berkeley. Professor Dickeman has done ethnographic work in New Guinea and on Native American cultures. She has taught at Merritt College, University of California, Berkeley and the University of Kansas. Dr. Dickeman is a Fellow of the American Anthropological Association, and a member of the Council on Anthropology and Education and the Board of Directors of the Southwest Intergroup Council. She was Editor and Assistant Editor of the* Kroeber Anthropological Society Papers *in 1955-56. Professor Dickeman frequently conducts workshops for teachers on teaching about ethnic cultures and has contributed to the books* Culture and Poverty: A Critique *and* With All Due Respects: Thoughts on Community and Diversity in The Southwest.

1

Teaching
Cultural Pluralism

In a provocative analysis of the growth of the American school bureaucracy, Michael B. Katz describes some significant characteristics of the
school system which emerged during the 1880's and have persisted till
today. American public education was and remains "universal, tax-supported, free, compulsory, bureaucratically arranged, class-biased and
racist."[1] All of these characteristics are, as Katz demonstrates, closely
interrelated. They derive from the historic and continuing functions of
public education in this society. It follows that if we hope to reform one
of these aspects of the institution, we may have to consider its ties to the
others as a part of a functional whole, and the possibility that more
extended reform may be required to achieve our goals.

I am concerned here with the elimination of racial and cultural bias
from the school system. But an effective attack on that problem requires
an understanding of the process by which our schools became racist
institutions, and the reasons why they are still characterized, for the
most part, by a pervasive racism today. Currently, a wide variety of
attacks are being made on the schools' failure to recognize cultural and
racial diversity, from curricular reform and experiments in teaching
method to teacher recruitment. Yet many of these attempts will, I
believe, remain only superficial, and will end by giving merely the
appearance of change, unless the dimensions of the problem are first
understood.

American schools are racist by design. Their racism is part of a larger philosophy, an ethnocentric dedication to the remodelling of citizens to conform to a single homogeneous acceptable model. That dedication, that definition of the function of schools, was formed in the period from 1830 to 1880, during which a modern, industrial class-stratified society was emerging, in which the ethnic diversity of this country was considerably increased by the immigration of large numbers of Europeans who formed a new mass of urban poor. Of course this nation was already incredibly diverse: upon the original variety of Indian cultures had been imposed European, African and Mexican-Spanish traditions. Cultural, religious and racial differences already existed. But in 1830, most of that diversity existed far outside the centers of growing industrial power. Non-Europeans were either slaves or Indians (either enemy or contained), and most Mexican territories had not yet been incorporated. The mass importation of Oriental labor had not yet begun. At the least these non-North Europeans were distant rural dwellers. This diversity could be ignored. Economic and social power was firmly in the hands of a small White minority of predominantly Anglo-Saxon and Germanic descent. It was the influx of a large laboring class of diverse languages, religions and values into the growing urban centers which created a problem for the emerging White power structure.

But what should have been a major dialogue for a growing democracy failed to take place. To what degree is conformity necessary for a federal system of representative democracy? In what areas is a consensus of values required, in what areas may cultural diversity persist and even be an asset? These questions were never explored. Instead, the dominant elite opted for the perpetuation, indeed the creation, of a homogeneous ruling class. Our failure as a nation to explore this critical issue has left us, one hundred years later, not only with no clear answers to which we as a people can agree, but with the consequences of a century of evasion and of generations of educational racism.

What instead developed was a mass system of public indoctrination. That system had two functions: first, to create a lower, laboring class which was docile and controllable, and which adhered sufficiently to the values and myths of the American ruling class that it was not likely to question its place in society. The second was the function of selection. Every society, to survive, must possess methods for the replacement of its elite. If that elite does not provide enough members to replace itself, and this is especially the case in an expanding society, new members of the upper castes and classes must be drawn from the lower ranks. The schools' function was, then, to select those few, as needed, who possessed adequate loyalty and sufficient conformity in attitudes, values, behavior and appearance, to be adopted into the expanding middle class.

It is predictable that in those periods of our history when there have been major needs for recruitment into the middle class, when rapid expansion of the industrial and service sectors of the economy has required large numbers of new, responsible dominant Americans, there has been a relaxation of barriers, and the degree and amount of mobility have increased. A shortage of Anglo-Saxons during the period of rapid growth of the urban public sector of the economy at the turn of the century made possible the entry of large numbers of Jews, Irish and Italians into city services, politics and the professions, including teaching. But in periods of economic decline, the doors of entry into the middle class constrict. A decreased demand for new replacements since the Second World War, coupled with massive migrations into urban centers, has meant increased difficulty of entry for racial minorities, for lower-class European-Americans and for women, with a consequent rise both in ethnic discontent and disillusionment, and in various expressions of racism on the part of both dominant and subordinate groups. In all this the schools have played their part.

Thus the public education system has become the major social sorting mechanism in this society, and the major means of instilling social control. In so doing, it seems to have become, as well, the major agency involved in the creation and evolution of modern middle-class values, far more influential, I suspect, than such commonly indicated sources as the mass media. The characteristics of the system listed by Katz appear, in this light, not at all surprising. That agency whose function is indoctrination and control of all but the reliable elite has of necessity to be compulsory. In order to impose values and behavior from the top down upon large masses of diverse individuals, rigid bureaucracies with hierarchical chains of command had to be created. Any institution whose major clientele is the poor must, of course, be free and tax-supported. And as the prime screening agency in a society which demands a homogeneous elite, the public school system has, surely, to be institutionally, designedly racist. It could not be otherwise.

When I propose that the schools are by nature racist, I do not mean to suggest that either the designers or the perpetuators of this bureaucratic system were or are consciously so. On the contrary, probably few of those involved in the creation and maintenance of the public educational system have been aware of this aspect of their actions. Many social functions, in any society, are best carried on by individuals who are thus unaware of the larger patterns in which they play a part. And for good reason: the unconscious actor is less likely to question either the system as a whole and its consequences or his own role in it. For this reason, institutional or unconscious racism may indeed be the preferred method of ensuring that the school bureaucracy carry out its functions.

That this system grew out of the needs and perspectives of a dominant power structure there can be no doubt. But that that power structure should have known, or knows today, all of the reasons for all of its behavior, or all of the implications and operations of the institutions which it creates and supports, would contradict all we understand about the nature of human social systems. The point here is not the level of awareness on the part of participant bureaucrats. The point is rather that it is and has been the school's function to be racist.

As these functions of the schools were crystallizing in the late nineteenth century, at the same time an ideology, a mythology was taking shape in this country. All mythologies serve to interpret reality in ways useful to the perpetuation of a society. In this case an ideology arose which interpreted the existence of ethnic diversity in America in ways supportive of the sociopolitical establishment. Probably the schools played an important role in the creation of this ideology. Certainly they came to serve as the major institutions for its propagation. It is important for us to examine this mythology in some detail.

The core concept of the American mythological system is the notion of individual opportunity. In the land of opportunity each individual, given equal access to the acquisition of necessary skills, is able to rise to the level of his own innate ability to fulfill his potential through free movement upward. The public schools, we are told, are the major means through which individual potential is actualized, by providing maximal training for all who can profit from it. Upon this educational base, the competitive forces of a free society ensure that the striving of individuals will place them where they are most suited and most effective. Unequal in talent, but equal in opportunity, we are all presumed to be striving upward toward positions which are at once the most personally satisfying and the most socially rewarding. The best man, then, always wins, and we may all become President if we only have the talent for it, for in this mythic system, talent is the only variable. Absent from this myth is, interestingly, the notion that some individuals may not want or value upward mobility.

A corollary of this mythical premise is that the upward striving of individuals from various ethnic groups results in a "melting pot." Diversities are left behind. They play no role in either helping or hindering advancement, but are irrelevant, given the American skills acquired in schools and the opportunities of the American social landscape. What remain are only the diversities of last name and of acceptable religious and food preferences, trivial in themselves but important as testimonies to the success of the system and the validity of the myth.

To be convincing, however, this explanatory system must confront a salient fact: individuals of all ethnic backgrounds are not equally distributed throughout all levels of our society. This fact requires explanation if the myth is to retain credibility. The explanations are simple, and there are two from which to choose. In the first, an observation of limited truth has been enlarged into a total generalization regarding American history: the movement of individuals upward into the dominant society is dependent in part upon the date of arrival of their ethnic group in this country. Thus, we are told, certain Anglo-Saxon and North European groups, because they arrived earlier in large numbers, have moved upward sooner, but are followed by those later arrivals, Mediterraneans and East Europeans for example, who, given the same length of time in which to take advantage of America's societal opportunities, take their places in their turn alongside the members of earlier groups. It is the proponents of this explanation who maintain that all need only wait their turn to succeed.

An alternate version is proposed by those less convinced of the inevitability of upward advance. This explanation of differential success rests on the assumption of innate racial differences in ability. According to this version, differences in the distribution of ethnic groups throughout our society are a consequence of differences in the distribution of talents between such groups. The most significant thing about both of these versions, largely ignored in the continuing argument between their proponents, is their unquestioning acceptance of the basic assumption that there indeed exists equal opportunity for fulfillment for all groups and individuals, and by extension, that opportunities for upward movement are the same today as they were in the expanding society of the late nineteenth century. Each of these assertions is, of course, absurd.

Needless to say, the historical and sociological accuracy of this myth leaves much to be desired. Individuals do not have equal access to the opportunities and rewards of American society. And the prime reason for this is that our society does not treat individuals as such but primarily and initially as members of ethnic groups. The classification and ranking in which this society engages is essentially on the basis of group characteristics, both biological and cultural, which determine initial placement in a hierarchy of classes and castes. And that ranking began, for those not native to this country, in the racist and culturally biased immigration laws, labor recruitment practices and slave importations which defined their placement in the hierarchy long before they set foot on our soil. It is only secondarily that a person who is able to remove himself from affiliation with such a group is accorded, to some degree, treatment as an individual.

Listening to America, we must be struck that, in spite of what our mythology tells us regarding the treatment of all as individuals, our language reveals a proliferation of terms for ethnic groups suggesting a concern with their existence which borders on the obsessive. "Majority," "minority," "ethnic," "race," are the polite terms of social discourse. But it is the specific terms of derogation that have done the linguistic dirty work in this country: "nigger" and "kike" and "okie" and "hunky" and "spik" and all the others. Everyone knows that these groups are ranked. They are ranked on the basis of the degree to which they possess a certain cluster of desirable traits, biological and cultural, which are usually said to have characterized the founding Anglo-Saxon. Thus, biologically, those least "Nordic" or "Anglo-Saxon" in appearance stand lowest on the ladder. Those biological traits chosen for sorting criteria are those most easily observable about the face and head, precisely those which are most useful for rapid classification of anonymous individuals in a wide variety of social encounters: skin color, eye color, hair color and form, and the structure of nose and lips being primary. This scheme has, of course, no validity as a biological construct. It is strictly social in origin and in function. All of the enormous individual diversity in these traits is classified, not in terms of any scientific understanding of human biology, but in terms of an ideal type, an ideal "Nordic" concept which exists in the minds of the members of the dominant society. In terms of this ideal, the blond, blue-eyed, wavy-haired, narrow-nosed and narrow-lipped are the all-American good guys. The greater deviance from this ideal type on the part of individual or group, the lower his or its rank in the American social hierarchy.

In addition, there is a cluster of sociocultural traits involved, which contains such obvious matters as language, including dialect and accent, religion and dress, and more subtle matters such as manners, body posture, family structure, values and attitudes. Again, the classification is in terms of a presumed Anglo-Saxon Puritan ideal of questionable historicity: inner-directed, individually responsible, morally upright, rational and emotionally restrained, ambitious but socially unostentatious, competitive, cleanly, prudent of time, money and self. Against this Boy Scout in long pants our society measures all claimants to status and power.

Thus in actual operation, though not in its mythology, our society ranks groups on the basis of their distance from a hypothetical North European middle-class norm. And the function of this ranking is to determine the degree of opportunity for upward mobility to which the members of each ethnic group will have access. Consequently the lower the rank, the more unequal the opportunity, the less likely will be entry into the dominant society and the greater the individual luck and striving which will be required to achieve it. It is clear enough, then, that the access of ethnic group members to power and status has little to do with the date of their arrival. American Indians, Blacks and Mexican-Ameri-

"What of the theory of the 'Melting pot' "? How many of these immigrants who arrived at Ellis Island in 1908 "stuck to the bottom of the pot"?

cans are not new arrivals on the American continent. They are simply bio-socially lower in rank. If Germans preceded Irish and Irish preceded Italians in achieving middle-class status in urban America, that is not primarily a statement of immigrant history, but rather one of racist preference.

Nor is any theory of racial or genetic disability necessary to explain the differential distribution of ethnic group members in American society, or their differential performances in school, once we understand that we are looking at a mass system programmed to provide unequal access. Indeed such theories are pitifully irrelevant and unprovable until that time when our society does provide equal treatment for individuals of diverse backgrounds and talents. This it has never yet done.

Then what of the theory of the melting pot? This notion can only persist as long as Americans focus only on the dominant society, the middle and upper classes. There, it is true, a predominantly Anglo-Saxon and North European society has been leavened by those individuals who, as the product of exceptional effort and special circumstance,

11

provide the individual exceptions, and by those members of ethnic groups which were allowed entry into the dominant mainstream. But the notion of the melting pot ignores that half of our society which has never been melted in, but rather, as Reverend Jesse Jackson once remarked, has stuck to the bottom of the pot. Most Americans are now aware of the presence of so-called racial minorities in large numbers at the bottom of our society. Most of us are less aware of the large numbers of unassimilated or partially assimilated Whites, often still European in language and values, who exist in our urban centers, and the large numbers of rural Whites on the lower rungs of our social ladder. These too, to one degree or another, are social rejects, serving the dominant society as scapegoats when needed, whether as "hardhats," "polacks," "okies," "arkies," "hillbillies," or "poor white trash," but otherwise ignored. They demonstrate clearly enough that even with all or most of the racially desired traits, cultural failures to conform may spell permanent social inadmissibility into middle-class ranks.

No better set of cultural data exists, for the confirmation of this exposition of American ideology, than the content of the American public school curriculum. An examination of this curriculum reveals not only the operation of the mythology, but at once the function of the public schools in its definition and perpetuation, its transmittal to the young. For the last hundred years at least, school texts, in picture and story, in history and literature, have presented this myth to the young. The actors in these texts have been and still are almost exclusively members of the dominant society, Anglo-Saxon, White, English-speaking, depicted with dress, manners, customs and family roles all deemed acceptably middle class. In those cases where it is essential to refer to and explain the existence of ethnic differences, reference is made to the myth of equal opportunity and the melting pot, or for those at the bottom, assurance is given that the lower orders are happy in their places, the slave on the plantation, the worker in the factory, the Indian roving his reservation.

This curriculum makes a loud and important statement to every child who is subjected to public education, a statement with a double edge. On the one hand it presents him with a model to which he must try to conform, a Uniform Code of Success. It tells him that in order to enter the dominant middle class, he must acquire those characteristics presented by the happy family in the little white house in the suburbs. But it tells him more than that. It informs him that he must abandon whatever differences he possesses, whatever ethnic identity that has characterized his home and family, if he hopes to succeed. That heritage, says the curriculum, is irrelevant. It was never a result of accident or oversight that text and lesson designed by the dominant elite omitted the existence of cultural diversity. Rather, it was and is an intentional and necessary assertion that any such divergence from middle-class homogeneity is unacceptable, and therefore philosophically simply nonexistent. A textbook is a philosophical statement.

In their study of formal education on the Pine Ridge Sioux reservation by the Bureau of Indian Affairs, Wax, Wax and Dumont described the "vacuum ideology" which pervaded the school administration. By this term they referred to the assumption held by school personnel that Indian homes and minds were essentially empty, lacking in pattern, tradition or value, in short, cultureless. The authors give many examples of that ideology in the words of school officials. One will suffice here:

> His home has no books, no magazines, radio, television, newspapers; it's empty! He comes into the school and we have to teach him everything.[2]

Urban readers will recognize this as but another version of the notion of the "culturally deprived," as the authors remark. They suggest that this ideology functions as a rationalization for educational failure. Undoubtedly this is so. But the point made here is that the primary function of this concept, whether applied to reservation Indians, urban Blacks, or others, is both older and deeper. It is to teach the student that nothing which he brings to the school, none of his sociocultural heritage, matters. It is evident not only in curriculum but in many other aspects of school structure and operation that educational institutions are, and have been for some time, the major agencies in this society engaged in the planned denial of cultural pluralism in America.

Another message is implicit in this curriculum. Of all the children exposed to the presented model, holding it as a mirror before themselves, their families and their communities, some must conclude that they can never fully conform, never fully achieve consonance with the ideal. For at least the biological aspects of the model are largely unalterable. Consequently, these children are informed of their future status. They are told that their success can only be partial, their rank always less, however successful they may be in the adoption of behaviors and attitudes and linguistic norms. And this, too, is a function of the curriculum, to preserve the racial and ethnic status quo, to inform those who are unacceptable that their aspirations must be limited, that they must resign themselves to their group fates. The content of the curriculum, in cooperation with many other parts of the school system, carries out the two major functions of schools, inculcating in the majority of its pupils an acceptance of the American social system, building into them enough allegiance that they will take their places in the employed and employable lower classes as loyal and manipulable citizens, and selecting for upward mobility those few who are acceptable and needed, those "out-standing exceptions" who will be pointed out as demonstrations of the validity of the school's ideology.

I have said that the school demands of the pupil a denial of his heritage, if he is to succeed in American terms. This has important consequences for the personalities and life histories of future members of the middle class.

One's ethnic heritage is of course imbibed at home, in one's family and local community. It is transmitted primarily through ties of kinship, secondarily through those of peer group and ethnic group loyalty. These are, of course, the earliest, most profound and affect-laden interactive networks of the young child. But the American ideology emphasizes personal, individual success, as we have seen, and it does so for a functionally significant reason. To succeed, to move into the dominant class, the individual must abandon most of the cultural traits of his home, except for those few, stripped of all real symbolic significance, which the dominant society deems tolerable. Those behaviors, values and attitudes which he must abandon are those emotionally imbedded, acquired as they were in the context of infancy and early childhood. To do so, he must disrupt his ties to his group of origin. What is demanded, then, is a rejection of his affiliation with kin and community, of his ties to his group of birth. What this means is a rejection of those emotional bonds with family and community which would compete with his loyal-ties to the dominant society. And this rejection is demanded of all Americans not already born into the middle class.

When we recall that most adult members of the middle class living today either went through this experience themselves, or are the sons and daughters of those who did so, we begin to understand the impor-tance of this personal experience in the shaping of American society. Terms such as "fink" and "tom" are much abused and certainly contain a large amount of viciousness. But they contain a core of valid sociologi-cal meaning, which refers to the process of alienation demanded of the upwardly mobile American. The "fink" as a social type may well be a peculiarly American creation, a creation in which the schools have played a major role.

The betrayal of the family is an essential prerequisite for American success. It should come as no surprise, then, that recent research on the Black family reveals that those Black youths who reject their parents have greater chances of future success.[3] Yet there is, strikingly, nothing in our mythology, and little in American literary or sociological dia-logue, which recognizes and attempts to deal with this incredibly painful experience. And certainly nothing in the school curriculum. Rather, we seem engaged in a mass repression of a major personal trauma, which only those, mostly of the younger generation, who are born into the middle class have been spared.

A choice thus confronts most American pupils from the moment they enter the classroom. Either they must betray family and heritage or they must settle for socioeconomic failure. How students respond to this crucial set of alternatives is, I believe, the most significant determinant of school performance, far outweighing such other variables as innate ability, linguistic background and pre-school environment. This choice forced upon the child clarifies the dropout phenomenon as a response to the educational process. The individual dropout is one who has refused to engage in the process of self-alienation. The reasons for such a decision are surely many. Some individuals are more likely than others to feel the demand for conformity as a personal violation. Some, with stronger family ties, may find it less easy to reject them. And of course the aspirations and rank of parents influence the degree of rejection demanded of the child. Some young people, involved more fully in the life of the community, may perceive earlier than others the degree to which the promised success will be ephemeral or unlikely. These, then, refuse, and state their refusal by withdrawing from the scene of emotional and philosophical conflict. This is, of course, an interactive process. The school communicates to the student the consequences of his failure, and he receives the message. "Pushout" is, as others have suggested, closer to the truth.

Are notions of genetic inferiority, or of cultural deprivation required, then, to explain the fact that those most biologically and culturally different from the middle-class ideal have the highest dropout rates? That is as is intended. Through this process the school stamps upon such individuals the label, usually irreversible, "unfit for upward mobility." Those who cannot content themselves with this label and its socioeconomic consequences will be dealt with by those other institutions of social control which take over where the school leaves off: the welfare agencies, the police and the prisons. The school can do no more for them.

American character structure, then, has its roots not only in the general qualities of mass society but in the specific nature of U.S. history. This character structure and its origins have significant implications for the functioning and personnel of the public school system. Teachers, of course, are crucial to the resocialization process for which the schools are designed, since it is they who have most direct contact with the subjects of that process, who most directly present the model to them. Teacher recruitment methods must therefore identify and select those individuals who can be certified as trustworthy in the enactment and propagation of the American ideology. And so they do. It is not

"Teachers are the primary and in many cases the only models presented to the child as representatives of the end result of the socialization process which he is to undergo."

accidental that teacher recruitment has always placed as much if not more emphasis on comportment, dress, speech, morality and manners, even on politics and hobbies, than on educational qualifications. These are far more important to the task at hand than any educational credentials, for the primary task, as we have seen, is not education but resocialization.

As the first significant individual with whom the child interacts, beyond the family and community, the teacher remains for many succeeding years one of the three most significant classes of individuals in interaction with the child, predictably in conflict in most cases with family and peers. Teachers are the primary and in many cases the only models presented to the child as representatives of the end result of the socialization process which he is to undergo. The uniformity of teacher personnel is thus a far more necessary and significant part of their role than what they do within the classroom. They communicate to the child, in cooperation with the curriculum, what he must be in order to succeed. This person, this speech, these manners and values, this appearance are the marks and means of success. That teachers of early grades have been largely women is perhaps not so much related to the needs of early child care as we might think. What better design than to present to the child a surrogate mother, to whom he can shift his allegiance while abandoning his allegiance to his true mother, if the purpose of the classroom is resocialization?

It has long been recognized that teaching is an important avenue of entry into the middle class, and that most teachers are recruited from the upper lower class and the lower middle class into the profession. This too is functionally important, because it guarantees loyalty to the newly won, and never fully secure status. In fact the general financial and status insecurity of teachers throughout the history of public education may be an important part of this structure. Members of the profession can be relied on neither to examine nor to question the purposes of the school, certainly not to explicate to their students the process of resocialization involved or to relate their own painful experience of rejection to the task in which they are engaged. Given middle-class status on the basis of a new and painfully acquired conformity, they have too much to lose.

A quality of educational institutions often commented upon, which may be termed the personality of the institution, is surely related to the character of its teacher personnel. I refer to the aura of rosiness, of unreal prettiness and cuteness which so often pervades the school. Not only in the area of social relations has our curriculum traditionally denied the ugly truths of life. The painful, the brutal, the existence of conflict and evil have been rooted out of the standard curriculum,

"A school free of ethnocentrism and racism must be a school new in function, profoundly new."

whether in literature, history, biology, geography or social studies. Surely we may ask whether there is not some relation between the rosy utopia of smiling faces which the school projects, and the function of the classroom as a place in which the student is initiated into the most traumatic social conflict of his early life.

The analysis of the schools outlined above has concentrated on the content of curriculum and on teacher personnel. It could be extended greatly. Teacher training, recruitment of personnel into administrative roles, the training and functions of counselors, systems of tracking and other methods of student classification, teaching methods, systems of accountability, disciplinary procedures and the operation of truancy laws, even the design and arrangement of classrooms and the architecture of schools ... all these contribute their part to a total system designed for the purposes described above. The moral is clear. If we are to root out racism from the schools, and introduce an awareness of ethnic diversity, we must recognize that we are engaged in what is, historically, a subversive task. While some school systems have declared in favor of major reform, most have not, and we will fail in effectiveness if we underestimate the overwhelming weight of the structure which we are opposing. A school free of ethnocentrism and racism must be a school new in function, profoundly new.

An evaluation of current attempts at reform is revealing. Most recent reforms designed to eliminate cultural and racial bias have lacked a foundation in an adequate understanding of the role of that bias in the public school system, and in society as a whole. They have resulted, mostly, in merely minor adjustments in the message of the schools. Most such reforms seem to be modifications of the racial uniformity of the success models presented to the child. This has been done most commonly through revision of text materials, and through increased recruitment of minority staff members. Most textual changes of commercial publishers have substituted only biological, not cultural variety. Dick and Jane in blackface or brownface retain all the usual middle-class social and behavioral traits. This, of course, is not cultural pluralism at all, but a reiteration of the old ideology that one can succeed even though possessed of deviant biological traits, if one adopts the requisite culture. None of the problems of cultural diversity, alienation and ethnocentrism discussed above have been recognized here.

This is not to minimize the important gains that may be reflected in the presentation of a black or brown or yellow middle class, if that is indeed an accurate reflection of a new reality. That those who have been willing and able to conform culturally and socially have been denied admission on the basis of racial traits is certainly a large part of the problem, that part most correctly referred to as racism. But it ignores the larger problem of the irrelevance of cultural pluralism to the concerns of the dominant society, and the consequent violations of generations of ethnically diverse students.

A similar school response to the demands of minority groups is seen in the inclusion of new minority heroes in the pantheon of leaders to whom the school child is exposed, and whom he is taught to revere. Martin Luther King now appears on the classroom wall and in the calendar, along with Washington and Lincoln. Again, there is no doubt that this change is beneficial for the self-respect of minority students, and for the enlarged comprehension of Whites. What concerns me is that it may become merely an extension of the old deception. Those "successes" admitted to the list of American culture heroes are precisely those who conformed to middle-class standards of behavior. Their presence again tells the student what he must do, and what a limited range of alternatives there exists, in order for him to succeed . . . even as a civil rights leader! Most aspects of his cultural and historical heritage and his personal life experience still have no place in school or society. Significant by their absence are those ethnic group heroes whose concern for social justice was expressed through other than middle-class means, or included a demand for recognition of their distinctive backgrounds. Even more significantly omitted are all those whose heroism consisted of a determination to survive and preserve their individual dignities in the face of a total society dedicated to the denial of their self-respect. Julian Bond was once asked whom he considered the greatest Black man alive. He replied, "The greatest black man alive today is a man of indeterminate age, with or without a family, with or without gainful employment, with or without any prospect for a future brighter than his past, who manages yet to wake up every morning with the notion that another day must be endured." This response extends to all minority members and to all those living in poverty in this country.

If the traditional family structures, roles, behaviors, religious beliefs and other values of American ethnic communities are absent from most schools, equally missing are the folk literatures, arts and music of all these groups, which have given expression to their experiences. A large part of these cultural expressions deals with the experiences of poverty, discrimination, inter-group conflict and pressures for conformity. They form a peculiarly American record of suffering, of which the blues is the foremost but by no means the only example. They form the true corrective to the unreal blandness, the dishonest sweetness of the traditional classroom. Until this experience enters the schools as a significant American record, students will continue to lack the means of relating themselves and their backgrounds to the goals of formal education. Their feelings of irrelevance and alienation will not disappear until the school positively and consciously validates their life styles and histories in this way.

Teachers may naturally fear the introduction of such matters into the curriculum. They know intuitively that to recognize is to sanction, and fear that in sanctioning these diverse cultural backgrounds they will imply an abandonment of all the standards and goals they have set themselves, to provide students with the skills necessary for effective functioning in the dominant society. This is not so. Rather, teachers will be forced to question which aspects of school indoctrination are truly necessary and appropriate, which goals are valid, and which constitute merely coercive demands for needless conformity. They will also find that students do not have the anticipated difficulty in moving between two cultural contexts, the school and the home, as long as both of these contexts are recognized as in some sense real and true. Americans have been engaging in what linguists refer to as "style-switching" for a long time. If they have not all been as effective at it as they might be or as the school has wished, that is because they have heard, and correctly, that the adoption of a new life style implied a derogation of the old. If teachers can trust this, can dare to engage in this experiment, they will discover that clear gains in student performance will be one of the significant outcomes.

How is this to be done? On what resources can teachers call, to relate their classroom goals to the cultural pluralism of their students and their students' communities? I wish to suggest that teachers have available to them, and must begin to use, four types of resources. That which has received most attention is of course the use of curricular materials, especially texts. While an important resource that needs further development, I believe that it is neither the most important nor the easiest for teachers to utilize. Teachers have regrettably little control over their curricular materials. Our discussion does underline the need for vigorous teacher demand for more accurate representations of ethnic history and culture in reading materials and other areas. It emphasizes the importance of pressure which has begun in some areas to end state control of text selection and allow increased teacher freedom in the selection and development of materials relevant to the needs of their classes. But I think that this area is least likely to undergo rapid reform. Lack of teacher influence over commercial textbook publishers is only part of the problem. With inadequate knowledge of the specific ethnic cultures and histories of this society, and this is true of all of us, teachers are greatly overburdened by the demand that they reeducate themselves and familiarize themselves with available materials. Without some more effective system of teacher leaves, and opportunities for retraining and redesign of curriculum than most teachers are provided, the pressures of time and job militate against any rapid improvements here.

There are, however, three other resources available to the teacher which, though largely ignored in most school systems, are far more readily available and more easily utilized. They are the students, the members of the local communities, and the teacher herself. The success and power of methods which recognize within the classroom the realities of the student's life, his fears and hopes and obsessions, have been recorded many times since Sylvia Ashton-Warner first presented her method of organic reading and writing.[4] The work of Herbert Kohl is an outstanding example.[5] But perhaps it has not always been clear to the teaching profession that such methods are not merely techniques for the teaching of reading and writing skills, or of literature. They are methods of relating the student's own life concerns and life style to all class activities, and as such, they convey to the student that the classroom is a place where he can learn to express, understand and evaluate the personal and social facts of his existence. What I propose, then, is not just organic reading and writing, but a total system of organic learning, in which students continually project into the classroom and into the curriculum those events and selves, those problems and conflicts which they need to master, while the teacher continually guides them in the direction of a more general recognition of the historic roots and the wide implications of their personal concerns.

"*Parents, grandparents and other community members as resource persons can speak with conviction of life . . .*"

In school districts characterized by ethnic diversity, the use of student generated concerns and the discussion of student experience within the classroom has an added power. It forces all students to focus on each other's ethnic identities and their consequences. By so doing, the classroom demonstrates that respect for diversity which it wishes to teach the students. But even in schools not populated by such diversity in the usual sense of the term, there is greater opportunity than is usually recognized to achieve the same goal. As has been remarked, the unacknowledged diversity within the dominant, largely White, society is great. The same is true of communities classified by the dominant society as containing a single "minority" group. It is through an exploration of these individual fates that the student can lay the groundwork for the understanding of ethnic communities and histories other than his own.

But the social fates of America's ethnic communities are manifested far more clearly in the lives of their adult members than in their children. These adults have a role to play equally important, perhaps more so, than the role of paraprofessional aide. In fact much of the success of some paraprofessional programs may be due to the subtle ways in which adult community members play this role. Brought into the classroom as representatives of the American experience, they can communicate to students the extent of diversity and the consequences of it in vivid and meaningful ways. Parents, grandparents and other community members as resource persons can speak with conviction of life in rural communities, recent urban migrations, dustbowls and detention camps, the meaning of the ghetto and the slum, and of the ways in which individual and group have retained loyalty and identity through language, religion and custom. I do not mean to underestimate the difficulties which will have to be overcome in such attempts to involve community resource people in the classroom. Centuries of distrust may have to be overcome, for most Americans have a justified suspicion that little which goes on in the classroom reflects their own concerns. These suspicions will not be overcome by teachers lacking in a deep sense of respect for others, nor those fearful of confronting the tragedy of the American condition. But those who succeed will do a major service in reducing the alienation of school from community. They will, likewise, do something to bridge the gap between generations in this country. A good part of the American saga still lives in the memories of older Americans. Their alienation is in part a product of their conviction that that saga is irrelevant to the lives and identities of the young.

Finally and most critically, there is the teacher, who paradoxically becomes the single most reliable and available resource person in the classroom. For if teachers as finished products have often been distressingly uniform in appearance, behaviors and values, our backgrounds are not. Coming as we do from a range of ethnic and cultural identities, and by the mere fact of recruitment primarily from the lower and lower middle classes, we have available to us, however forgotten, repressed or ignored, the experiences of self and family in the context of pressure for assimilation and upward mobility which are the subject of this essay. When teachers begin to recognize that their own ethnic heritages are valuable, that their own family histories are relevant to learning and teaching, the battle is half won. Indeed, I am convinced that without this recognition and acceptance of self, the teacher will remain unable to communicate to his class or to the surrounding community the respect necessary for the creation of contact between life and learning. Respect flows from empathy (and is not to be confused with approval, as we Americans sometimes do). But the very nature of the processes of teacher selection and pressures for teacher conformity have tended to reduce the qualities of empathy and respect in traditional classrooms. Without them, the teaching of cultural pluralism will remain artificial and ineffective. Only through the recognition of his or her own alien-ation, his own family tragedies and achievements, can the teacher make valid contact with those of others.

Using these resources, each teacher may begin to create, in that small sphere in which he or she is influential, a series of intercultural transac-tions, in which teacher and students begin to define with and for each other the significance of their lives and histories. So doing, each teacher serves as a translator and guide, assisting students with the aid of their communities to a comprehension of the value of formal learning, of all the technical and analytic skills which the school has to offer, for the acquisition of a more powerful and broader understanding of their place in America, of the contexts and causes of their own fates, and ultimately of the possibilities and the means for change.

In such an intercultural classroom, the students' growing awareness of cultural pluralism is but the first benefit. Their own comprehension of the complex realities and problems which beset this country is a second. But the third is the creation of a motivation for learning founded not on artificial rewards of approval and prestige, but on the discovery of the relevance of learning to self.

FOOTNOTES

[1] Michael B. Katz, *Class, Bureaucracy and Schools: The Illusion of Educational Change in America* (New York: Praeger, 1971), p. 106.
[2] Murray L. Wax, Rosalie H. Wax and Robert V. Dumont, Jr., *Formal Education in an American Indian Community*, 1964. Supplement to *Social Problems*, Vol. II, No. 4 (Spring, 1964), p. 67.
[3] John H. Scanzoni, *The Black Family in Modern Society* (Rockleigh, New Jersey: Allyn and Bacon, 1972).
[4] Sylvia Ashton-Warner, *Teacher* (New York: Simon & Schuster, 1963).
[5] Herbert Kohl, *Thirty-Six Children* (New York: New American Library, 1967).

BIBLIOGRAPHY

Ashton-Warner, Sylvia. *Teacher* (New York: Simon & Schuster, 1963). Still one of the best introductions to the organic method of teaching in an intercultural setting, this report on the teaching of English in a New Zealand Maori infant room can be taken as a model for the use of the method in other cultural settings and in other areas of the curriculum. Ashton-Warner's approach is in great contrast to most intercultural experiments in this country, which have tended to prescribe content, and hence to define for the students their own subculture, rather than allowing children to generate content out of their own needs and experiences.

Catro, Janet. "Untapped Verbal Fluency of Black Schoolchildren" in Leacock, Eleanor, ed. *The Culture of Poverty: a Critique* (New York: Simon & Schuster, 1971). An honest and exciting account of an experiment in teaching language skills through the involvement of students, and the students' own subculture, in creative drama, role-playing and games. This is a clear demonstration that no sacrifice in standards need occur when teaching standard English through an organic method. Included is the script of one result of this experiment, a school spring festival involving students and community members, which can serve as a model for teachers in other schools.

Fuchs, Estelle. *Teachers Talk: Views From Inside City Schools* (Garden City, New York: Doubleday & Co., 1969). There are few studies of what the school does to the teacher. This one focusses on the problems, and pressures for indoctrination, to which the beginning teacher is subjected. It should provide both the beginner and the experienced teacher with an awareness of the dangers of institutionalized educational systems, and of the possibilities for resistance and reform.

Katz, Michael B. *Class, Bureaucracy, and Schools: the Illusion of Educational Change in America* (New York: Praeger, 1971). Like Katz's previous writings, this small book is a departure from most educational history, because it dares to raise questions about the covert functions of the institution, rather than accepting its stated ideology as fact. There is no better introduction for teachers wishing to relate their own current classroom problems to a historical perspective.

Kohl, Herbert. *Thirty-six Children* (New York: New American Library, 1967). Kohl's application of organic teaching methods to a New York ghetto school, though it concentrates primarily on the teaching of language skills, is an excellent source of ideas and insights for application to American classrooms.

Kohl, Herbert. *The Open Classroom: a Practical Guide to a New Way of Teaching* (New York: The New York Review, 1969). This small Bible for teachers who want to begin to make teaching a meaningful and creative process is written by one who understands the constraints and anxieties within which teachers function. A compassionate and courageous guide to the reform of self and classroom.

Rosenfeld, Gerry. *"Shut Those Thick Lips"; a Study of Slum School Failure* (New York: Holt, Rinehart & Winston, 1971). This study of a Harlem ghetto school by a teacher trained in anthropological analysis provides the best available demonstration of what social science can offer the individual actively involved in education. Rosenfeld's analysis includes not only the school bureaucracy, but the students, the surrounding community, the ideology of the institution and the teacher's own responses to the teaching situation. Far more than another radical critique or personal account, this book is a model for those wishing to understand their own schools and students in more meaningful terms than those of traditional ideology or personal outrage.

Wax, Murray L., Wax, Rosalie H. and Dumont, R. V., Jr. *Formal Education in an American Indian Community.* Supplement to *Social Problems,* Vol. II, no. 4 (Spring 1964). An outstanding study of the failure of education for American Indians, this analysis of the school bureaucracy and the classroom on an Indian reservation identifies many of the sources of classroom problems in intercultural contexts. Of special value is the authors' discussion of the "vacuum ideology" of the schools and the students' response to it.

Geneva Gay

GENEVA GAY is Assistant Professor of Curriculum and Instruction and Acting Chairman of Afro-American Studies at the University of Texas at Austin. Professor Gay received her B.A. and M.A. degrees in social studies and history at the University of Akron, and her Ph.D. from the University of Texas. Dr. Gay was formerly a high-school social studies teacher and has participated in NDEA Institutes at Georgetown and Purdue Universities. She is a member of a number of honorary and professional organizations, including Phi Alpha Theta, Kappa Delta Pi, Pi Lambda Theta, and the Association for Supervision and Curriculum Development. Dr. Gay has served as an ethnic studies consultant to a variety of institutions, including the University of Michigan and the Texas Education Agency. She is a consultant and coauthor of the Scott, Foresman elementary social studies series, Investigating Man's World, *and has contributed to the books* Language and Cultural Diversity in American Education *and* Curricular Concerns in a Revolutionary Era. *Her articles have appeared in* Educational Leadership *and* Texas Outlook.

GENEVA GAY

2

Racism in America: Imperatives for Teaching Ethnic Studies

Introduction

Racism, in all its destructive splendor, permeates every aspect of American life. It is one of the most crucial problems we now encounter. As the Joint Commission on Mental Health of Children exclaimed:

> Racism is the number one public health problem facing America. The conscious and unconscious attitudes of superiority which permit and demand that a majority oppress a minority are a clear and present danger to the mental health of all children and their parents.... Its destructive effects severely cripple the growth and development of millions of our citizens, young and old alike. Yearly it directly and indirectly causes more fatality, disability, and economic loss than any other single factor.[1]

It is this White problem which causes the racial strife and polarization currently plaguing the country, not the Black, Mexican American, Native American, or Puerto Rican "problem" so often blamed. Schools and teachers are as guilty of perpetuating this demonic disease as are all other institutions and individuals actively engaged in practicing "the American way of life." Until these facts are realized and accepted, without attempting redemption through rationalization, we can expect to see little substantive progress toward achieving harmonious racial relations among the diversified ethnic groups within our culturally pluralistic society. The first step is to understand the realities of what is, regardless of how ugly and disturbing they may be.

27

The study and analysis of racism in America, if seriously and conscientiously pursued, should begin with a frame of reference or a mind-set that is reality-based. Martin Luther King warned that "to live with the pretense that racism is a doctrine of a very few is to disarm us in fighting it frontally as scientifically unsound, morally repugnant, and socially destructive. The prescription for the cure rests with the accurate diagnosis of the disease."[2]

Teachers and students alike must accept the fact—and clearly understand its implications—that the United States is and always has been a racist society. Although the term "racism" is relatively recent, the concept is as old as the nation and is as American as the flag and apple pie. It is deeply woven into the entire ideological foundations of American life, and is perpetuated by all of the institutions of the society. Social studies teachers who wish to dispel myths about America's history and culture by "telling it like it was and is" must help their students understand the fact that racism is, unequivocally, an American heritage.

Another "reality" to keep in mind is that racism pervades the whole society and affects us all. It is hard for most Whites to accept the fact that they are racists. This is due in part to the distorted conceptions they hold about what is meant by racism. They interpret racism to mean such blatant, bigoted, and extremist behavior as lynchings, night riders, church bombings, and burning crosses on lawns. Quite the contrary is true. Some of the most devastating kinds of racism are subtle acts committed, out of habit, by people who have no conscious desire or intent to relegate ethnic minorities to perpetual states of inferiority, oppression, and suppression.

Guilt complexes have no useful role in the study of racism. For one to parade his guilt feelings about the racist acts he has committed, once these are exposed, is a waste of time and energy which serves to no one's avail. It does nothing constructive towards ridding society of this menacing disease or changing the behavior of the individuals who spread it. Instead, guilt can become an effective scapegoat or substitute for real action. Nor does it help matters to shift the blame to the victimized. The reality is that racism is created and maintained by Whites, and it is the Whites who must accept the responsibility for bringing about change.

Search for a Definition of Racism

Despite the outcries and numerous indictments by ethnic minorities charging the United States with practicing racism; despite the retaliations and defensive statements of WASPs; despite the revelations of governmental and educational commission reports; despite the treatises

of scholars and researchers analyzing the racist nature of the United States, the meaning of racism remains somewhat vague and ambiguous. Members of ethnic minorities, who are experts on racism from a practical and experiential standpoint since they are the recipients of its ill-effects, are hard-pressed to define it definitively. When asked to define racism they are quick to respond, "I don't know if I can put it into words, but I *know* racism when I see it." Scholars, theoreticians, and commissioners tend to resort to reporting testimony of the victims of racism, citing examples of discriminatory actions, and the effects of the disease, instead of defining it in specific, operational terms. And, one is still left wondering what exactly is this thing called racism.

Definitions of racism are as numerous and varied as are the people who have studied this social disease. However, several characteristic features are recurrent in the various analyses now available on the subject. General agreement prevails that racism in America is individual and institutional; intentional and unintentional; overt and subtle; is an activity predicated on an idea or an attitude; is insidious and pervasive; ascribes to the inherent superiority of Whites over people of color; is learned and culturally sanctioned; and involves the exertion of power, authority, and/or control by Whites over other ethnic groups.[3]

Racism is defined here as *any activity, individual or institutional, deliberate or not, predicated upon a belief in the superiority of Whites and the inferiority of ethnic minorities, which serves to maintain White supremacy through the oppression and subjugation of members of ethnic minority groups.* It is the extension of an attitude into an action. Although the focus of attention is on *behavior,* attitudes are of crucial importance for they are the motivational forces which determine the nature of the actions one takes. If racism is perceived systematically, attitudes become one of the interdependent elements in the process which culminates in various acts of oppression and repression. Attitudes and actions are inseparably bound to each other.

Thus, one who believes Native Americans are less civilized than Whites may be considered by some to be merely prejudiced. However, his behavior will reflect that belief and thereby carry this attitude beyond the realm of mere prejudice. The White housewife who allows her children to call her Black domestic by her first name is being racist if she does not extend to her children like prerogatives with members of her bridge club. Educational institutions are practicing racism when they prescribe White curricula, and ignore and/or teach distortions about the cultural experiences of ethnic minorities. A person who is apathetic toward or tolerates the injustices rained upon minorities by social institutions is racist by his *failure* to act. In each of these instances some behavioral manifestation is exhibited which succeeds in projecting and perpetuating the superiority of "Whiteness." Behavior, in this sense, encompasses action, inaction, and nonaction.

Kinds of Racism

The idea that racism is insidious and permeates all aspects of American society may cause consternation for many serious students of American culture, and teachers who wish to develop appreciation for cultural diversity by including systematic analyses of racism as part of their social studies curricula. How can anyone ever expect to pinpoint evidence of racism or design programs and strategies to combat it if he must analyze *all* sectors of society? Is not the task too monumental to be feasible for any one person to undertake? Procedurally, if we think of the expressions of racism as falling into three major categories, we have a frame of reference which will make the task more manageable, if not easier. We call these individual, institutional, and cultural racism. The definition suggested above is inclusive of all three.

Individual Racism

Individual racism is in some ways analogous to race prejudice. It is the belief that ethnic minorities are inferior to Whites because of their racial identity, and the corresponding behavioral patterns which serve to perpetuate these attitudes and positions. The "norms" that are used as evaluative criteria are those ascribed to by White Anglo-Saxon Protestants. Whites are considered superior to Blacks, Mexican Americans, Native Americans, and Asian Americans in physical, intellectual, moral, emotional, and cultural traits.

A person who allows his behavior relative to ethnic minority group members to be determined by stereotypic attitudes and beliefs he holds toward them is a racist. Such behavior may be covert or overt. Although covert racism is much harder to detect than overt racism both are equally destructive to human potential. Thus, the White store clerk who sees every Black child who enters his place of business as a potential thief and *watches and waits* for him to steal something is being racist. He is acting out the belief that Blacks are by nature dishonest and prone to thievery. The White citizen who, upon observing a group of White youth, thinks and/or comments to a companion, "What a nice looking bunch of kids"; but when he sees a group of Black youth, senses a threat of impending danger and/or comments, "I wonder what they are up to now," is being racist. The teacher who expects less performance from her Black, Chicano, and Puerto Rican students than her White students is also racist. A belief deeply embedded in her perceptual framework says that Blacks, Puerto Ricans, and Chicanos, as racial groups, do not have the same intellectual potentials as Whites. She exposes her racism with such apparently simple and innocent statements as, "What else can you expect of them given their poor home environment?" The White liberal who argues vehemently at rallies for Blacks', Chicanos', and Native Americans' claims to reparations, yet stands and listens silently to a friend or family member's negative racial characterizations of ethnic minorities without rebuttal, is contributing to individual racism. Similarly, the homeowner in Dallas, Texas, who rushes to sell his house when a Mexican American moves in next door because the property value will decline; the parents in Pontiac, Michigan, who shout ugly insults at Black youth and burn school buses transporting them to previously all-White schools; the school teacher who insists that Native American children cut their hair so that they will look "normal"; the other teacher who is anxious to teach in Black schools because of her overwhelming desire to help educate Black youth, yet appeals to her Black fellow teachers for names of experienced Black "girls" or "gals" that will be dependable, trustworthy domestics; and the night riders who burn crosses on people's lawns, are all guilty of committing individual racism.

Institutional Racism

Any institutional activity which creates racial inequalities, and results in the subordination and oppression of minorities, whether it be intentional or the result of "business as usual," is institutional racism.[4] Blatant acts of institutional racism, such as separate educational, social, and recreational facilities, poll taxes, and literacy tests, have been largely eliminated as a result of litigations and legislation. It is the subtle acts remaining that are so debilitating. This form of racism is apparent in all the major institutions—educational, political, religious, economic, legal, health and welfare, and communications. These institutions are created by individuals for their benefit, and they operate under the auspices of customs, laws, mores, habits, and other cultural sanctions. Therefore, institutional racism is an extension of individual racism and indicative of the racism inherent in the culture.

Institutional racism appears in many forms. Colleges and universities which proclaim to treat all applicants for admission equally, irrespective of ethnic identity and judge them on the merits of their qualifications, yet continue to use standardized tests as the evaluative criteria are committing institutional racism. The judicial system which grants a personal bond of $1,000 to a White confessed and thrice-convicted felon accused of murder, but denies bail to a Black man accused of selling a marihuana cigarette to an undercover agent, and allows a Mexican American who has been declared mentally incompetent to be tried and convicted of first degree murder, is guilty of practicing racism. So is the economic system which lays claim to "free enterprise," but disqualifies ethnic minorities because of their racial and ethnic identity, and exploits them as consumers; the communications system which habitually paints negative stereotypic views of Blacks, Chicanos, and Puerto Ricans in newspaper reporting and advertising; the political system which spends billions of dollars annually to put a man on the moon, but allows poverty and starvation to continue to exist in this land of plenty. Thus, institutional racism is a "fact of American life," whether committed by design or effect, by intent or ignorance, by bigotry or naiveté. In its subtle form it is extremely difficult to detect and to determine who is at fault.

Cultural Racism

A third form of racism is that which involves the elevation of the White Anglo-Saxon Protestant cultural heritage to a position of superiority over the cultural experiences of ethnic minority groups. It involves elements of both institutional and individual racism. The idea that "White is right" prevails in this expression of racism. Only those values, attitudes, beliefs, traditions, customs, and mores ascribed to by Whites are considered acceptable and normal prescriptions of behavior. Anything else is labeled deviant, abnormal, degenerate, and pathological. If this belief were to remain in the realm of attitudes, it would be merely ethnocentrism. It becomes cultural racism when Whites use power to perpetuate their cultural heritage and impose it upon others, while at the same time destroying the culture of ethnic minorities.

Several examples serve to illustrate how racism is deeply entrenched in the values, language, history, customs, religion, and psychology of mainstream America. The professed "brotherly love" which is supposed to transcend racial and ethnic identities to embrace all mankind is expressed as the "White man's burden," which, in turn, has been used to rationalize imperialism, slavery, and other kinds of exploitation; the genocide committed against Native Americans in the name of the manifest destined right of Whites to settle the western frontier; the audacity of some state legislatures to pass laws making Mexican Americans White; the portrayal of "Black" in everyday language usage as something bad, evil, dirty, and undesirable, while "White" connotes purity and goodness; standards of beauty which glorify white skin, blond hair, and blue eyes; the statement that Columbus still "discovered" America even though Native Americans lived here long before his arrival; the situations where Africa continues to be remembered as the "dark" continent and Africans as "primitives," Indians as "savage," and Chinese and Japanese as "dirty and clannish"; the democratic principles of "equality" and "liberty and justice for all" which did not extend to Blacks who were held in human bondage, or Japanese placed in concentration camps; the list of *American* "heroes" children study in school, all of whom just happen to be White; and all the national holidays which pay homage only to Whites and their accomplishments.

These and many other similar attitudes and actions permeate the totality of the American Experience. They combine to form a value system that is inherently racist. All major institutions are built upon these racist ideologies. They, in turn, are responsible for socializing individuals and transmitting culture, thereby creating individual racism and perpetuating cultural racism. The result is that over the years a complex, interlocking system of racism has evolved which is deeply ingrained into the entire fabric of America.

Manifestations of Racism

Racism takes many forms. It is evident in the textbooks we read, the schools we attend, the language we speak, the churches where we go to worship, the songs we sing, the politics of the nation, the press and television, the laws of the land, and the day-to-day activities in which we are involved. It is one of the most distinctive characteristics of American culture.

A few specific examples of racism in operation are presented below. They are illustrative of the evidence available documenting the manifold existence of racism, and are suggested here as a means of further clarifying the operational dynamics of racism. Each of the vignettes presented herein includes a description of an attitude, behavior, and/or situation which seems to be harmless, or even complimentary to ethnic minority groups, and an explanation of the implicit racist messages.

SCENE 1

In response to the question, "What are your general attitudes toward Blacks?", a White college sophomore commented that "There is nothing wrong with the Black race except that the majority of them will not accept the standards, rules, and ways given to them by the Whites, and I do believe these rules are equal and fair for both Black and White."

The racism implicit in this statement is the arrogant assumption commonly expressed by Whites that they know what is best for Blacks as well as Chicanos, Native Americans, and Asian Americans. The key words are "accept" and "given to." This person is expressing a belief in the superiority of White culture over Black culture, the rightness and redeeming qualities of White values and norms, and, thus, perpetuating the image of the "great White father."

SCENE 2

The setting is a conference on bilingual education for Mexican American students. Ms. X has just finished describing the teacher training program which she helps to direct. She explains that if teachers want to work effectively with Chicano youth they should learn to speak Spanish and familiarize themselves with Mexican American culture. She claims to have accomplished both. The speech ends and discussion begins.

Participant A: Asks a question in Spanish.
Ms. X: Answers the question in English.
Participant A: Asks for further clarification, again in Spanish.
Ms. X: Continues to answer in English.
Participant B: Asks Ms. X why she did not respond to the questions in Spanish.
Ms. X: Explains that since the *majority of the people speak and understand English* she wished to reach the greater number.

In this particular instance the audience was comprised largely of Mexican Americans. *They were the majority!* Ms. X's apparent oversight in view of her avowed sensitivity to cultural diversity and knowledge of Mexican American culture suggests that as far as she was concerned "White was still right"—that is, the numerical turnabout was insignificant. Although temporarily outnumbered, Whites still reigned supreme, English was superior to Spanish, and the "people" really meant "Whites."

SCENE 3

A group of students and teachers are attending a meeting in the library of a large urban high school which was only recently desegregated. The topic of discussion is, "How to Improve Human and Racial Relations."

Student A (Black):   "In class we are made to feel like we weren't even a part of the group."
Student B (Chicano): "That's right. Teachers ignore our presence and try to pretend like everything is the same way it was before we came here."

Student C (Black):	"Yea! When we tell them (teachers) that we are 'Black' and want to be called 'Black,' they are always talking about, 'but you aren't really Black. Your skin is brown.' And then when we start discussing Blacks in class, they start in on 'the Negro problem'—always 'the Negro problem'!"
Teacher:	"It makes no difference to me whether my students are black, white, brown, green, red, yellow, or purple. They are *students* and I treat them all the same. After all, we are all human beings. Why can't we forget about color entirely and just treat each other like human beings?"

The teacher who applauds her immunity to racism with the testimonial that "I see no color. My pupils are all the same to me." should realize that to her minority students this is a declaration of racism. How can this teacher, or any teacher for that matter, look at a student and not see his color? What she is really saying is, "I have been looking at you all this time and I have never really _seen_ you." Such statements as "I see no color," "you people," "they," and "them," when used by Whites in the presence of minorities to refer to other members of that group, are racist because by not using a definite label they succeed in depersonalizing and dehumanizing the people, thereby stripping them of their concrete identity. They become "things"—unnamed objects—instead of people. For the Black student his humanness is inextricably interwoven into his Blackness, and to deny one is to deny both. The teacher who is blind and sees no color is also deaf and hears no differences. The fact that she limits "Blackness" to color indicates a lack of insight and sensitivity to the cultural experiences of her students. Both are racist deeds. Undoubtedly, this teacher, and others like her, will use their WASP norms to determine instructional processes and selection of curriculum materials in the classroom. The result is that no attention will be given to either cultural diversity, cultural relativism, or cultural pluralism.

SCENE 4

A party of twelve arrives at a restaurant for dinner. The group includes both men and women, a Black woman, and a "distinguished guest." Several members of the party are acquainted but others have yet

"For the Black student his humanness is inextricably interwoven into his Blackness, and to deny one is to deny both."

to be introduced. After everyone is seated the person (Mr. A) in charge of planning the event begins to introduce the distinguished guest (Mr. B) to the rest of the group. He proceeds to introduce each member as he comes to him. When he gets to the Black member (Ms. X) and those seated nearest her (Mr. C to the left and Mr. D to the right, both of whom are White), he says:

Mr. A: "Mr. C, I would like you to meet Mr. B."
Mr. C: "I am honored to meet you Mr. B. I have wanted to for a long time."
Mr. B: "Nice to meet you, too."
Mr. A: (Skipping over Ms. X.) "Mr. D, may I present Mr. B, the one who . . ."
Mr. D: "It's a great pleasure."
Mr. A: (Takes Mr. B, the "distinguished guest," by the arm and begins to leave.)
Mr. B: "I don't think I have met this young lady." (Referring to Ms. X.)
Mr. A: "Oh! I'm so sorry, I forgot. I thought you two already knew each other."

Three things are too apparent in this incident for Mr. A to have made a simple mistake or to have forgotten his social graces. First, as he introduced this particular guest (Mr. B) he *did not* limit the introductions to only those present who had never met him before. Second, everyone was introduced in order of the seating arrangement and the sequence was never broken until Mr. A got to Ms. X. Third, his explanation is contradictory. How could he "forget" to introduce her and at the same time "think she already knew" the man? Why did this mistake, exception, or confusion occur with *only* the Black guest? What Ms. X heard Mr. A really saying was this racist message: "This honor (being personally introduced to the distinguished guest) is reserved for Whites only; and I forgot you were even here, or I wish to forget that you are here, since you don't count anyway!"

SCENE 5

Mr. X frequently shops for his wife. Since she uses large amounts of a particular brand of soup in her cooking, Mr. X often buys it in large quantities. Two out of three times, as Mr. X goes through the checkout counter to pay for his purchases, the clerk will say, "This is for the restaurant, isn't it?"

This statement seems like an innocent query of a friendly and/or curious clerk. However, implicitly it is a racially-loaded statement. Mr. X is Chinese. Thus, the underlying message is that "all Chinese are cooks"!

SCENE 6

Checking the television weekly prime time programs for something interesting to watch, the viewer sees a Black man who is the personal aide of a police chief and a brilliant part-time law student; an infallible Black policeman; a Black personal secretary to a private detective; a Black many-talented teacher; a Black mechanical genius who is also an expert at the art of disguise; and two cunning Black men at a junkyard. Between shows he may pause to observe this scene:

> The popular comedian, Bill Cosby, struggles to climb atop a mouthful of large white teeth. Having completed this amazing feat, he flashes a wide grin of victory and proudly announces that he is "Mr. Tooth Decay." Just as he begins to enjoy his work of spreading cavities, he is confronted by a man-size tube of Crest toothpaste, with its superior fighting and whitening power. A fight follows. Cosby loses the battle and is kicked out of the mouth.

The initial reaction to this and other examples of contemporary television advertising is appreciation and applause. Finally, the lily-White image projected by television for so long has been broken! Blacks and Chicanos can now be seen on commercials *and* prime time programs. However, if the viewer looks a little closer, he will find that (1) there are still very few, if any, Chicanos, Native Americans, and Asian Americans appearing as regulars in television programming; and (2) while the number of Blacks appearing on television has increased, the image they portray has not changed radically from the days of their predecessors— Step'n Fetchit, Bojangles, and Amos and Andy. Their predecessors "made it" by portraying stereotypic views of Blacks as shuffling, stupid, superstitious, childlike creatures. Now Peggy ("Mannix"), Barney ("Mission Impossible"), Linc ("Mod Squad"), Pete ("Room 222"), and Mark ("Ironside") are still loyal and devoted, and serve their masters faithfully. The costumes have changed but the roles remain the same—servility. These Blacks are no longer stupid, but neither are they "average." They are now "superspades." Both portrayals are reflections of the racist thinking of White Americans about Black Americans. Blacks must be exceptional in order to receive any resemblance of acceptance in White society.

The subtle racist message of the commercial described above involving Bill Cosby is apparent in the symbolism. The Black man as "Mr. Tooth Decay" suggests that Blackness is evil. The superior strength and inherent goodness of Whiteness is symbolized by the Crest toothpaste success in overpowering the menacing threat and the evil of Blackness.

SCENE 7

A social studies class is discussing the westward expansion of the United States. The students ask the question, "What happened to the Native Americans as White settlers pushed westward?" Reading in their textbooks they find this description:

> For years the Indians had been driven farther and farther to the west by the frontier of the white man's civilization. Promises of permanent rights to large tracts of land were given to many Indian tribes. ... However, the promises were not kept, and as the Indian lands were gradually used for other purposes, the Indians themselves were forced into smaller and smaller reservations.[5]

In their supplementary readings they find that Native American chiefs were often summoned to the nation's capital to discuss treaty relations with various presidents of the United States. They find that on one such occasion, when Shahaka, Chief of the Mandan Indians of Missouri, visited Thomas Jefferson on December 30, 1806, the President remarked:

> My friends and children ... we consider ourselves no longer of the old nation beyond the waters, but as united in one family with our red brothers here. ... We are now your fathers; and, you shall not lose by the change.
> ... remember, then, my advice, my children, carry it home to your people, and tell them that from the day that they become all of the same family, from the day that we become fathers to them all, we wish, as a true father should do, that we may all live together as one household, and that before they strike one another, they should go to their father and let him endeavor to make up the quarrel.*

These descriptions of the White man's relations with Native Americans reek with racism. In the first passage the phrase, "by the frontiers of the white man's civilization," is suggestive of manifest destiny. Furthermore, those "unkept promises" were in actuality "broken treaties"; Whites dared to "promise land to the Indians" that was rightfully theirs anyway; and Indian lands were not "gradually used for other purposes," they were *taken* by Whites. In the second passage Jefferson's words, "my children" and "we are now your fathers," epitomizes the American image of "the Great White Father" and the "White Man's Burden" relative to people of color. Racism is also evident in Jefferson's references to Whites and Native Americans being members of the same family, while at the same time he instructs Shahaka to go tell "your people"!

---

* From *Red Men Calling on the Great White Father,* by Katharine C. Turner. Copyright 1951 by the University of Oklahoma Press.

SCENE 8

Ms. D. enters an expensive jewelry store. As she browses around, a sales clerk approaches:

Clerk: "Good afternoon. May I help you?"
Ms. D: "I was interested in this ring. May I take a closer look?"
Clerk: "Sure. It's a fine stone. Would you like to purchase it?"
Ms. D: "Well, I don't know . . ."
Clerk: "Do you work?"
Ms. D: "Sure."
Clerk: "Fine. Then we could arrange some easy credit terms for you."

The clerk in this episode makes two assumptions about the customer's economic status that are typically racist. He assumes that she does not work (notice he said, *"Do* you work?" not *"Where* do you work?") and that she is incapable of paying for the item in cash (his ready reference to credit!). His behavior is racist because it is indicative of Whites' belief that Blacks are lazy (Ms. D is Black!), and the economic exploitation of Blacks by Whites through the use of "easy credit."

SCENE 9

Every school year hundreds of children across the nation—Black, Chicano, White, Native American, Asian American, Puerto Rican—assemble in auditoriums on various occasions to pay homage to America's heroes and heritage. Frequently, the programs begin with the pledge of allegiance to the flag and the singing of:

. . .

America! America!
God shed His grace on thee,
And crown thy good with brotherhood,
From sea to shining sea!

O beautiful for pilgrim feet,
Whose stern impassioned stress
A thoroughfare for freedom beat
Across the wilderness.

. . .

O beautiful for heroes proved
In liberating strife,
Who more than self their country loved,
And mercy more than life.

For members of ethnic minority groups America is not nearly as beautiful as the picture painted in this revered song. Its image has been blemished too often by racism. Blacks wonder what happened to the "brotherhood" when they were enslaved. Native Americans wonder where was this praised "mercy and love" when they were dying of starvation and exposure during the "Trail of Tears." Mexican Americans wonder about their "heroes" who have been lost forever in the pages of American history.

These illustrations are but a few of the numerous manifestations of racism. They are indicative of the categories and kinds of materials readily available to classroom teachers for their use in helping students develop skills in detecting and understanding the operations of racism in its many forms.

Suggestions for Studying Racism

If social studies teachers are to help their students study racism analytically and systematically, they must begin by creating a state of readiness or frame of reference that is reality-bound. Both teachers and students must have a clear understanding of what racism is and what it is not. During this preparatory stage students, and teachers alike, must dispel the myth that racism is a Black, Chicano, or Native American "problem." They must develop "White consciousness" in the sense of understanding the fact that racism is a "White problem," and all its implications and ramifications. Whites are the creators and perpetrators of racism, while ethnic minority group members are the suffering recipients of its devastating effects. They must understand that racism flourishes under the auspices and sanctions of America's "democratic" principles and institutions.

Frequently, racism is confused, and used interchangeably, with prejudice, stereotypes, and ethnocentrism. These concepts are closely related but they are not synonymous. In making distinctions between them and understanding the interrelationships that do exist, it should help students to know that racism goes beyond mere attitude or action. It is inclusive of both.

Productive discussions about racism are also hampered by the mistaken belief that institutions hold a monopoly on the practice of racism, or that for a person to be a racist he must behave in such ways that he obviously means to do harm to others because of their racial identity. These assumptions are dangerously misleading and serve only to complicate the task of studying racism realistically and with an open mind. They are unrealistic because they ignore another whole dimension of the problem. *Some of the most insidious kinds of racism are committed by individuals who have no conscious intent of doing harm to ethnic minorities and are totally unaware of what they are doing.*

Therefore, during the readiness stages of the instructional process, time should be devoted to developing realistic perceptions about racism by bringing students into confrontation with themselves—their attitudes, beliefs, and behavior—relative to ethnic minorities. Undoubtedly, they will feel that everyone else except themselves is racist. Developing skills in values clarification, systematic analyses, reflective self-analysis, and perceptive awareness through the use of simulation, role playing, socio-drama, inquiry, and multi-media materials are useful tools for bringing students to the realization that racism pervades all of society and affects us all. Teachers must become as actively involved in reflective self-analyses and the other "awareness" processes as the students. Both should begin these processes with questions generated by the examples of racism described above, such as: Have I ever done something like that? What do I really see, think, and/or feel when I interact with Blacks, Chicanos, Puerto Ricans, etc. in person or observe them on television, in magazines, newspapers, etc.?

It is imperative that both students and teachers understand the differences between absolute reality and perceptual reality if they are to understand the effects of racism. Absolute reality is that which exists independent of any exterior forces, such as numerical quantities and material objects. Perceptual reality is relative to individuals' particular circumstances. *What one perceives to be true is reality to him.* A White person may say something or do something which means nothing in particular to him, while to a member of an ethnic group it is a racially significant message. For example, often teachers, in the normal course of events, refer to their students as "boys and girls." Black males respond violently to this usage because, to them, it has all kinds of racial overtones. It is wise to remember that when a minority student says to a teacher, "To me, you are a racist," not to dismiss it as untrue or become defensive because you (the teacher) have been accused unjustly of a crime you did not commit. Rather, explore with him, "What do you mean?"; "What have I done or said to make you think that I am racist?"; then explain that "I didn't know that I was doing that," and "When I said/did . . . , to me it meant. . . ."

Once the students are no longer threatened by the mere mention of the word "racism," the classroom atmosphere is conducive to open discussion, and the group has agreed upon an operational definition, they are ready to pursue the study of racism in depth. The following suggestions are specific techniques or activities social studies teachers can use to facilitate the further development of students' conceptual knowledge and application of their analytical skills in studying racism:

1. Compile a list of criteria to be used in detecting racism in individuals, institutions, and American culture.

2. Have students view their own classrooms and teachers as fields of study. The students would function similarly to anthropologists who do research by becoming participant-observers in their field of study. They would study the classroom for evidence of racism by looking specifically at attitudes and actions of teachers and students, and classroom activities.

3. Compile a list of questions to be asked about specific institutions to determine if there is evidence of racism. These lists would vary with institutions, but some may be general enough to apply to all institutions. Included would be such questions as: How many minority group members are included? What positions or jobs do these minorities hold? Is minority representation in the various aspects of the institutional structure disproportionate to their number at large?, etc. After the lists have been compiled they can be used as guidelines to investigate institutional racism.

4. Make a set of criteria for analyzing the content of textbooks. Follow this exercise through to its ultimate conclusion by finding out whether the textbooks are racist and producing a different version to correct the mistakes or eliminate the racism. For example, one set of criteria may deal specifically with how textbooks treat Native Americans via pictures and other graphic illustrations, and choices of words. If the students find the books to be racist, they can write descriptions of Native Americans' history and culture which are nonracist. This could be done generally or with specific incidents such as the California Gold Rush, the "Trail of Tears," or "Custer's Last Stand." The idea here is to tell the story from the Native Americans' point of view, including what happened and why *they* believed it happened. This technique could also be used with other ethnic minorities—that is, teaching about racism by studying America's history and culture through the perspectives of the various victimized ethnic groups.

5. Do an analytical study of the English language and how it perpetrates racism. Look for common expressions that are a part of everyday usage (e. g., blackball, black cat, blackmail, etc.) and see the images of "black" and "blackness" they portray. Examine how these portrayals stigmatize Blacks and contribute to the formation of racial attitudes.

6. Examine newspapers, magazines, and news reporting to see if they treat information about minorities differently from Whites. Ask such questions as: Is the ethnic identity of the people generally given? What kind of news about minorities receives prominence? Is this different from news about Whites? How is this prominence shown (frequency of reports of crimes as compared to social items and human interest stories, placement of news items about ethnic groups in relation to the rest of the news, etc.).

7. Television advertisements, movies, conversational dialogues, and children's literature (e.g., "Mother Goose," "Dr. Seuss," etc.) may be examined similarly to newspapers and magazines. "Black History: Lost, Stolen or Strayed," a film narrated by Bill Cosby and produced by the Columbia Broadcasting System, presents an excellent explanation of how movies have helped to implant stereotypic images of Blacks in the minds of Americans. This movie could be a useful training tool to be shown to students prior to beginning their own analyses.

"... teaching about racism by studying America's history and culture through the perspectives of the various victimized ethnic groups."

8. Examine how America's efforts to actualize certain "democratic principles" affected the conditions of ethnic minority groups. For example:

Principle	*Effect*
A. Provide for the national defense	Relocation of Japanese Americans in 1942
B. Freedom of choice	Laws prohibiting mis-cegenation
C. Manifest destiny	Genocide committed against Native Americans
D. Equal protection of the laws	Jury trials of members of ethnic minorities
E. Law and order	Excessive police power for the containment of ghettos and barrios

9. Use the school as a major case study to examine racism in its many manifestations. Include analyses of institutional, individual, and cultural racism all within the context of the school environment:

   A. Institutional Racism
      1. Educationally—Examine curricular materials and content, grouping and tracking, intelligence tests, teaching methodologies, etc.
      2. Economically—Determine who are the cooks, janitors, administrators, counselors. Are there any minority supervisors? How do the money and supplies your school receives compare with those of other schools? Etc.
      3. Politically—Find out who are the decision-makers. Who desegregates? Who are the administrators and counselors? How are rules made? Etc.

45

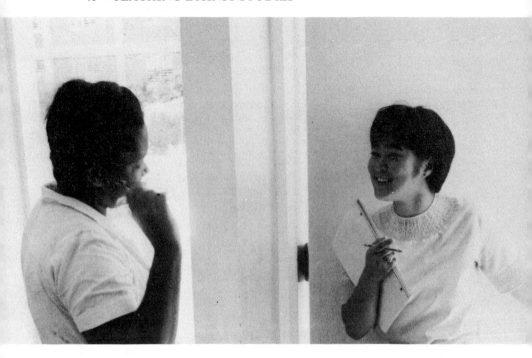

"Understanding the cultural experiences of America's ethnic minorities and the true nature of the American Experience is inseparably bound to understanding racism."

    4. Justice— Examine disparities in discipline. Who drops out? Who is expelled? Who enforces rules? Etc.

B. Individual Racism—Examine how teachers, administrators, and students behave toward minorities, expressions of racial attitudes, who receives school "honors," etc.

C. Cultural Racism—Examine how textbooks treat the cultural experiences of ethnic minorities. What are the school holidays? What "American heroes" are honored at assemblies? Whose pictures adorn the halls and walls of the school? Etc.

Understanding the cultural experiences of America's ethnic minorities and the true nature of the American Experience is inseparably bound to understanding racism. This duality is a prerequisite to effecting behavioral change so as to create a truly open society that embraces human diversity and cultural pluralism. Thus, the inclusion of racism in social studies curricula is imperative to achieving relevance and realism, honesty and authenticity in teaching ethnic minority studies. These should be first among the priorities of social studies teachers as they strive to help their students become more effectively functioning citizens and self-actualizing, perceptive individuals in our culturally pluralistic society.

FOOTNOTES

[1] Whitney Young, Jr., *Beyond Racism: Building an Open Society* (New York: McGraw-Hill, 1969), p. 87.
[2] Martin Luther King, Jr., *Where Do We Go from Here: Chaos or Community?* (New York: Harper and Row, 1969), p. 97.
[3] For further information on definitions and analyses of racism see: Stokely Carmichael and Charles V. Hamilton, *Black Power: The Politics of Liberation in America* (New York: Vintage Books, 1967); James A. Jones, *Prejudice and Racism* (Reading, Mass.: Addison-Wesley Publishing Company, 1972); Louis L. Knowles and Kenneth Prewitt, *Institutional Racism in America* (Englewood Cliffs: Prentice-Hall, 1969); *Racism in America and How to Combat It* (Washington, D. C.: U. S. Government Printing Office, January, 1970); Barry N. Schwartz and Robert Disch, *White Racism: Its History, Pathology and Practice* (New York: Dell Publishing Company, 1970); Robert W. Terry, *For Whites Only* (Grand Rapids: Eerdman's Publishing Company, 1970).
[4] Terry, *For Whites Only*, p. 131.
[5] Landis R. Heller, Jr. and Norris W. Potter, *One Nation Indivisible*, with supplement (Columbus, Ohio: Charles E. Merrill Publishing Company, 1968), p. 352. For a summary analysis of textbooks' treatment of Native Americans see Rupert Costo (Ed.) and Jeannette Henry (Writer), *Textbooks and the American Indian* (San Francisco: The Indian Historian Press, 1970).

BIBLIOGRAPHY

Brown, Dee. *Bury My Heart at Wounded Knee: An Indian History of the American West* (New York: Bantam Books, 1970). A history of the genocide committed against Native Americans by Whites from 1860 to 1890 as seen from the standpoint of the victims. This author relies heavily upon reports of council discussions and treaty negotiations to document the incidence of greed and malice inflicted upon Native Americans.

Daniels, Roger and Kitano, Harry H. L. *American Racism: Exploration of the Nature of Prejudice* (Englewood Cliffs: Prentice-Hall, Inc., 1970). This book analyzes the nature of racism and discusses racist practices inflicted upon different ethnic groups prior to and after World War II. Primary attention is focused on the racism experienced by Japanese Americans. The authors develop their arguments around the premise that "relocation camps can happen again," and explain why this is conceivable.

Deloria, Vine, Jr. *Custer Died for Your Sins* (New York: Avon Books, 1969). Written by a Native American, this book examines the myths and stereotypes Whites have built up about Native Americans; the spheres of influence which manipulate the lives of Native Americans, especially Congress, churches and social scientists; and the future of "Indian Affairs."

Jones, James M. *Prejudice and Racism* (Reading, Massachusetts: Addison-Wesley Publishing Company, 1972). An excellent treatment of racism—concise yet comprehensive. Well written and vividly illustrated. This book is particularly useful in conceptualizing racism, definitively and operationally. It offers definitions, illustrations and interpretations of racism in its various manifestations—individual, institutional, and cultural. A *must* for teaching about and studying racism.

King, Larry L. *Confessions of a White Racist* (New York: Viking Press, 1969). A personal exposé of one man's awakening to the realization of his own racism, and the enduring struggle with his conscience to understand the ramifications of it. It is not only about one man's struggle; it is also about *White Americans and their racist attitudes* in general.

Knowles, Louis L. and Prewitt, Kenneth. *Institutional Racism in America* (Englewood Cliffs: Prentice-Hall, 1969). This book gives an explanation of the ideological roots of racism in America, and an analysis of the racism perpetrated by political, economical, legal, religious, health and welfare, and educational institutions. A classic study which presents descriptive accounts of the operations of racism in these American institutions.

McWilliams, Carey. *North From Mexico: The Spanish-Speaking People of the United States* (New York: Greenwood Press, 1968). This book discusses the cultural heritage, problems surrounding settlement, myths, and stereotypes about lifestyles, prejudices and discrimination, and political activism of Mexican Americans of the Southwest. Special attention is given to Mexican Americans in Texas, New Mexico, and California.

Monte, Anita. *Racism* (New York: Pocket Books, 1972). One of the volumes in the *Problems of American Society* series, this book presents fifteen articles, drawn from a wide range of materials, depicting racism in situational contexts. It argues that racism is the destructive force which is ripping American society apart. Using firsthand accounts of the victims of racism, it explains how racism has developed and has been reinforced by institutions. Good resource book for students.

Moore, Joan W. *Mexican Americans* (Englewood Cliffs: Prentice-Hall, 1970). One of the volumes in the *Ethnic Groups in American Life Series*. The author presents excellent information on several topics relative to the Mexican American experience in American life. Among these are White perceptions of Mexican Americans; American institutions in the Mexican experience; the family, language, culture, and politics of Mexican Americans.

Schwartz, Barry N. and Disch, Robert. *White Racism: Its History, Pathology and Practice* (New York: Dell Publishing Company, 1970). An anthology of historical and contemporary writings which documents the existence of racism. The articles, written by both Blacks and Whites, cover a wide range of diversified materials.

Stalvey, Lois Mark. *The Education of a WASP* (New York: Bantam Books, 1970). This book tells the story of the author's awakening to the realities of the extent and depth of racism in American society. In the process the author examines existing social attitudes and prejudices, and the platitudes of White liberals.

Steinfield, Melvin. *Cracks in the Melting Pot: Racism and Discrimination in American History* (Beverly Hills: Glencoe Press, 1970). This excellent collection of readings is arranged in such a way as to give an overview of racism in order to create an accurate perspective, and to provide insights into the racist practices inflicted upon ethnic minority groups. It provides insights into how racism has influenced, provoked, or encouraged territorial acquisitions, presidential utterances, immigration laws, constitutional crises, barbaric brutalities, and brought American society to the brink of self-destruction.

Terry, Robert W. *For Whites Only* (Grand Rapids: Eerdmans Publishing Company, 1970). Terry discusses the racism of White liberals. He suggests "White consciousness" as an alternative for racism. His major premise is that the race problem is a White problem, rooted in White attitudes and White-controlled institutions. He also discusses strategies and tactics Whites can use to rid society and themselves of racism.

Wilhelm, Sidney M. *Who Needs the Negro?* (Garden City: Anchor Books, 1971). The author argues that Blacks are in danger of being annihilated by Whites since they are no longer a useful commodity. As long as the presence of Blacks was an economic asset, they were not in danger of extermination. Now that this is no longer the case, due to technological advancements, Blacks are perceived as liabilities.

Yette, Samuel F. *The Choice: The Issue of Black Survival in America* (New York: Berkley Medallion Books, 1971). Yette argues similarly to Wilhelm that the primary issue facing Blacks is the question of survival since America has declared them an obsolete people. He develops his hypothesis by setting forth a series of government measures and proposals that appear to be leading toward Black genocide. Although the argument may be somewhat extreme, this book *should not be* discounted in a thorough analysis of racism in American society.

Young, Whitney M. *Beyond Racism: Building an Open Society* (New York: McGraw-Hill, 1968). Young presents a thorough examination of racism in its various manifestations and proposes an action program that will enable America to become a truly open society. He also explains why individuals and institutions are mutually responsible for bringing about change so as to prevent further violent racial crises and confrontations.

Zilversmit, Arthur. *Lincoln on Black and White: A Documentary History* (Belmont, California: Wadsworth Publishing Company, 1971). This collection of readings, one in the *American History Research Series,* provides original documents for analyzing Lincoln's attitudes toward Blacks. These documents offer a wealth of materials for testing the hypothesis: "Lincoln was a White supremacist."

David Ballesteros

DAVID BALLESTEROS is Dean of the School of Arts and Sciences at California State University, Sacramento. Dean Ballesteros holds B.A. and M.A. degrees in Spanish from Redlands University and Middlebury College, and a Ph.D. in Latin American Studies from the University of Southern California. He is a former high school teacher, and has taught at California State University, San Diego, Arizona State University, and the Universities of Oklahoma and Texas. Dean Ballesteros was formerly the Director of Teacher Corps at the University of Texas at Austin. He has served as a multicultural education consultant to a number of institutions, including the Department of Health, Education, and Welfare and the State of California. Dr. Ballesteros was awarded a Spanish Government Grant in 1957-58, and was a United States Office of Education Fellow in 1969-70. His publications include A-LM Guide, Spanish Level One (coauthor), and articles in Hispania, The National Elementary Principal and NCRIEEO Newsletter (National Center for Research and Information on Equal Educational Opportunity). Dean Ballesteros is a specialist in multicultural education, community-based education, and the training of teachers. He is active in a number of professional organizations concerned with the problems of bilingual education, including the National Education Task Force de la Raza, and the Association of Mexican American Educators.

DAVID BALLESTEROS

3

Social Justice
and Minorities

1976 marks the bicentennial anniversary of the founding of the United States of America. The founding fathers advocated, promoted, and insisted that the new Constitution be a document that would bring *freedom, justice, equality,* and the *pursuit of happiness* to its new citizenry. After two hundred years the American dream is far from being realized, particularly for the minorities. Through economic development and land expansion the United States has inherited diverse groups of people whose potentials and contributions have not yet been recognized.

There are serious problems within our society today. Minority groups are equated with these problems. Misconception, ignorance, suspicion, and fear about minority persons prevail. This is why it is so important that teachers keep constantly aware of cultural and linguistic differences and promote understanding among their students to lessen these anxieties. The real problem in our society today is not the "Black Problem," nor the "Indian Problem," nor the "Mexican American Problem"; it is the "Anglo Point-of-View Problem." This viewpoint determines what happens in our schools and communities—what emphasis will be given or denied racial, cultural, and language values.

The late Commissioner of Education, James E. Allen, in a speech on September 2, 1969, talked about specific steps which communities may find constructive in dealing with some of the underlying causes of student unrest. One of the suggested steps included: "The introduction of Black, Brown, and other ethnic studies into existing courses and through additional offerings—developed collaboratively by students,

51

teachers, and administrators—to increase understanding, rather than fear, of cultural differences."

When referring to minorities a large percentage of persons think black. This may be true for a good part of the country, but for other parts of the United States one must also think brown, red, yellow, white. And in many cities of the Southwest minorities are brown and nothing else. There are approximately ten million Spanish-speaking persons in the United States, two-thirds of whom are Mexican Americans. Mexican Americans (or Chicanos) are the second largest ethnic minority in the United States and the largest in the Southwest. Together the Brown and Black populations make up one-sixth of the total United States population and a majority in several major cities, which potentially comprises a significant political coalition.

Minorities have contributed more than their share in defending our country in wars. The proportion of Blacks and Mexican Americans drafted during the Vietnam War exceeds that of their numbers in the general population. During World War II, the Korean War, and in Vietnam, Blacks, Chicanos,[1] Indians, and Japanese Americans distinguished themselves fighting and dying thousands of miles from home. Perhaps a positive effect of the wars has been the returning of these veterans, demanding the rights and privileges at home for which they fought in Europe and Asia. This *pursuit of happiness* includes decent housing and jobs, a more equitable welfare system, participation in the political and legal processes, a relevant education, but above all to be treated as a bona fide citizen, a person, a human being.

The Cycle of Poverty

No one can say that the problems of the poor have not been researched, studied, examined, handled, committeed, sloganized. There is hardly a letter of the alphabet that has not been used to form an abbreviation for an agency. Businesses have invested personnel and resources on job training programs designed to diminish poverty. Church groups have been conspicuous in the attempt to enliven the conscience of the country about conditions related to poverty and race. Foundations are encouraging innovative programs to alleviate poverty and prejudice. But, unfortunately, this activity, this flood of concern engages but a minute percentage of the total population in the United States.

There is discrimination in all aspects of employment in both the public and private sectors. This includes hiring, rate of pay, and opportunity for promotion. Qualifications and tests for jobs often serve to eliminate minority workers from jobs which they are capable of performing, by imposing standards, language, and experience requirements that are unrealistic and unrelated to the work to be done.

Poverty is not restricted to minorities. There are poor whites in Appalachia and in the cities. But, the majority of persons from minority groups seems to be caught in this cycle of poverty. A report by the United States Office of Education concerning the urban student and his environment cites characteristics of homes in which economically disadvantaged students live:[2]

1. He and his family are apt to live on a diet which is less than adequate—if not insufficient. And he is likely to manifest inadequate health and energy levels for a sustained effort on demanding tasks, e.g., reading as taught by the school.
2. He lives in a world in which the mortality rates of women and babies in birth are higher and the life expectancies of men are lower than for other Americans.
3. Economically, he lives in a world in which unemployment, underemployment, and the inadequate welfare check are common facts of life. He learns, too, as his family already has, that his family's economic status is all too often a direct offshoot of racial discrimination. For even if he does finish high school or college, he will earn less than his white counterpart with the same years of schooling.
4. He lives in housing which is apt to be in poor condition—and it may very likely be overcrowded.
5. His family will probably pay more for this housing than it is worth simply because there is really nowhere else to go. A new home or a better apartment would be out of the question on his family's income—quite apart from the discrimination barrier.
6. Within his immediate experience, if not directly within his family, there may be problems resulting from divorce, separation, or desertion by one or the other of his parents. And, although only touched upon peripherally or implied, he will probably gain a knowledge of the problems associated with drug addiction, prostitution, and theft within his neighborhood—if not within his immediate family.
7. Within his family—and particularly if it is an extended family—he will develop a tough self-reliance, learn to cooperate, probably receive a prompt reaction in terms of physical discipline for stepping out of line, tolerate a high degree of noise, and experience considerable casualness in terms of daily routine.
8. The concepts, language, and problem-solving techniques he acquires will be primarily geared to his survival in the neighborhood and the necessary interactions in and demands of his family.

"The concepts, language, and problem-solving techniques he acquires will be primarily geared to his survival in the neighborhood . . ."

Being poor is a burden. Being a member of a minority in our society is a burden. Being a minority and poor is a double burden that few are able to successfully overcome under present welfare systems. In human terms this means that a Mexican American woman in West Texas, with four children at home and a husband in the hospital for a prolonged stay, has her claim for assistance denied because there is no caseworker who speaks Spanish and she cannot properly fill out the application form (in English) with its legalistic terminology. It means that a Black woman who has had the misfortune to have an illegitimate child must submit to periodic inconvenient "raids" by welfare officials who search under the bed for a man in the house. It means that Puerto Rican families in New York, unaware of the avenues of appeal, receive their winter clothing allowance in February, after their children have already missed two months of school because they have no coats or shoes. It means that a Black tenant farmer in Mississippi will receive his $60 a month for his family *if* he does not register to vote, or attend any political meetings.

It is the favorite game of the "Haves," especially those of conservative political persuasion, to revile the "Have-nots" and to decry welfare spending. Some of the more widely accepted myths about Welfare have been refuted by recent Department of Health, Education, and Welfare statistics:[3]

Myth—Welfare families have lots of children to get more money.
Fact—A typical family has a mother and three children. She gets $35 extra for another child.

Myth—The rolls are full of able-bodied loafers.
Fact—Less than 1% are unemployed males.

Myth—Welfare is only a dole (money).
Fact—Many services as well as money are given.

Myth—Give them more money and they'll spend it on beer and cars.
Fact—Most spend extra money on food, clothes, and better housing.

Myth—Most welfare children are illegitimate.
Fact—Less than one-third are born out of wedlock.

Myth—Once on welfare, always on welfare.
Fact—The average family is on welfare for two years.

Myth—Most welfare families are Black.
Fact—Only 46% are Black.

Myth—Why work when you can live it up on welfare?
Fact—Average payment for a family of four ranges from $60 a month in Mississippi to a high of $375 in Alaska.

In all states payments are below the poverty level.

Another commonly held *myth* is that only poor people receive welfare. The fact is that one of the biggest welfare programs in the country is through the Department of Agriculture which hands out millions of dollars each year to wealthy farmers and corporations for *not* growing crops. Indeed, the farmers' lobby is so strong that the poor are used to dispose of the agricultural surpluses through the "commodities" programs. This "in kind" assistance, in lieu of a cash grant, is one more way in which the dignity inherent in freedom of choice is denied the poor. How many Chicanos would eat that much peanut butter if they had a choice?

Another *myth*, widely believed, but which needs closer examination, is that there is much cheating going on among those who receive welfare. Of course, there are some who are receiving grants that they are not entitled to; however, the number of cases and the amount of money involved is virtually negligible as compared with the misrepresentations which middle- and upper-class American citizens include in their income tax reports. The amount of money lost to the government through income tax evasion is many times more than that lost through welfare cheating, not to mention the number of millionaires in this country who pay absolutely no tax at all.

Minorities have been increasingly forced to resort to Public Assistance. The Social Security Act, which set up our federal programs of income maintenance, is primarily based on an insurance concept, tied in with employment. The major portions which include retirement benefits (Old Age Survivors and Disability Insurance), Unemployment Insurance, Workmen's Compensation, and Medicare usually work to the disadvantage of the minority person, since the types of work which he has been allowed to do—domestic work, farm laborer work—have not been covered by these benefits. With the advancing technological gains and high unemployment rate, many find that they are without the proper training background on which to base future security.

They must then deal with the various welfare offices—those bureaucratic nightmares of administration—which often are more concerned with their maze of rules and regulations than with the needs of the people whom they are serving. The appeals procedure is an example of this confusion. When an applicant is turned down, or a recipient has aid terminated or reduced, often through lack of understanding on the client's part or language barriers, the appeal must be made first of all through the same office, through the same caseworker, the same supervisor where the problem arose in the first place.

The Office of Economic Opportunity Legal Aid services made people aware that they did have rights under the system and pressed for their claims. As increasing numbers of welfare clients began to realize that

they were not receiving what was legally theirs, and getting the runaround from caseworkers and officials, they began organizing to present their case as a group. Out of this developed, since the late 1960's, the Welfare Rights Organization (WRO), with its national office based in Washington, D.C. With the help of Office of Economic Opportunity lawyers, many WRO chapters demanded and got their rights. Tactics are used ranging from open conflict aimed at changing the system to collaboration with officials in redistributing the resources. The Welfare Rights Organization has helped many individuals, but more importantly, it has been instrumental in changing the attitudes and practices of public officials toward welfare recipients.

It is clear that the present system of public assistance is not functioning properly. Federal efforts at eliminating poverty through the Economic Opportunities Act had only limited success. It is estimated that by 1976 there will still be 21 million people in this country living below the poverty line with inadequate health, housing, and education.[4] A new approach is needed. Reform of the present system has been periodically undertaken, with the result that there has been little basic change in benefits or administration.

The one approach that seems most feasible is the guaranteed annual income, through a Cash Assistance Grant, similar to the Family Assistance Plan proposed by the Nixon Administration in 1971. Administered by the federal government, equally in all states, this would provide a minimum income for every family, or individual, to be supplemented by earnings if the recipient is able to work. It would go a long way in correcting some of the deficiencies existing in the Aid to Families with Dependent Children program, provided that the amount is sufficient for a decent standard of living. In contrast to the present system, it would encourage families to stay together and provide incentives for work. It must consist of cash grants, and eliminate the "in kind" aid, so that the recipient is provided with a greater degree of personal freedom and dignity in determining how to allocate his personal resources.

"If we had used violence we would have won contracts a long time ago, but they wouldn't have been lasting because we wouldn't have won respect. Wages are not the main issue in the strike. If wages were the issue our organization would disappear after recognition and an increase in pay. No, what is at stake is human dignity. If a man is not accorded respect, he cannot respect himself and if he does not respect himself, he cannot demand it."[5] These words from Cesar Chavez, director of the United Farm Workers Organizing Committee (UFWOC), imply more than economic survival for the agricultural worker. As a leader of the farm workers' movement Chavez has also become the spiritual leader for the advancement of the Mexican American cause, *la causa.*

America can certainly give the farm worker the minimum wages, the unemployment compensation, the health and social benefits, and the right to negotiate collectively. It is a shame that the hands that labor so hard to satisfy this abundantly-fed nation are in economic distress, they themselves lacking the basic staples. Our national poet, Carl Sandburg, understood the cries of the worker:

> Those who have nothing stand in two pressures:
> Either what they once had was taken away
> or they never had more than subsistence.
> From these hands pour a living cargo of overwhelming
> plenty from land and mill into the world's markets.
> Their pay for this is what is handed them
> Or they take no pay at all if the labor market is glutted
> > next month maybe
> > next year maybe
> > the work begins.[6]

There is a growing concern among *la Raza* and many others for the rights, dignity, and freedom of the migrant farm worker. Migrant needs—low income, irregularity of employment, exemption from social

legislation, inadequate education—are not seasonal, but a full-time operation.

Mexican Nationals take jobs away from United States Mexican American citizens. This is particularly true of green card holders along the border towns. The United States government grants them the immigration documents from which they derive the designation "green carders" despite the fact that there is no proof that they intend to establish residence in this country and, in fact, every evidence that they do not. There have been many allegations that commuters have been used as strike breakers in labor disputes in the United States. And there is substantial evidence that their daily migration depresses wages and creates unemployment for Mexican Americans who live along the border. The United States Attorney General is required by law to refuse entry to commuters if domestic workers are available. The evidence suggests that this law is not enforced. For the United States government to encourage the commuter practice is simply a failure to take care of its own people and therefore a failure to do justice to them, and justice is above charity.

It was the grape boycott that shook the conscience of the plight of the Mexican farm worker in the rich San Joaquin Valley in California. Today the grape represents the blood and sweat, the life and bread of many migrants. It is the grape that unites Chicanos to improve the economic, educational, and social conditions of *la Raza*. The significance of the grape strike, *la huelga*, aside from the farm workers' attempt to unionize and to receive equitable pay for their labor, is symbolic of the Mexican American quest for a full role in our society.

Along with a new concept of income maintenance for those unable to support themselves must come greater efforts to aid those working poor, by raising the minimum wage level and enlarging the coverage to many of the jobs in which the unskilled worker finds himself. Social Security, Workmen's Compensation, and Unemployment Benefits must be expanded also so that the jobs that many minorities have traditionally been allowed to hold will have the dignity of recognition and worthiness associated with them.

Legal Rights

"Justice restrained is justice frustrated, justice delayed is justice denied, and justice denied is an abridgment of human respect and dignity, violative of human decency, and a basis for the sowing of distrust, discord, and a foothold for hate."[7]

Minorities have always suffered violations of their constitutional rights, and have not had full or ready access to all of the processes involved in the administration of justice. Recurring complaints are made with special frequency by minorities of police brutality, denial of bail, excessive jail and prison sentences, harassment in registration to vote and in voting, exclusion from juries. Minorities do not have sufficient members of their own groups to represent them before the tribunals of justice. Therefore, is it any wonder that they have deep mistrust and suspicion about the administration of justice?

Harassment of Blacks and Chicanos, particularly the young, by police, rather than physical brutality, is a major conflict in many communities. A particular problem confronting these youths is the police practice of arrest on suspicion. This has been described as arresting everyone in sight or within reach when a crime has been committed. The result of this is that many young men accumulate long arrest records without ever having been tried or convicted of a crime. An arrest record, with or without convictions, is difficult to overcome in educational or employment opportunities.

Although discrimination in jury selection is prohibited by the Constitution and proscribed by various civil rights acts, violations are still flagrant today in certain states. Discrimination in jury selection is also reflected by the jurors themselves. How can juries with only selected segments of the population be intimately familiar with the conditions of local minorities and make impartial judgments of their acts? Serving as a grand or trial juror is the only opportunity most citizens have to participate actively in the administration of justice. Some say that it is hard to find "qualified jurors" among minorities (draft boards do not have trouble finding qualified Blacks and Chicanos to fight in wars). Undoubtedly, when the composition of juries changes so will the results. A jury system is fair only if the jury selection is fair and only if the jury truly reflects a cross section of the people. When this fails, then the miscarriages of justice result, such as have been witnessed in the deep South.

In some areas minorities have testified that their rights to vote have been compromised by means ranging from outright intimidation to restrictive laws which make registration difficult. In certain Texas communities, Chicanos described a variety of attempts to lower the Mexican American turnout. First, elections are held when people are away harvesting the crops. They allege that welfare recipients are intimidated, that police ticket cars for minor defects on election day, and that election officials attempt to confuse the voters by asking questions like "Where is your property?" instead of "Where do you live?", thus making some eligible voters believe they must own property in order to vote.

The Mexican American Legal Defense and Educational Fund (MALDEF) is a legal organization representing Mexican Americans to bring about social change through the judicial process. Before its founding, only a handful of cases had been tried to adjudicate the constitutional rights of Mexican Americans. Because few Mexican Americans have been in the Courts, the judiciary is not familiar with the social, economic, and political problems of this group. So, the task of MALDEF has been in part to educate the judiciary. Matters litigated by MALDEF include education, employment, voting rights, police misconduct, media, immigrants, and farm workers. The inability to communicate between Spanish-speaking American citizens and English-speaking officials has complicated the problem of administering justice equitably.

Two extreme examples of violations of constitutional rights involving United States citizens were (1) during the Great Depression of the thirties, local authorities in the United States organized and helped finance the shipment of tens of thousands of Mexican Americans back to Mexico, as a device to relieve themselves of welfare support and to ease the terrifying problems of unemployment of domestic workers; (2) the roundup of Japanese Americans during World War II and placing them in relocation camps (a euphemism for concentration camps) as a means to prevent "subversive" activities. Because of tax claims, many Japanese families never recovered their land upon return. The Japanese encampment was a reversal of the fundamental premise: innocent until proven guilty.

The Treaty of Guadalupe Hidalgo (1848) guaranteed property, civil and cultural rights to the Spanish-speaking persons annexed to the United States as a result of the United States-Mexico war. As stipulated in the treaty, the Mexicans who chose to remain in conquered territory were guaranteed the rights—property, political, social—that are given to all American citizens. It should never be forgotten that, with the exception of the Indians, the Mexican Americans are the only minority in the United States who have been annexed by conquest—the only minority, Indians again excepted, whose rights are specifically safeguarded by a written provision.

Under the superior military and political forces of the United States government, through outright conquest and unenforced treaties, Indians and Spanish-speaking people in the Southwest have lost vast amounts of land. Today, nearly four centuries after the Spaniards first settled New Mexico, problems growing from land grants are a source of continuing controversy, despite efforts for the past 100 years to straighten them out.

Resolutions have been introduced to create a special House Committee in Congress to investigate land grant claims in the Southwest. The proposal calls for a "full and complete investigation and study into the legal, political, and diplomatic status of lands which were subject to grants from the King of Spain and from the government of Mexico prior to the acquisition of the American Southwest as a result of the Treaty of Guadalupe Hidalgo."[8]

"The Japanese encampment [during World War II] was a reversal of the fundamental premise: innocent until proven guilty." Many Japanese-Americans were compelled to sell their businesses.

The idea of uniting the land grant organizations—with the ultimate aim of returning all the grant land to its legal owners—came with the creation in 1963 of the Alianza Federal de Mercedes led by Reies Lopez Tijerina. Although the land is the issue, Tijerina's real concern—in and out of prison—has been poverty, lack of education, discrimination, denial of civil rights to Spanish-speaking Americans.

Quality Education

Through walkouts, protests, boycotts, and sit-ins, minority students are demanding a relevant education. What do these students want? They want an education. They want freedom. They want equality in opportunities. They want books and curriculum revised to include their ethnic contributions. They want instructors, counselors, and administrators from the same ethnic background or persons who at least have empathy toward their needs. They want quality education, which, after all, is the stated goal of our educational institutions.

Contributions of the various ethnic groups in this country should be integrated in all aspects of the school experiences: history, geography, art, music, literature. Multicultural education means not only the integration of students and staff but also the integration of the curriculum. Ethnic studies must not be treated as an isolated program or be taught only in certain parts of the school year, but should be taught on a continuing basis to *all* students.

Parity must have priority in deciding the fate of minority students. In planning and implementing programs, the community, students, faculty, and administrators must work together if curriculum is going to be relevant and viable. The United States Office of Education Urban Education Task Force supports the principle that parents and local community residents must be participants in the educational process if effective changes in education are to be achieved in the schools. The role of the community must be expanded in part because of the relative failures of school boards, school administrations, and teacher organizations to meet local educational needs. In addition, the community has a legitimate role in education decision making on the basis of American traditions and its ability to make valid contributions.

Setting criteria for measuring equal educational opportunity can no longer be the province of the established "experts." The policy makers must now listen to those for whom they say they are operating, which means, of course, that they must be willing to share the powers of policy making.

Cultural genocide occurs very early in the lives of minority students. The use of achievement and aptitude tests for selecting people and sorting them out has persisted down through the years and is unquestionably most prevalent in our public school system today—even, of course, right down to the preschool and kindergarten levels where "readiness tests" have become so predominant in delaying the entrance of children to kindergarten and the first grade. This widespread use of tests for purposes of selection, for deciding from kindergarten on up who will succeed and who will fail, is indicative of the kind of competitive culture that characterizes all of our social institutions, including our schools.

Placement in Educable Mentally Retarded (EMR) and remedial classes is tantamount to a life sentence of illiteracy and public dependency. We must look into other factors beyond mental ability that might produce a low test result: poverty, hunger, linguistic and cultural background, motivational learning styles, psychological effect of poor clothing and living conditions. It is of paramount importance that no child be placed in an EMR class unless it is clear beyond reasonable doubt that he suffers from an impairment of ability to learn. Until we find better means of measuring the potential of students or intervene in the administration of such tests, there should be a moratorium on testing for the non-English and limited-English-speaking students.

A stereotype by the majority culture can become a tremendously damaging element for the minority student, since the perpetuated stereotype often becomes a self-fulfilling prophecy. There is additionally the danger that the student himself will come to believe the stereotype and begin to act the assigned role, thus fulfilling his part of the self-fulfilling prophecy. It is easy to see how a teacher or a counselor who believes a minority student to be a poor scholar will soon have the student behaving accordingly.

We must become acquainted with institutions and agencies—along with their administrative heads—which have long neglected minority students. In order to effect changes in curriculum it behooves us to identify our targets:

1. Teacher-training institutions
2. State education departments
3. Teacher certification agencies
4. Local boards of education
5. Commercial companies—textbooks and tests

Once the decision makers (targets) have been identified, a coalition of the various ethnic groups and interested groups can perform a very important service in making demands to implement relevant programs for minority students.

Puerto Rican and Mexican American students who begin school in our educational system without speaking English run into the hundreds of thousands. The trend has been to force these students to repeat grade levels and to postpone all serious academic work until they learn English. This latter approach commonly leaves the Spanish-speaking student three to five years behind his Anglo counterpart by the time he is a teenager. The United States Civil Rights Commission report on the Mexican American states that there is a strong relationship between grade level repetition and low student achievement. Thus, the State of Texas, which has the highest proportion of grade repetition for Mexican Americans in the first and fourth grades, also has 74 percent—the highest proportion—of Mexican American eighth graders reading below grade level.[9]

Most Chicano students are still isolated in schools which are predominantly Mexican American, situations caused by de facto segregation or gerrymandered school boundaries. While the segregated Anglo American student is equally deprived of a heterogeneous environment which

Minority students "want instructors, counselors, administrators from the same ethnic background or persons who at least have empathy toward their needs."

could lead to increased educational development, he is rarely confronted with a school environment which directly rejects the culture of his home environment: lifestyles, clothing, food, family relationships, holidays, physical appearances.

The effect of federal, state, and local aid for schooling the disadvantaged makes but a small alteration in the basic system of support, which is unequal to begin with. Perhaps the greatest tragedy in the financial chain is that, when additional dollars finally filter down to the inner-city schools, they are often squandered on traditional approaches that have consistently failed the inner-city student. The record of spending on compensatory education programs—instead of on enrichment programs—is an outstanding testimony to the futility of doing more of the same things that have not worked in the past. Federal, state, and local programs must change institutions, not only students.

Existing teacher-preparation courses have not provided the experiences which will enable a teacher to teach successfully in schools having predominantly minority students, much less to teach ethnic studies. Objectives to better prepare the teacher to do an effective job with minority students include:

1. The teacher will come to understand his own attitudes, anxieties, insecurities, and prejudices through a program of sensitivity development.
2. The teacher will understand the nature of the student's environment and culture (including language) through a program of teacher interaction in the school community.
3. The teacher will become knowledgeable of learning styles of his students and competent in effective teaching skills and techniques.

The notion of cultural superiority has seriously harmed the United States in its dealings with other nations. Whereas European students grow up with the notion of cultural diversity and frequently learn a second and third language in the course of their formal schooling, schools in the United States commonly isolate the students from cultural exchange.

The need for recognizing the bilingual-bicultural student as a positive force in our society is beyond question. It is rather paradoxical that in the Southwest some schools have forbidden students to speak Spanish, while at the same time we give lip service to the wisdom of learning foreign languages. Millions of dollars are spent supporting programs that teach a foreign language to monolingual English-speaking students in our schools and colleges. Spanish is one of the more popular electives.

Bilingual education serves five positive purposes for the student and the school:

1. It reduces retardation through ability to learn with the mother tongue immediately.
2. It reinforces the relations of the school and the home through a common communication bond.
3. It projects the individual into an atmosphere of personal identification, self-worth, and achievement.
4. It gives the student a base for success in the field of work.
5. It preserves and enriches the cultural and human resources of a people.

We as educators must take a positive approach to see that programs are designed to make students succeed, not fail, that programs include students, not exclude. I am hoping that in the decade of the '70s we will begin talking about minority students not as disadvantaged, but as *advantaged,* which means that they must be given the opportunity to develop their full potential within their experience base.

Conclusion

Although I have focused on the case of the Mexican American in this chapter, it is obvious to the reader that injustices are equally applicable to other minorities in this country.

The examination of social justice should be in the heart of the curriculum along with social participation activities. In the promotion and practice of cultural democracy, we as teachers must make it clear that all minority groups have made a contribution to this country, and that this land, *our land,* was built by many different persons representing distinct cultural and linguistic traits. We must institute a philosophy that argues that an individual need not lose his identity with his ethnic group in order to succeed in our society, one that argues recognition of the worth of the individual's heritage, one that respects the value system of his culture.

Awareness and Social Action Questions

Social justice can be integrated in the various aspects of the curriculum. The teacher and students can research the problems and assets of minorities, invite resource persons to the classroom to further aid in understanding our multicultural society. Students can assess their own behavior to see if it is in line with their own ideals and values. Assignments in the school and community can help students translate their beliefs into action.

The following are examples of discussion and action questions:

1. Why does it take militant action to fight for one's rights? Can this be done in a peaceful manner?

2. React to the statement of the housewife: "If farm workers are paid more, I will have to pay more for fruits and vegetables."

3. Social injustices may be by commission or omission; name some books, periodicals, and films in the school library which stereotype minorities. What social science texts currently used by the school system omit contributions of minorities?

4. Can an ethnic minority candidate win in a predominantly Anglo neighborhood? Are there or have there been minorities elected in your community? If so, where did their support come from?

5. In many state prisons, e.g., Attica, the inmate population is heavily minority, far out of proportion for the state as a whole. What factors account for this?

6. Is low income the only reason that keeps minorities in ghettos and barrios? Investigate real estate brokers, developers, and financial institutions in dealing with housing for minorities. Is your community integrated? What effect does this have on busing? What are some alternatives to busing?

7. It is incongruous that such a rich nation like ours has so many people on welfare. Investigate practices in the local community that keep people on welfare. How do other countries handle welfare? Do you know where the welfare office is in your city? Who is eligible to receive public assistance in your state? How do you apply? How much would your family receive each month if you were on welfare?

8. Are judges appointed or elected in your community, county, state? How many are of distinct ethnic groups? What is the practice of grand and petit jury selection? Obtain the list of jurors within the past year to check for ethnic minorities.

9. Land expansion by the United States has been done by wars, treaties, purchases, and outright possession with the resultant action that minorities like the Indians and Mexicans have suffered. Under what condition was the land in your community obtained? Who were the former owners? Who owns most of the land now? What percentage of the land is owned by minorities?

10. How are test results used in your school system? How do they affect minority students? What percentage of minority students drops out of school? What percentage goes to college? Ask the school counselor to talk to the class about uses of tests and counseling practices among minorities.

FOOTNOTES

[1] During World War II and the Korean War, 17 Mexican Americans received the Congressional Medal of Honor. For more on this subject see Raul Morin, *Among the Valiant* (Los Angeles: Borden Publishing Co,, 1963).

[2] *Task Force on Urban Education,* U.S. Department of Health, Education, and Welfare, Office of Education (Washington, D.C., 1969).

[3] *Findings of the 1971 AFDC Study,* U.S. Department of Health, Education, and Welfare (Washington, D.C., January, 1972).

[4] Robert S. Benson and Harold Wolman, *Counterbudget,* The National Urban Coalition. A Blueprint for Changing National Priorities, 1971-72 (New York: Praeger Publishers, 1971), p. 48.

[5] Joan Levin Ecklein and Armand Lauffer, *Community Organizers and Social Planners* (New York: John Wiley and Sons, Inc. and Council on Social Work Education, 1972), p. 34. For more on Cesar Chavez, see cover story in *Time,* July 4, 1969.

[6] Carl Sandburg, excerpt from *The People, Yes* (New York: Harcourt Brace Jovanovich, Inc.). Reprinted with permission.

[7] Speech by Mario G. Obledo, Mexican American Legal Defense and Educational Fund, before the Commission on Mexican American Affairs Archdiocese of San Antonio, University of Texas Medical School, September 25, 1971.

[8] *Land Grant Problems in New Mexico* (Albuquerque *Journal,* 1969), p. 23.

[9] *The Unfinished Education,* Report II of Mexican American Educational Series, United States Commission on Civil Rights (Washington, D.C., October, 1971), p. 31.

BIBLIOGRAPHY

Adoff, Arnold (ed.). *Black on Black: Commentaries by Negro Americans.* New York: The Macmillan Company, 1968. Includes penetrating and highly readable analyses by Blacks of the American racial dilemma. Provoking recommendations for the resolution of our racial conflicts.

Cahn, Edgar S. *Our Brother's Keeper: The Indian in White America.* New York: World Publishing Company, 1969. A series of accounts told by Indians themselves to expose the shocking economic, political, and cultural exploitation of the first Americans.

Cloward, Richard A., and Piven, Frances F. *Regulating the Poor: The Functions of Public Welfare.* New York: Pantheon Books, 1971. Authors argue that public assistance or "relief" serves the economic and political order so that during periods of mass unemployment and disorder welfare is expanded and during periods of stability the program is contracted to rush recipients into the labor force.

Committee for Economic Development: A Statement by the Research and Policy Committee. *Education for the Urban Disadvantaged.* New York, New York, 1971. This policy statement reflects two areas of interest: (a) a concern for the equality and effectiveness of education and (b) ways of alleviating poverty in the United States, especially among the urban disadvantaged.

Dorsen, Norman (ed.). *The Rights of Americans, What They Are—What They Should Be.* New York: Pantheon Books, 1970. The book's aim is to give the reader a complete survey of what is currently going on in every area of law that has an effect on personal freedom.

Douglas, William O. *Points of Rebellion.* New York: Random House, 1970. A short, direct, easy-to-read book by the liberal Justice of the Supreme Court. Douglas argues that young people and minorities are right to rise up against widespread poverty, segregation, inequitable laws, and inadequate education.

Galarza, Ernesto. *Spiders in the House and Workers in the Field.* South Bend: University of Notre Dame Press, 1970. Documents long drawn out legal battles between Cesar Chavez Farm Union and grape growers. Study is important to the understanding of today's farm policies and political manipulations and exploitation of not only the Chicano, but all poor people in America.

Harrington, Michael. *The Other America.* Baltimore: Penguin Books, 1963. Classic work describes how the poor in the United States are alienated and excluded from the mainstream of American life.

Haslam, G. (ed.). *Forgotten Pages of American Literature.* New York: Houghton Mifflin Company, 1970. Literary contributions by writers of various ethnic groups. Book corrects social injustice of omission of these authors in most American literature texts.

Jackson, George. *Soledad Brothers: The Prison Letters of George Jackson.* New York: Bantam Books, 1970. Letters give vivid account of conditions in Soledad State Prison in California and how the brothers considered themselves political prisoners.

Mexican Americans and the Administration of Justice in the Southwest. Washington, D.C.: U.S. Government Printing Office, 1970. The Commission on Civil Rights documents that American citizens of Mexican descent in five southwestern states (Texas, California, Arizona, Colorado, New Mexico) are being denied equal protection of the law in the administration of justice.

National Elementary School Principal. (November, 1970), V. L, No. 2. A special issue on the education of the Spanish-speaking with articles by leading Mexican American and Puerto Rican educators.

Ogawa, Dennis. *From Japs to Japanese: The Evolution of Japanese-American Stereotypes.* Berkeley: McCatcham Publishing Corporation, 1971. This work describes the evolution of attitudes toward Japanese from World War II to the present. A delineation of the stereotypes, an examination of their salient dimensions, and an analysis of their functions are the primary concern of this work.

Ryan, William. *Blaming the Victim.* New York: Vintage Books, 1971. This book reveals how the blame is put on the victims of poverty, instead of the real villains of our society: racism and elitism which also affect our so-called liberals.

Barbara A. Sizemore

BARBARA A. SIZEMORE is Associate Secretary of the American Association of School Administrators, Arlington, Virginia. Ms. Sizemore received her B.A. and M.A. degrees from Northwestern University in Latin and Elementary Education. She is currently completing a Ph.D. in educational administration at the University of Chicago. She is a former elementary and junior high school teacher, and principal of Forrestville High School in Chicago. Ms. Sizemore has been an Instructor at Northeastern Illinois State University, a Staff Associate at the University of Chicago, Midwest Administration Center, and Director-District Superintendent of the Woodlawn Experimental Schools Project in Chicago. She has spoken at numerous national educational conferences, including the National Policy Conference on Education for Blacks sponsored by the Congressional Black Caucus of the United States Congress, and the Study Commission on Undergraduate Education and the Education of Teachers. Ms. Sizemore has served as a consultant to many organizations, including the Governor's Office of Human Resources (State of Illinois), and the National Panel on High Schools and Adolescent Education. Her articles have appeared in Educational Leadership, *the* Notre Dame Journal of Education *and* Phi Delta Kappan. *She contributed to the books* Racial Crisis in American Education *and* Black Self-Concept: Implications For Education and Social Science.

BARBARA A. SIZEMORE

4

Shattering
the Melting Pot Myth

The 1950's brought a non-violent black revolt stimulating all liberty-loving citizens to support Martin Luther King, Jr., in his attempts to achieve his dream. The 1960's ushered in black nationalism which rose from this frustrated drive for equality through integration, and the fiery oratory of Malcolm X championed a new separatism which summoned Stokely Carmichael's demand for black power. Black America was spurred to a new understanding of the American dilemma described by Harold Cruse in this way:

> ... this dilemma rests on the fact that America which idealizes the rights of the individual above everything else is, in reality, a nation dominated by the social power of groups, classes, in-groups and cliques—both ethnic and religious.[1]

Cruse pointed out that the three main power groups—Protestants, Catholics and Jews—neither wanted nor needed to become integrated with each other, for their very power resided in the collective strength of the group.

According to Cruse, black intellectuals and artists had missed the boat when they allowed the illusion of integration and the individual pursuit of achievement to blind them to the potential power of the black masses. He attacked the goal of integration, labeling it cultural negation, and recommended a cultural, economic and political movement as a correction of this inaccurate conception of reality.

73

Stating that ethnic groups in the United States constitute a "motley collection of refugees from Fatherland poverty who worship daily at the altar of white Anglo-Saxon Protestant superiority," Cruse accused this Anglo-Saxon ideal of effectively dissuading, crippling and smothering the development of a democratic cultural pluralism, and questioned the policy of integration through the imposition of this ideal which stigmatized the cultures of other ethnic groups.[2] Called the silent majority, these "unmeltable ethnics" aroused the national interest in the 1970's and during the presidential election campaign of 1972. Responding to their interests, the President emphasized aid to parochial schools, anti-busing and anti-abortion legislation and strict constructionism.

This chapter contends that ethnic groups do exist and have never melted. It will attempt to (1) trace the origin of the melting pot and define the concepts used in these explanations, (2) specify the relationship between the melting pot theory, the capitalistic process and culture, (3) describe the separatist ethnoreligious models used by excluded groups to achieve power within the framework of capitalism, and (4) relate these findings to educational institutions and programs.

The Melting Pot and the Spirit of Capitalism

The melting pot myth emerged from the need to force the many immigrants into the white Anglo-Saxon Protestant cultural mainstream. According to Brossard, this need arose out of responses to nativism, the intense opposition to an internal alien minority group. Nativism stood for a particular nationalism which affirmed a common American culture and society and called for a reduction in non-American elements and a curtailment of foreign domination of American culture and society.[3] Job competition stands out as the chief agitator of nativistic movements. Describing the Irish immigration in Boston, he says that native workers protested against Irish competition and struggled to define what an American was not.[4]

Brossard asserts that the Irish received a nativist response for seven basic reasons: (1) their high visibility, (2) their labor concentration, (3) their preferences for the professional services of their own group, (4) their magnified native self-consciousness, (5) a collective social prejudice directed against them, (6) servile notions defining a native American elite, and (7) their religion.[5] The institutionalization of the melting pot theory was necessary in order to destroy competing cultural ideals.

The next step was legitimation. Berger and Luckmann define legitimation as the process of explaining and justifying symbolic universes which are bodies of theoretical tradition that integrate competing meanings and encompass the institutional order in a symbolic totality.[6] The Protestant Ethic and the spirit of capitalism provided the symbolic universe for the legitimation of the melting pot theory.[7] It advanced the notion that individual hard work earned success, and this impulse toward success must find expression in capitalistic terms.

Based on a philosophy of avarice, the spirit of capitalism promoted the idea that the individual's duty was to increase his capital. Honesty, industry, and frugality were virtues in so far as they were useful in this pursuit. The acceptance of white Anglo-Saxon Protestant ethnocentrism was the key to access to opportunity. Consequently, individuals from other ethnic groups believed that it was necessary to embrace these values and to conform.[8] Some changed their names, broke away and dropped all connections with the old ethnic community. But, most immigrants were excluded from effective participation in the interdependent competitive model[9] of capitalism through the economic paradigm of supply and demand in labor as Brossard has indicated; therefore, the preservation of the group power was an imperative to maintenance of the group's gains. Therein lay the contradiction between conformity to the white Anglo-Saxon Protestant ideal and the preservation of ethnic differences.

If A represents groups with power and B represents groups with no power, the social order could be described as one where A has power over B (A/B). Under capitalism when A wins, B loses and vice versa.[10] Inherent in the model there will always be losers. The question, then, is not "Will there be unemployment?" but rather "Who will be unemployed?" A's problem is how to keep B powerless, and B's problem is how to achieve power and parity. Since capitalism required losers, the myth of the melting pot was necessary to promote the belief in individual mobility through hard work and competition.

According to Weber,[11] capitalism was encouraged through a new conception of religion which taught that the pursuit of wealth was a new duty. The creed of Calvin changed the moral standards and converted a frailty into an ornament of the spirit, canonizing vices as economic virtues. Capitalism was the social counterpart of Calvinist theology.

Weber explained that the doctrine of predestination was the most characteristic dogma of Calvinistic theology. Some men were chosen for eternal grace and others were damned to everlasting death. This inhumane doctrine created a feeling of inner loneliness in the single individual who was forced to follow his path alone to meet a destiny which had been decreed for him from eternity. Calvinist theology prepared one to accept this place in the society. The perseverance of the individual in this place and within the limits which God had assigned to him was a religious duty.

The individual was forced to attain the goods necessary for survival yet to struggle for profit free from the limits set by his needs. These ends controlled the form and direction of his economic activity. Weber posits that the capitalistic economy of the present day is an immense cosmos into which the individual is born, and which presents itself as an unalterable order of things in which he must live. It forces the individual involved in the system of market relationships to conform to capitalistic rules of action. So the earning of more and more money became an end in itself and man was dominated by it.

However, many new immigrants were Catholic and unencumbered by the Protestant Ethic. Their ethic was one of intention. A single good or bad action was credited to the doer determining his temporal and eternal fate. A man was not an absolutely clearly defined unity to be judged one way or the other, but his moral life was normally subject to conflicting motives and his action contradictory. To the Catholic the absolution of his church was a compensation for his own imperfection.[12] While the church taught the new immigrants to work hard, to obey the law, to respect their leaders, and to concentrate on private, familial relationships, its focus was not upon immediate and intense responsibility, but upon the long-term, quiet processes of growth. Hence, the Catholic assertion has been more conservative, more easygoing with a tough view of authority.[13]

Other newcomers were Jewish and their religion dictated the preservation of the highest human values for the sake of God for whom they are witnesses and for His Law of the world.[14] The committed Jew enters into a B'rith, the Covenant, the partnership with God. The Talmud teaches that God has provided legitimate pleasures for man's enjoyment, and God will hold man strictly accountable for every one which he has ungratefully declined.[15] The Jewish ethic is characterized by a deep love for personal freedom, a fierce trust in the goodness of human nature left to itself and unimpeded by governments, a longing for a socialism without totalitarianism, a libertarian and often anarchic vision of a perfect society and a condemnation of civilization for its tendency to breed discontents.[16]

Apart from religious tenets, however, the basic axiom of capitalism is that land, factories, machines, offices and other assets are owned privately, by a small group of people who use their control to organize the work process and sell goods and services in order to make profits for themselves.[17] Food, housing, clothing and medical care are among these goods and services. As the development of the forces of production (tools, buildings, equipment, technology and organizational techniques) increases, the potential social surplus (that part of the total material product of a society that is left over after the basic requirements needed to maintain the people at a subsistence level of living has been met) that can be produced increases. One group produces the surplus and another appropriates it.

The Melting Pot and the Concept of Culture

The Melting Pot, a play by the British-Jewish writer Israel Zangwill, was first performed in 1908, and depicted America as God's Crucible, the great melting pot. Moynihan and Glazer say that the melting pot did not happen even in the play. Their account of the play was that the drama was concerned with Jewish separatism and Russian anti-Semitism "with a German concert master and an Irish maid thrown in."[18] Zangwill, himself, was engaged in one of the deterrent processes to "melting" in that he was a separatist and a Zionist. They conclude that the merging of the varying streams of population differentiated from one another by origin, religion and outlook was deferred.

On the other hand, Krug argues that it was the general effectiveness of the melting pot theory which made a balkanization of America possible. He postulates that America owes a debt of gratitude to the inventors of the melting pot theory, for otherwise a young nation like the United States could not have absorbed such a large and unprecedented influx of immigrants from so many countries, speaking so many languages, worshipping in so many different ways, and still survive as a united country.[19] Krug seems to avoid the needs of capitalism in his analysis while Handlin makes these observations:

> Becoming an American meant therefore not the simple conformity to a previous pattern, but the adjustment to the needs of a new situation. In the process the immigrants became more rather than less conscious of their own peculiarities. As the immediate environment called for the succession of fresh institutions and novel modes of behavior, the immigrants found themselves progressively separated as groups.[20]

Additionally, during the great immigrations capitalism was expanding at an astounding rate. There was a great need for unskilled labor to build canals and railroads. Two hundred thousand miles of paved highways were laid in 1910.

Another Krug assertion is that the stress on American unity and the conscious attempt to ignore or to minimize the ethnic backgrounds of the children of the immigrants made it possible for thousands of able sons and daughters of the newcomers to rise rapidly to positions of prominence in business, government, education and the professions. Handlin has much to say on this issue:

> In the end, all was tinged with vanity, with success as cruel as failure. Whatever lot their sons had drawn in this new contentious world, the family's oneness would not survive it.[22]

Moreover, Erickson indicates that there is evidence to suggest that the subcultural orientation is psychologically preferable to the emphasis on the societal mainstream. Further, he says that membership in well-integrated subgroups may be necessary for full participation in the larger world.[23]

An ethnic group is any group of the same race, religion and/or nationality who shares a common and distinctive culture. However, Moynihan and Glazer define ethnic groups as interest groups. They say that the ethnic group became a new social form, not a survival from the age of mass immigration.[24] According to their study and in agreement with Handlin, ethnic groups are continually re-created by new experiences even after distinctive language, custom and culture losses. They show that these interest groups carved out work niches and experiences for their own and passed the fruits of these labors to their children through inheritance.

Krug's position is that the public schools were the basic workshops for democracy for immigrant groups. He says that the members of the various ethnic and religious groups learned to live and work together and subsequently these schools made it possible for Jewish, Polish, Italian and German children to attain positions of prominence in all walks of life. Yet, he concedes that these same schools did not work as well for blacks, the Spanish-speaking and Indians. He admits readily, too, that the melting pot theory is irrelevant for non-white ethnics.[25] He does not emphasize the fact that capitalist expansion no longer needed unskilled labor, and, thus affected the position of non-whites in the economy. Additionally, the concept of culture may be useful in developing an explanation of the plight of these ethnic groups as well as the concept of racism.

Wax uses Barth's[26] definition of ethnic groups as categories of ascription and identification by the actors themselves and thus having the characteristic of organizing interaction between people. But, Wax does not use culture as a defining concept. He says:

"Indianness" is a socio-political rather than a cultural identity.

He says that it is misleading both to Indian and non-Indian students to portray Indianness as if it were a matter of preserving the traits of an aboriginal and static culture.[27] In adopting this stance, Wax comes close to Moynihan and Glazer's definition of interest groups. Yet, something is missing when culture is excluded.

If the schools reflect the society and the culture, then certain cultural imperatives may operate as causes of social problems.[28] In man's attempt to preserve and reproduce himself, he has been in constant conflict with

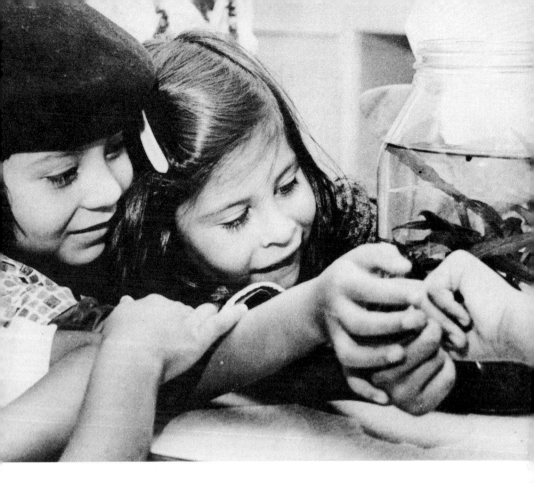

". . . ethnic groups are continually recreated by new experiences . . ."

the land, nature and other men. Sékou Touré defines culture in this context:

> Creative action springing from a universal imperative and culture, which is its reflection subject and effect, both constitute universal realities. Wherever there is the necessity of creation, we find culture. As the expression of the relationships between man and society, between man, society and nature, culture poses in the most pressing terms of the problem of the dialectic of the general and the particular. Culture is an expression, in particular, specific forms, of a general problem—that of the relationships linking man to his environment.[29]

These relationships are greatly affected by differentiations in the structure of the object world with regard to orientation to the polarity of gratification and deprivation.[30]

Egos interact with social objects called alters and with non-social objects. Social objects have expectations which are oriented toward egos producing a complementarity of expectations. This system can be analyzed in terms of the degree of conformity of ego's action with alter's expectations and vice versa, and the contingent reactions of alter to ego's action are sometimes called sanctions.

The effect of these sanctions is determined by ego's need-dispositions and the ability of alter to gratify or deprive. There, then, is a double contingency inherent in such an interaction. Ego's gratifications are dependent on his selection among available alternatives and alter's reaction will be determined by ego's selection. This double contingency produces the precondition for cultural patterns. Foreign groups emigrated to the United States. They brought with them their cultural patterns, language, customs, religion and more. Their needs threatened the cultural patterns of the Americans already here. Thinking of the foreign groups as egos and the WASP Americans as alters, Parsons and Shils shed light on their situation through their discussion of the double contingency.

> If punishment or reward by alter is repeatedly manifested under certain conditions, this reaction acquires for ego the meaning of an appropriate consequence of ego's conformity with or deviation from the norms of a shared symbolic system. A shared symbolic system is a system of "ways of orienting," plus those "external symbols" which control these ways of orienting, the system being so geared into the action systems of both ego and alter that the external symbols bring forth the same or a complementary pattern of orientation in both of them. Such a system, with its mutuality of normative orientation, is logically the most elementary form of culture. In this elementary social relationship, as well as in a large-scale social system, culture provides the standards (value-orientations) which are applied in evaluative processes. Without culture neither human personalities nor human social systems would be possible.[31]

Thus complementarity of expectations in the processes of human interaction is central in the analysis of the cultural patterns. The foreign-born found that alter demanded conformity to the A group norm, but they also found that individually they were powerless. The very cultural patterns which formed their source of unity also threatened their right to participate. This was the dilemma of these groups.

Nativist responses did not deter B groups from their search for a way out. The cost of assimilation was too great; therefore, most excluded groups opted for routes to inclusion, or full participation in the social order with preservation of their ethnic differences, one of which was the right to be Catholic or Jewish. The obstacles to the attainment of inclusion are the institutions which perpetuate, promote and preserve the symbolic universes of the dominant group. In this social order, where so many groups with varying cultural patterns reside, pluralism and desires for inclusion confound the double contingency and the complementarity of expectations. Pluralism is here defined as the condition of cultural parity among ethnic groups in a common society.

The melting pot theory was to be operationalized in the schools through education, one of the two great equalizers in the society. However, schools financed through the property tax are unequal and reproduce the hierarchical social division of labor. Children of affluence receive more years of schooling than children of poverty. Both the amount and the content of their education greatly facilitate their movement into positions similar to their parents.[32] The other great equalizer, the progressive income tax, was to place the burden of government on taxpayers according to their ability to pay. Yet, millionaires pay no income taxes. FHA finances middle-class homes. Lockheed goes on welfare. Oil millionaires profit from government subsidy, as do farmers, some of whom are U.S. Senators.

The Power-Inclusion Model

The great myth that the public schools were effective mobility vehicles for white American immigrant groups has been a notorious diehard. Greeley shows a difference of more than twenty percentage points between the children of northern Italian immigrants and those of southern Italians.[33] Handlin describes the schools for immigrants in graphic terms:

> Mostly the teachers kept their distance, kept flickering the hope that a transfer might take them to a nicer district with nicer pupils from nicer homes. When that hope died, bitterness was born; and there was thereafter more savagery than love in their instruction.[34]

Obviously, one individual could not buck such a system without support. Most B groups have used a separatist model to provide it. This separatist model for group mobility and full citizenship in the American social order has been called a Power-Inclusion Model. It has two strategies, violence and nonviolence, and five stages. See Figure 1, p. 82.[35]

The first stage is the separatist stage, during which the excluded group defines its identity. This is consistent with Barth's definition of ethnicity. This process includes the emergence of the pseudospecies declaration, "We are the chosen people made in the image of God." The unchosen are given special names, such as goyim, devils and pagans. It is during this stage that social or group identities are carefully delineated and religion is used to emphasize the "we" or "in" group feeling from which

FIGURE 1*

POWER-INCLUSION MODEL FOR EXCLUDED GROUPS

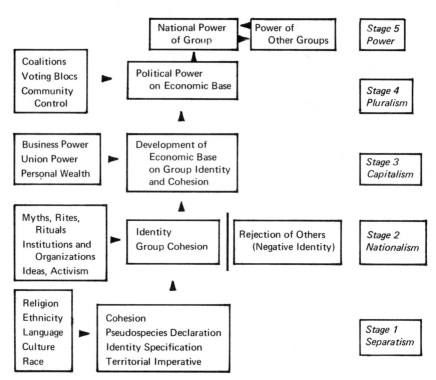

cohesion results. The identity-separation phenomenon is difficult to analyze, for it is an ongoing process. The stages of identity formation probably occur before the inclusion process but provide the necessary impetus for movement into it. The process cannot begin until identity is defined. But once this definition occurs, cohesion can develop. This cohesion is further enhanced by the attachment of a group to a land base. The separatist stage is characterized by three developments: (1) the pseudospecies declaration, (2) the identity specification, and (3) the territorial imperative. Separatism is the condition of separation which occurs when one group decides voluntarily to separate from other groups.

The second stage is the nationalist stage, in which the excluded group intensifies its cohesion by building a religio-cultural community of beliefs around its creation, history, and development. The history, religion

---

* Barbara A. Sizemore, "Is There a Case for Separate Schools?", *Phi Delta Kappan*, January, 1972, p. 282.

and philosophy of the nation from which the group comes dictate the rites, rituals and ceremonies utilized in the proselytization of the old nationalism. Because of rejection by white Anglo-Saxon Protestants and the ensuing exclusion from full participation in the social order, the excluded group embraces its former or future nation. For the Irish Catholics, it was Ireland; for the Polish Catholics, Poland; and for the Jews it was Zion-Israel. This intense nationalistic involvement increases separatism.

Through this model, ethnic groups plug their form of nationalism into Americanism (the common core of myths and language provided by the White Anglo-Saxon ideal) and become Irish-Americans, Italian-Americans, German-Americans. The nationalism of these groups is paraded annually on holidays such as March 17, St. Patrick's Day. So intense was the involvement of the nationalistic stage that such vestiges still remain. As group cohesion and solidarity increased, development of the negative identity occurred. The negative identity of other pseudospecies is "perversely based on all those identifications of finding and defending a niche of one's own."[36]

The third stage of progression toward inclusion is the capitalistic stage. The cohesion developed in the separatist stage and magnified in the nationalist stage, added to the rejection of others created in the second phase, produces a need which can be the foundation for an economic base for the group. The negative identity is the mechanism for relegating other groups to the loser category and nationalism and religion provide the dynamics necessary for the maintenance of group cohesion and solidarity for the creation of the necessary work niche and economic bloc.

Such work niches and blocs are discussed by Moynihan and Glazer who demonstrate that the best jobs demand skills and training which tend to be kept within the "in" group.[37] Therefore the problem is not simply discrimination against the blacks or any one group, but against all outsiders. In other words, there are Irish and Italian skilled workers in part because Irish and Italians were prominent in contracting and construction and they dominated the unions. Nationalism and separatism have contributed to an ethnic base for business and jobs.

According to Weisskopf,[38] capitalism has historically been characterized by great inequalities in the distribution of income and wealth. He says that the only legitimate claim to income arises from the possession of one's own labor-power and from the ownership of the physical means of production. In advanced capitalist nations, labor income typically accounts for about three-quarters and property (capital) income for about one-quarter of the total national income. The distribution of capital ownership in a capitalist society is necessarily unequal, "for if every individual shared equally in the ownership of capital, the fundamental distinction between the capitalist and the worker would vanish." The idea is to accumulate enough capital to become an owner of property and the means of production. The route up is through the control of jobs (wages and salaries).

This control over jobs (unions), as stated before, depended on certain skills passed through family background socialization and on-the-job training. Access to these was through the ethnic group. Maintenance of accumulated capital was passed on to the next generation through inheritance; consequently, endogamous practices were imperative.

The fourth stage is the pluralistic stage, during which the group utilizes its cohesion-rejection powers to form a political bloc on its economic base in order to thrust its interests into the foreground of the political arena. Here the "interest group" concept of Moynihan, Glazer, and Wax combine with the culture concept of Touré, Cruse, Carmichael and Hamilton, and Krug. It is in this stage which gives the illusion of parity, one man, one vote. But political power is dependent upon financial backing. Without an economic base, a group is dependent on another for this need.

An example is the UFT fight against community control in the famous Ocean Hill-Brownsville case. Rogers reports that the majority of teachers, principals, and district superintendents as well as headquarters officials in the New York City school system are Jewish.

"There may be as many as 35,000 Jewish public educators in the New York City school system, and they set the tone as much as the Irish do in Boston."[39]

Consequently, the largely Jewish UFT combined its economic clout with its political bloc and forced the city of New York to dismantle its plans for real community control. The decentralization pattern which resulted is being duplicated throughout the country as providing real community decision-making.

In fact, in the black man's drive for integration which started in housing, the white response was separation. Since identity cohesion is an important variable in four stages of the power-inclusion model, the particular ethnic group involved in integration responds to this need. When an ethnic group is approaching or is in the nationalistic phase where identity cohesion is great, the rejection of others will be intense. Resistance to desegregation may be fierce and violent. When the ethnic group is approaching or in the capitalistic phase, where identity cohesion and rejection have formed a strong economic base, resistance may be immediate but nonviolent. In integration of housing, for example, this group could afford to relocate or to prevent the invasion.

When a group enters the pluralistic stage, integration may be a threat to its cultural institutions, but the group's high degree of participation in decision-making offers abundant opportunities for control of the rate of integration. Resistance might be delayed and nonviolent. Once in the Power phase, the group is then ready to control the conditions which provide impetus for integration. Stokely Carmichael and Charles Hamilton[40] indicate that coalitions are not viable when blacks are not equal partners. In this capitalistic society, no partner without capital is equal.

The fifth stage is the power stage, sometimes called egalitarian and/or democratic. In this stage the economic and voting blocs and coalitions guarantee that the interests of the group have as much chance of winning as those of other groups at this level of participation. This is still utopian. Power is still held by white Anglo-Saxon Protestants but both Jews and Catholics are trying to get it.[41]

Implications for Education

The idea of the melting pot is as old as the republic, say Moynihan and Glazer, but through time the number and kinds of immigrants involved changed, and the confidence that they could be fused together waned. Their evidence is the history of immigration exclusion and quota laws which created successive and selective barriers to certain groups of people.[42] The barrier of racism operates effectively for blacks, the Spanish-speaking and the Indians. Racism is the inherent belief in the superiority of one's own race, and, as Dickeman points out, "[it] is part of a larger philosophy, an ethnocentric dedication to the remodelling of citizens to conform to a single homogeneous acceptable model."[43] The educational system was created to maintain the A/B relationship, to promote the Protestant Ethic and white Anglo-Saxon ethnocentrism as the symbolic universe with which all groups must conform, and to socialize A groups as distributors of the capitalistic surplus and B groups as the consumers.[44]

To change the schools so that they become institutions for education instead of indoctrination, several cultural, racial and religious ethics must be taught. Democracy must be practiced and capitalism must be understood. Superficial, band-aid approaches such as sensitivity training, curriculum revision and teacher recruitment will not suffice.

Roles must be re-defined and dialogical processes must begin. The new teacher will be a subject-actor, the administrator a facilitator, the student an actor-subject. The teaching-learning process must be seen in a new light and given more meaningful interpretations tailored to the

"The teaching-learning process must be seen in a new light and given more meaningful interpretations tailored to the needs of the specific client and his unique problems."

needs of the specific client and his unique problems. The essence of this new methodology is dialogue according to Paulo Freire who says:

> Authentic education is not carried on by "A" for "B" or by "A" about "B", but rather by "A" with "B", mediated by the world—a world which impresses and challenges both parties, giving rise to views or opinions about it.[45]

Teachers and students are both subjects in this method, and they negotiate over the mediating objects. Ideas such as poverty can be mediating objects as can racism or ethnocentrism.

Hierarchical decision-making models will no longer serve since they impede dialogue. An aggregate model is required to facilitate dialogue and to increase the chances for mutuality of effort among the various constituencies: community, administrators, parents, teachers and students (CAPTS). Without such a model "B" groups fall constant prey to "divide and conquer tactics."[46] Such a model is the Community Control Decision-Making Model. See Figure 2.

FIGURE 2*

COMMUNITY CONTROL DECISION-MAKING MODEL

Approval	6	Community Board	Receiving	5 ▶ Veto ▶
Recommending	7	CAPTS Congress*	Accepting	4 ▶ Rejecting ▶
Coordinating Communicating	8	Administrative Staff	Organizing	3
Implementing	9	Professional Bureaucracy	Formulating	2
Evaluating	10	CAPTS Congress	Planning	1 ◀ Start Here

*Community, Administration, Parents, Teachers, and Students

The model has ten steps. First each group meets separately. A plan emerges. It is submitted to the other groups who discuss and negotiate. The negotiated plan is then sent to the professional bureaucracy to be formulated into an educational program. This formulation is then sent to the administrative staff for organization. The administrative staff then submits the proposal to the CAPTS Congress. There is a body of representatives from each of the constituencies. The CAPTS Congress either accepts or vetoes the proposal. If it accepts, it forwards it to the community board which receives or vetoes. If the Congress rejects the proposal, it starts over again in planning. If the community board vetoes the

* Barbara A. Sizemore, "Is There a Case for Separate Schools?", *Phi Delta Kappan*, January, 1972, p. 283.

proposal, it starts again also. If the community receives the acceptance of the Congress, the proposal is ready for implementation and is sent to the Congress for recommendations, then to the administrative staff for coordination and communication. The proposal is forwarded to the professional bureaucracy for implementation and to the CAPTS Congress for evaluation. Each group meets separately again to discuss the method and the instruments to be used for evaluation. These are then negotiated and the evaluation takes place according to this negotiated plan.[47]

Such a decision-making process allows all groups to participate and becomes a tool for cultural pluralism and opportunity equalization. The evaluation procedure will sharpen diagnostic skills for all and will release new sets of knowledge about each constituency. Learning to initiate and execute dialogue will require skills in interviewing, microethnography, questionnaire construction, public opinion polling, test construction, categorizing and codifying. Careful study of selected characteristics of each constituency will lead to better program designs specifically geared to deal with a well-defined problem.

It is difficult for A groups to define B group problems. This failure at the definitional level results in solutions which are inadequate—the right solutions but to the wrong problems. The professional education of teachers seen as perennial students must begin with knowledge, information and skills which create a dialogue with people in order to define problems.

In designing a curriculum to deal with the economic, cultural and political aspects of the total social reality, the education of CAPTS must change in order (1) to create more accurate conceptual maps of reality; (2) to understand those who might want to interfere with the program of reform; (3) to establish a dialogue with the clients, the students; and (4) to provide better insights into the causes of things so that more alternatives will become available for the solution of problems. A liberal arts program with strong interdisciplinary courses including economics, anthropology and political science can bring much needed sets of knowledge to the teacher and administrator who can share with other members of CAPTS, yet strengthening the content of teachers' courses will not be enough.

Berger and Luckmann say that knowledge is socially distributed, possessed differently by different individuals, and can become highly complex. They argue that all symbolic universes and all legitimations are human products whose existence has its base in the lives of concrete individuals and has no empirical status apart from these lives. Consequently, social change must always be understood as standing in a dialectical relationship to the "history of ideas."[48]

In the American social order, it seems that knowledge is distributed by A groups to B groups. This strengthens the position of A over B. Knowledge can also be withheld. Berger and Luckmann posit that those in power are ready to use that power to impose the traditional definitions of reality on the population under their authority. They say "power in society includes the power to determine decisive socialization processes, and, therefore, the power to produce reality." The demands for changes in the educational institutions are for changes in this power arrangement. The hue and cry for community control is directed toward a correction of this A/B formula. These demands for power are derived from an ideology taken on by various groups because of specific theoretical elements that are conducive to its interests, as Moynihan and Glazer indicate. Every group in social conflict must achieve solidarity and ideologies generate that solidarity. The resistance to white supremacy and European superiority by blacks and to property owners by the poor is endemic to the struggle for community control since the schools financed by the property tax remain in the hands of the property owners who wish to obtain the best education possible for their own children with the lowest tax attainable for the maintenance of the status quo.

Curriculum changes emerge from evaluation data and the decision-making apparatus. These changes in content and substance, teaching and its methodology, the administration and its organization, all accommodate the inputs of the various ethnic, interest and excluded groups to

make the school a vehicle for cultural pluralism and to provide the conceptual maps necessary for understanding the total social reality. This understanding can lead to alternatives for full participation in the social order with the maintenance of ethnic differences. More important, these changes give B groups more control over ways of orienting to external symbols creating new behaviors geared into the action systems of both A and B groups.

In 1965, an attempt was made to effect such curriculum changes at the Forrestville High School in District 23, Chicago, Illinois. During this time a part of the black community was agitating for educational parks to enhance the possibilities for integration. Three experimental districts were implemented by the Chicago Board of Education and District 23 was one. A new high school was to be built to alleviate the overcrowding but controversy developed over the selection of a site. Part of the community wanted the high school located in the district. This would mean that it would be a segregated high school. These parents felt that there was nothing wrong with being black; that the community had few resources, the high school being one; and they did not want to lose it. Others felt that white financial support would be forthcoming only for white students and, if blacks expected their children to receive equal education, those children would have to be in schools where whites were.

An aggregate body of community representatives, administrators, parents, teachers and students (CAPTS) were concerned over the constellation of problems which plagued the school such as gang-related activities, low achievement, high dropout rates, poor facilities and the lack of equipment and materials. They felt that the controversy over integration skirted the educational issues; therefore, during three Saturdays in October, 1965, twenty teams of two visited over three hundred homes soliciting the views of parents regarding the location of the new high school. Seventy-eight percent of the parents wanted the new high school in the district and twenty-two percent wanted it located outside of the community. These data were delivered to the General Superintendent who then selected a site in the district. The new Martin Luther King High School was later constructed on this site.

Once this problem was resolved, CAPTS began to look at the problems of the community. Recorded observations reflected the following:

(1) More students wanted instrumental music than the facility could accommodate
(2) There were over thirty informal singing groups formed among the high school students
(3) Incoming freshmen had a median reading score of 4.8
(4) Sophomore boys had the highest dropout rate

(5) Two girls graduated for every one boy
(6) Approximately eighty percent of the attendance and discipline problems were attributed to freshmen
(7) Four out of every five students in the freshmen Civics classes cut because they felt the subject matter was boring and irrelevant
(8) Seventy-seven percent of the students in study halls cut study
(9) The high school district had been declared an urban renewal area and demolition was a daily occurrence
(10) The majority of the homes in the district were owned by absentee landlords
(11) Liquor stores were the predominant business on the 43rd Street strip
(12) Over sixty percent of high school males between the ages of 12 and 18 had had some encounter with the police

A meeting of CAPTS was called to discuss these data and what they imported for the planning of the new high school. At this meeting a committee was assigned to this planning.

The parents on the new school committee began to discuss the possibility of having larger music, art and drama departments in the new school. Teachers were resistant at first to the idea but gradually the new high school emerged. The performing arts was to be the core. Parents did not want it to be a singing and dancing high school. It had to be more. It had to respond to the students and their needs.

Five parents, three teachers and three students met with the architects to discuss these ideas. The stage was to be the center of the school surrounded by a television beaming station and an electronic shop where the students could learn how to design and repair television equipment. There were to be a radio station and a recording studio for students interested in related careers. The business department was to be located nearby so that students who wanted to be entertainers could learn the whole business because parents and teachers wanted to end the exploitation of black entertainers by agents and businessmen. Students majoring in the performing arts were to learn accounting, business law, income tax preparation and management necessary to control their talents.

There were to be a ballet room and a little theatre that was to offer opportunities for unique techniques in the use of sociodrama for teaching reading to those who despaired of ever learning how with books. Here the students were to use videotapes and cassettes to learn to read. Near the little theatre the sewing rooms were situated so that costumes for plays could be made. So located were the art rooms and the wood shops for making scenery for the theatre.

For students who wanted to be professionals, performing arts was to be the motivating dynamic. Independent study situations were built into the academic departments of mathematics, social studies, science, biology and language. A large library was located in the front of the school with private carrels and listening posts to accommodate independent learning. Every effort was made to maximize the use of the multi-media.

The Related Ideas Unit

Through the interaction of parents, teachers and students several new entries appeared in the curriculum. Black History and Black Literature were introduced in many classes as were African art and music. Courses were designed to provide orientation and group guidance for more relevant and meaningful services to the students. One of these was the "Related Ideas Unit"[49] which was an introduction to the basic structures of the high school subject areas. The general objectives were:

1. To establish a functional or organic approach to the total school program.
2. To build a social environment based on language, thought and activity.
3. To establish throughout the school environment the theory of functional or organic processes.

The specific objectives of the unit were:

1. To establish Forrestville as a community within a community.
2. To regard the division room activity as an important social unit of the Forrestville community image.
3. To develop in the classrooms the kind of socialization process that will enable the teacher to more fully realize his educational aims, and at the same time create a closer identification of the student with his high school and community.

The teaching-learning objectives were:

1. To help each student to develop realistic ideas about himself (social reality).
2. To help the student to see that what he does determines what he is.
3. To establish the Forrestville way as a process of doing something with the student, not to him, or for him.
4. To regard the student as his own ultimate subject of study.
5. To help the student to find meaning in
   a) what he is
   b) what he says
   c) what he does
   d) what happens to him
   e) what he may become
6. To make the student an active participant in learning about himself, others and his universe.
7. To draw out of the student his most cherished beliefs about himself and his social environment.

The unit was designed to help the student to think critically about himself, his society, his natural order and his values. It was not the aim to give the student a set of answers to these problem areas, but rather to increase his critical awareness. The student was to be confronted in every classroom with the Related Ideas Unit the first three weeks of school during the 1966-67 school year to develop a foundation for outside thought and discussion. As an outgrowth of the unit, basic freshman civics classes outlined programs for community study. Honors classes set up projects for the study of land distribution in the city of Chicago.

The unit utilized a basic ideas approach which consisted of a vocabulary and a schema for looking at the world. See Charts I, II and III.

Chart I

Man's Way of Looking at the Whole World

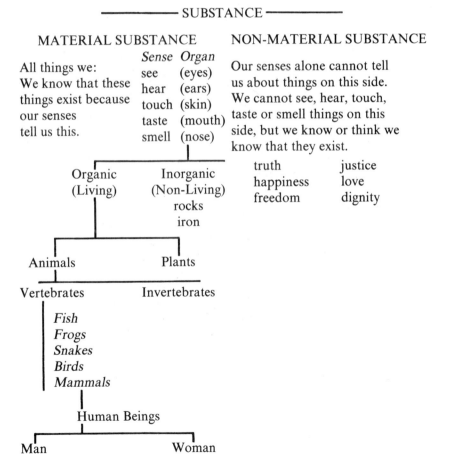

Chart II

Is man shaped by his social world or does man shape his social world?

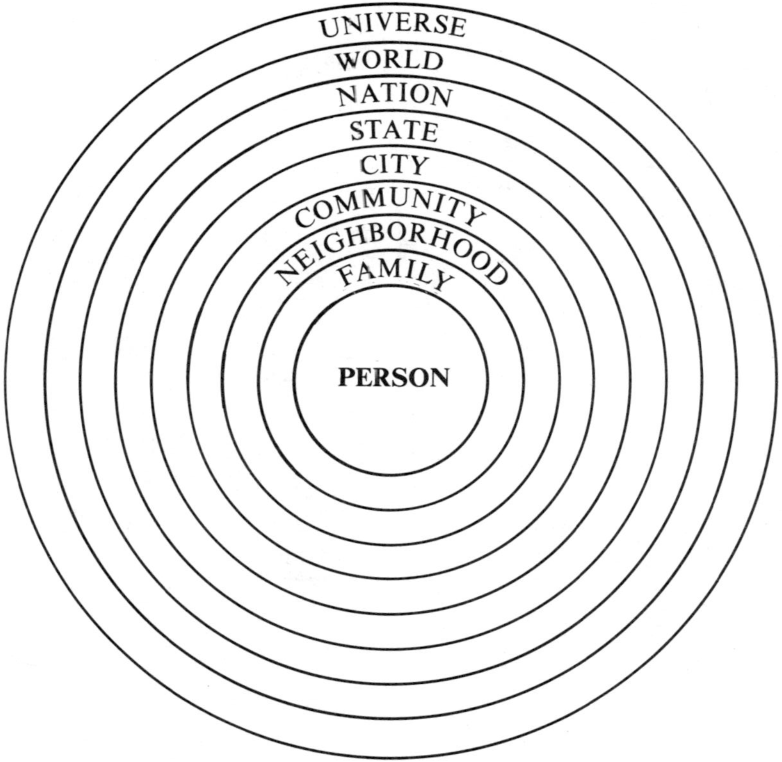

PERSON

FAMILY
NEIGHBORHOOD
COMMUNITY
CITY
STATE
NATION
WORLD
UNIVERSE

VOCABULARY

Person
Family
Neighborhood
Community
City
State
Nation
World
Universe

Is man shaped by ideas or does man shape ideas?

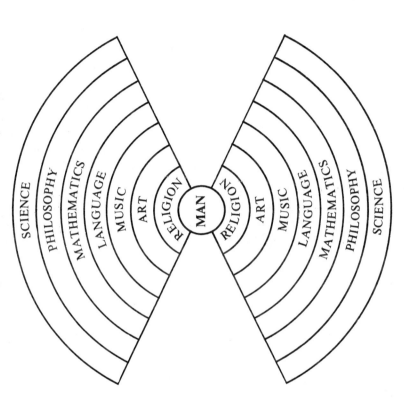

VOCABULARY

Man
Religion
Art
Music
Language
Mathematics
Philosophy
Science

Chart III

Man's Way of Measuring Himself

I. SCIENCES—(Methods of discovering and exploring phenomena)

    A. Physical science   Basic unit of explanation*
        1. Chemistry   (matter)
        2. Physics   (energy)
        3. Biology   (life)

    B. Social Science
        1. History   (time)
        2. Sociology   (group)
        3. Anthropology   (man)
        4. Religion   (god)
        5. Economics   (wealth)
        6. Psychology   (behavior)
        7. Mythology   (story)
        8. Geography   (place)
        9. Civics   (duty)

II. ARTS—(Methods of expressing thoughts and feelings)

    A. Performing Arts
        1. Music   (note)
        2. Art   (form)
        3. Drama   (play)
        4. Dance   (step)
        5. Athletics   (game)

    B. Communication Arts
        1. Language   (word)
        2. Mathematics   (number)

* The Basic Unit does not include every aspect of the academic discipline nor does it pretend to encompass the entire content of the subject or to exclude overlapping content areas.

The Related Ideas Unit had six stages developed by a teacher-student committee for teacher implementation:

STAGE ONE

1. Before classes arrive:
   a. Inspect your classroom!
   b. Secure all essential items and equipment necessary for the completion of your job.
   c. Rearrange the classroom if you desire to do so.
   d. Seating arrangements should fit some definite order.
   e. Place your name in the upper right-hand corner of the chalk board.
   f. Draw the form for assignment sheets on the chalk board.

STAGE TWO

1. Take attendance—have students make assignment sheets for your class.
2. Check program cards.
3. Allow students time to prepare interview reports.
4. Make seating charts.
5. Make sure that everyone has given a report and has had a report given about him.

STAGE THREE

Begin discussion on the nature of your particular subject. Allow the students to do most of the talking. Ask them how (course name) is related to what they have talked about in their divisions.

STAGE FOUR

(Spend as much time as needed to accomplish Stage Four.)

1. Elect or select class officers and/or clerical workers in a style most fitting to you and the nature of your class.
2. Pass out seating assignments. You select whatever means for assigning seats to the students.
3. (First period class teacher) pass out charts 1, 2, 3, have students look up definitions of these terms.

STAGE FIVE

All Academic Classes—Man's Way of Looking at Himself and Other Things

Objective: To foster a continuous discussion on this question in all classes.

Possible approaches—the classroom teacher might ask how the question was handled (if at all) in the previous class or classes.

Questions: How are these charts related to my life?

How are these charts related to my particular
subjects at Forrestville High School?

STAGE SIX

Teacher presents his own subject matter.
1. By pointing out the relationship of _____
   to the Related Ideas Unit.

This Related Ideas Unit is responsive to any ethnic and/or interest group. It permits dialogue and the negotiations of mediating objects. Culture as the specific form and expression of the relationships linking man to his environment permeates the entire program and is dictated by the participants themselves. No one pattern of culture can dominate when the mechanism for decision-making includes all participants. The values which dominate the construction of curriculum will respond to the needs of the students, their parents and that community instead of to the institution.

But, these efforts made during 1966-1967 at Forrestville High School were not sustained when the Martin Luther King High School was occupied. The curriculum reverted to the traditional experience and its symbolic universe. So that in 1973 there is only a trace of the performing arts thrust and no sign of collective decision-making.

Jules Henry stated that "American education is bleak; so bleak indeed that, on the whole, educators having long ago abandoned the ideal of enlightenment, concentrate on tooling up." For Henry, several factors constrict education: the political economy and its need for rampant consumption of the gross national product, wars, and the occupational systems which demand stupidity and vulnerability. The educational system must then aim at a steady state. He explains this state:

> All steady-state systems of culture are designed to develop a kind of equilibrium between, on the one hand, a spontaneity adequate to prevent a person's going to pieces when confronted with any novelty at all, and, on the other, a spontaneity so unfettered that he will propose new solutions . . .[50]

Hopefully, the shattering of the melting pot myth will unchain the schools so that the potential of cultural pluralism will be unleashed.

Men structure their social relations in a group or larger collectivity of people and share beliefs and orientations that unite members of the collectivity and guide their conduct. The large collectivity of people in this country called Americans share certain beliefs of white European superiority, male superiority and the superiority of people with money. These beliefs create excluded groups: non-whites, women and the poor.[51]

The professional education of teachers must be humanized by concern for the inclusion of these groups in the larger collectivity of people called Americans through aggregate models and cultural pluralism. Teachers must learn to be human. Students are demanding more from personal relations. They want to be people.

"Hopefully, the shattering of the melting pot myth will unchain the schools so that the potential of cultural pluralism will be unleashed."

There is no doubt that a democratic culturally pluralistic society is imperative. That fights must be waged on all fronts is accepted. Education can then be concerned with the meeting of men's needs of identity, stimulation and security based on their values of land, liberty and life. Once this occurs, the vital area of man's purpose and existence on this earth becomes the primary focus of his educational experience and the point position at the frontier of knowledge.

FOOTNOTES

[1] Cruse, Harold. *The Crisis of the Negro Intellectual* (N.Y.: William Morrow & Co., 1967), p. 7.

[2] *Ibid.*, p. 456.

[3] Higham, John. *Strangers in the Land* (N.Y.: Atheneum, 1971), p. 4. Quoted by Carlos Brossard in "Variants in Nativism: 1820-1900" (Unpublished manuscript, Harvard University, 1972), p. 1.

[4] Brossard, *op. cit.*, p. 3.

[5] *Ibid.*, p. 5.

[6] Berger, Peter L. and Thomas Luckmann. *The Social Construction of Reality* (Garden City, N.Y.: Doubleday & Co., Inc., 1966), pp. 85-118.

[7] Weber, Max. *The Protestant Ethic and the Spirit of Capitalism* (N.Y.: Charles Scribner's Sons, 1958).

[8] Handlin, Oscar. *The Uprooted* (N.Y.: Atlantic-Little, Brown, 1951), pp. 244-258.

[9] Deutch, Morton. "Cooperation and Trust: Some Theoretical Notes" in *Interpersonal Dynamics,* Warren G. Bennis, Edgar H. Steele (Eds.), (Homewood, Ill.: Dorsey, 1964), p. 506.

[10] Tax, Sol. "The Freedom to Make Mistakes" in Fred Gearing, Robert McNetting, and Lisa R. Peathe (Eds.), *The Documentary History of the Fox Project* (Chicago: University of Chicago Press, 1960), pp. 245-250.

[11] Weber, *op. cit.*, pp. 35-46 and 47-78.

[12] *Ibid.*, p. 116.

[13] Novak, Michael. *The Rise of the Unmeltable Ethnics* (N.Y.: The Macmillan Co., 1971), pp. 9-14 and 170-177.

[14] Berkowitz, Rabbi William. *Ten Vital Jewish Issues* (N.Y.: Thomas Yoseloff, 1964), p. 21.

[15] *Ibid.*, pp. 104-105.

[16] Novak, *op. cit.*, p. 175.

[17] Edwards, Richard C., Michael Reich and Thomas E. Weisskopf (Eds.). *The Capitalist System* (Englewood Cliffs, N.J.: Prentice-Hall, Inc., 1972), pp. 90-91.

[18] Moynihan, Daniel P. and Nathan Glazer. *Beyond the Melting Pot* (Cambridge, Mass.: MIT Press, 1963), p. 289.

[19] Krug, Mark. "Teaching the Experience of White Ethnic Groups" in James A. Banks (Ed.), *Teaching Ethnic Studies: Concepts and Strategies* (Washington, D.C.: National Council for the Social Studies 1973 Yearbook).

[20] Handlin, *op. cit.*, p. 186.

[21] *Ibid.*, p. 66. See Mildred Dickeman, "Teaching Cultural Pluralism" in James A. Banks (Ed.), *Teaching Ethnic Studies: Concepts and Strategies* (Washington, D.C.: National Council for the Social Studies 1973 Yearbook).

[22] Handlin, *op. cit.*, p. 258.

[23] Erickson, Donald A. "Freedom's Two Educational Imperatives: A Proposal" in *Public Controls for Nonpublic Schools,* edited by Donald A. Erickson (Chicago: University of Chicago Press, 1969), p. 161. See also "Contradictory Studies of Parochial Schooling: An Essay Review," *School Review,* 76 (Winter, 1967), pp. 425-436.

[24] Moynihan and Glazer, *op. cit.*, p. 17.

[25] Krug, *op. cit.*, See Mildred Dickeman, *op. cit.*,

[26] Wax, Murray L. "Cultural Pluralism, Political Power, and Ethnic Studies" (Unpublished manuscript). Quoted by Wax from Frederick Barth. *Ethnic Groups and Boundaries* (Boston: Little, Brown & Co., 1969), pp. 9-38.

[27] *Ibid.*, p. 3.

[28] Sizemore, Barbara A. "Making the Schools a Vehicle for Cultural Pluralism" (Unpublished manuscript prepared for TTT Conference, Chicago, Illinois, 1971).

[29] Touré, Sékou. "A Dialectical Approach to Culture," *The Black Scholar,* November, 1969, p. 13.

[30] Parsons, Talcott, Edward A. Shils and others. "Some Fundamental Categories of the Theory of Action: A General Statement" in *Toward a General Theory of Action,* edited by Talcott Parsons and Edward A. Shils (Cambridge: Harvard University Press, 1951), pp. 3-29.

[31] Parsons and Shils, *op. cit.,* p. 16.

[32] Bowles, Samuel. "Unequal Education and the Reproduction of the Hierarchical Division of Labor" in Edwards, Reich and Weisskopf, *op. cit.,* pp. 218-229.

[33] Greeley, Andrew M. *Why Can't They Be Like Us?* (N.Y.: E. P. Dutton & Co., 1971), p. 29. See also *The Education of Catholic Americans* by Andrew M. Greeley and Peter H. Rossi (Chicago: Aldine Publishing Co., 1966).

[34] Handlin, *op. cit.,* p. 248.

[35] Sizemore, Barbara A. "Separatism: A Reality Approach to Inclusion?" in *Racial Crisis in American Education,* edited by Robert L. Green (Chicago: Follett Educational Corporation, 1969), pp. 249-279.

[36] Erikson, Erik H. *Identity: Youth and Crisis* (N.Y.: W.W. Norton, 1968), p. 175.

[37] Moynihan and Glazer, *op. cit.,* p. 31.

[38] Weisskopf, Thomas E. "Capitalism and Inequality" in Edwards, Reich and Weisskopf, *op. cit.,* pp. 125-133.

[39] Rogers, David. *110 Livingston Street: Politics and Bureaucracy in the New York City School System* (New York: Random House, 1968), p. 161.

[40] Carmichael, Stokely and Charles V. Hamilton. *Black Power* (N.Y.: Random House, 1967), p. 96.

[41] Sizemore, Barbara A. "Is There a Case for Separate Schools?" *Phi Delta Kappan,* January, 1972, pp. 281-284.

[42] Moynihan and Glazer, *op. cit.,* pp. 288-289.

[43] Dickeman, Mildred. "Teaching Cultural Pluralism" in James A. Banks (Ed.), *Teaching Ethnic Studies: Concepts and Strategies* (Washington, D.C.: National Council for the Social Studies 1973 Yearbook).

[44] For an interesting discussion of this point see Jules Henry, *Culture Against Man* (N.Y.: Random House, 1963); and "Is Education Possible? Are We Qualified to Enlighten Dissenters?" in *Public Controls for Nonpublic Schools* by Donald A. Erickson (Chicago: University of Chicago Press, 1969), pp. 83-102.

[45] Freire, Paulo. *Pedagogy of the Oppressed* (N.Y.: Herder and Herder, 1970), p. 82.

[46] *Ibid.,* pp. 137-143.

[47] Sizemore, Barbara A. "Is There a Case for Separate Schools?", *op. cit.,* p. 282.

[48] Berger and Luckmann, *op. cit.,* pp. 107-118.

[49] The Related Ideas Unit and the Division Guidance Program were directed by Anderson Thompson, Assistant Professor, Center for Inner City Studies, Northeastern Illinois State University. Mr. Thompson was Assistant Principal of Forrestville High School.

[50] Henry, Jules. "Is Education Possible? Are We Qualified to Enlighten Dissenters?", *op. cit.,* p. 100.

[51] For more information on this point see Barbara A. Sizemore, "Social Science and Education for a Black Identity" in *Black Self-Concept,* edited by James A. Banks and Jean D. Grambs (N.Y.: McGraw-Hill, 1972), pp. 141-170.

 Larry Cuban

LARRY CUBAN is a teacher at Roosevelt High School (Washington, D. C. Public Schools), and is currently working on his Ph.D. at Stanford. Mr. Cuban is the former Director of Staff Development for the District of Columbia Public Schools and Director of the Cardozo Project in Urban Teaching. He has also served as Director of Race and Education for the United States Commission on Civil Rights.

Mr. Cuban has been an urban consultant to numerous public and private agencies, including the National Teacher Corps, the United States Office of Education, and the University of Washington. He served on the President's Advisory Committee for the Teacher Corps, and was a member of the United States Office of Education Summer Institute on Educational Renewal in 1972, a group which prepared a document on reform in the nation's public schools.

His articles have appeared in such publications as the Phi Delta Kappan, Social Education, The Los Angeles Times, Harvard Educational Review, Saturday Review, *and the* Journal of Negro Education. *He is the author of* To Make a Difference: Teaching in the Inner City, Black Man in America, Youth as a Minority *(NCSS), and* The Promise of America. *He is the coauthor and program editor of the Scott Foresman Spectra Program, which includes volumes entitled* Japan, India, Mexico, Kenya, *and* Russia.

LARRY CUBAN

5

Ethnic Content
and "White" Instruction

In those classrooms where earnest teachers are telling it like it is, pas-
sionate advocates of ethnic education will soon discover students yawning. Some programs have already reported lower enrollments, erratic
attendance, and youngsters "resting their eyes." As ethnic studies multi-
ply, boredom will drive students up the walls in frustration; worse yet,
apathetic students will encourage teachers and administrators to draw
inaccurate conclusions about ethnic education.

At issue here, I think, are some of the directions taken by ethnic
studies and their possible consequences for educating children. The
questions I raise here, and I want to be clear on this point, are directed
less at their academic validity than at the sloppy educational thinking
that has produced quickie programs in both black and white public
schools.

With racism in curriculum and instructional materials having been
revealed for all to see in the last few years, the main thrust behind ethnic
education has been to catch up on knowledge and "truth." Demands by
students and teachers to tell it like it is has triggered thunderbolts of
facts hitherto ignored or suppressed. This catch-up syndrome masks a
basic error in educational thinking: the belief that racism can be eliminated by filling up kids with information. By casting the issue into
familiar and manageable terms, educators of both races leap at the
obvious, ignoring a far more critical problem—"white instruction."

Reprinted from *Phi Delta Kappan,* January, 1972, Vol. 53, pp. 270-273, with the
permission of *Phi Delta Kappa* and Larry Cuban.

"White instruction" is a shorthand term to describe those traditional methods of telling, explaining, and clarifying that have been the mainstay of classrooms for the last millennium. I mean the teacher's view of the learner as a passive absorber of data. I mean the belief that acquisition of all the facts must precede analysis. I mean the credo that the function of the public schools is to instill certain values and attitudes. These articles of faith have been too long a design for failure.

To graft ethnic content onto white instruction will shrivel and ultimately kill a hardy, vital effort to reform what happens in the classroom. And that is what I feel is happening now. A brief look at some examples of the grafting process may be instructive.

Because of enormous gaps in ethnic knowledge, there is a logical and determined effort by teachers to communicate information to fill those gaps. Teachers of black history, for example, lecture students about heart surgeon Daniel Hale Williams, poet Jupiter Hammon, artist Henry Tanner, and blues singer Bessie Smith. Better informed teachers add an indictment of white political and cultural oppression. To assist teachers in communicating this data, there are bigger and blacker textbooks, myriad filmstrips, records, and workbooks.

Without reviewing the exhaustive criticism of traditional methods of instruction, without invoking Jerome Bruner's, John Holt's, or any other critic's words on how the educational ball game has changed (or should change) from the days when books were chained to tables and teachers had to lecture—without all of that, let me focus on just one crucial point: Traditional approaches to ethnic content lock students into the passive role of soaking up information.

This role, with all of its assumptions about the authority of the teacher as truth-giver, offers only a small margin of interaction. And that thin margin of interaction, hanging upon the teacher's willingness to enter into give-and-take discussion, shrinks even further because of another traditional article of faith: the dedicated belief in the proposition that students cannot analyze issues—especially ones dealing with ethnicity—until they have all the facts. It is difficult for laymen to fathom the typical educators' obstinate devotion to this proposition. Even though each of us makes judgments every day on the basis of fragmentary data; even though each of us, including children, goes through the steps of analysis—some more aware of each step than others but through them nonetheless—it is of no moment to many schoolmen. Step into classrooms and the traditional sequence of facts first; discussion later is painfully present. The possibility that fact presentation and analysis can occur simultaneously is not considered. For ethnic education, this curious belief tied to the view of the youngster as a consumer of information strengthens each delivery of missile after missile of facts.

On another level, for reasons unrelated to tradition and familiarity, conventional teaching approaches are used which further force students into acting like sponges. Consider who the teachers are in Puerto Rican, Chicano, or black studies programs. Since every school system must generate its own supply of ethnic studies instructors, two sources have been tapped.

Wherever possible, ethnic teachers, regardless of their competence and training, are dragooned into service; any white teacher, again regardless of competence or training, who once expressed interest is quickly recruited. Put teachers unprepared in terms of content into classrooms and their vulnerability often forces them to lecture and use any available textbook or workbook religiously.

Information is a smokescreen to hide shallowness. While this is usually the case with teachers dragged into service, for scholarly graduate students (a second source of manpower) who are unfamiliar with classroom management, content is also a convenient tool to quiet kids with a barrage of words, notes to take, and dates to remember. In both cases the defensive use of information protects teachers' esteem while deluging captive youngsters with facts.

What is disastrous about white instruction, of course, is that children who are thrown into a sea of information will not come out cleansed of self-hate and sparkling with ethnic consciousness. Thrown into such a sea, children drown. After all, how many times between the primary years and graduation and from how many teachers can students be informed of the brutality of slavery, the wickedness of Southern racists and white oppression without yawning? Even those teachers driven compulsively to preach about the iniquities of this country's treatment of minority groups must sense that their students—when they are of minority status—existentially know oppression and carry its history with them. And if that isn't apparent, then how can they ignore the explosion of information on ethnicity from the media that envelops students daily? Or the constant discussion of race in the streets? Buried deep, then, in the marriage between ethnic education and white instruction is a patronizing assumption about kids held by too many teachers: Unknowing, unthinking, and unaware, students can only absorb the Truth.

Less patronizing but just as simplistic (and inaccurate) is another belief that crops up in virtually every ethnic educational effort. Many programs are based upon the notion that information about ethnic experience will remedy identity problems and instill in children a proper appreciation of themselves. A school, the notion goes, can inculcate a sense of pride in a child about himself, his family, and his group.

Next to apple pie, waving the flag, and invoking images of Mom, there is nothing as sacrosanct as the belief that the schools inculcate the right values and attitudes. But *can* schools develop responsible citizens? Can they produce youths who respect the dignity of those less fortunate than themselves? Probably not.

If there are serious reservations about the capacity of schools to turn out men and women with minimal intellectual skills, areas in which measurement is possible, then reservations increase when schools claim that their graduates have certain values and attitudes, areas where evaluation is notoriously unreliable. A case in point is patriotism.

Patriotism is an expected attitudinal outcome of the educational process. The mandating of U.S. history, for example, is a conscious effort to force kids into at least three years of exposure to American history. National pride is the legislative as well as the educational objective. But the record of the U.S. history courses in instilling pride is, at best, ambiguous; at worst, utter failure. Dull books, dull courses, and low-level patriotism have been part of the harvest from mandated U.S. history.

If the teaching of American history isn't grim enough, turn to the experience of civics education. Here the value aims are no less grand than the making of "good" citizens who know their responsibilities to the group and to themselves. Yet study after study documents that instructional programs in civics have little or no impact upon the attitudes and values of students, much less upon their behavior.

The point is that the failure or, charitably, the uncertain outcomes of U.S. history and civics classes reveal the complexity of the interlocking influence of the school, home, mass media, church, and friends. Pride in group begins at birth and is constantly shaped by those forces. Family and church, for example, are where a Polish child gets his sense of being Polish—not the schools (unless, of course, Italian kids beat up Polish kids on the playground and the school—unintentionally—sharpens each crying child's sense of himself).

Witness the experience of the Catholic parochial school system. That exhaustive study, *The Education of Catholic Americans,* pointed to the complexity of trying to instill and maintain certain values.[1] Andrew Greeley and Peter Rossi pointed out that there were *some* changes in attitude and certain kinds of religious behavior the longer Catholic children went to school, but the study underscored the interrelationship of family, church, and school. The writers suggested that rather than causing the minimal level of religious allegiance they found in American Catholics, the schools may be a result of it.

I have dealt with this issue of values and attitudes because it is another article of faith that proponents of ethnic education have swallowed whole from white instruction. Transferred to these programs, what is supposed to happen is improved self-esteem, pride in race, and

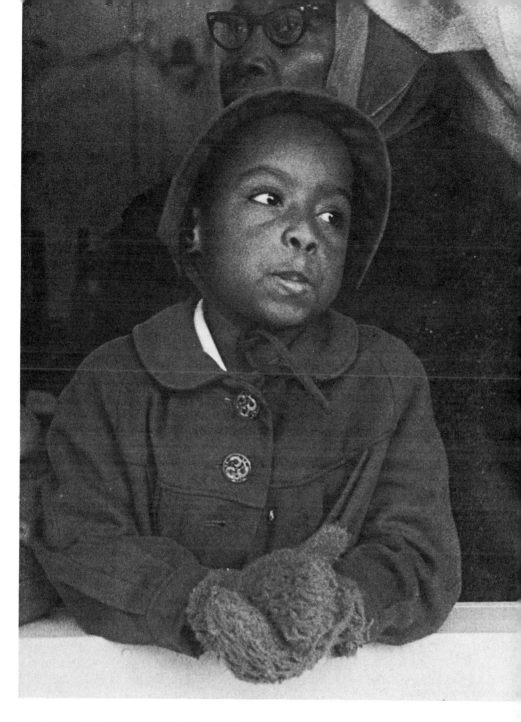

"... how a black parent reacts to his child's first questions about skin color ... is far more important than how much time that child spends in black studies programs."

deeper involvement in the community. The sorry performance of U.S. history and civics education and the ambiguous evidence from Catholic schools suggest that the growth of ethnic consciousness and a reversal of negative feelings about oneself would be doubtful outcomes of ethnic education. If, for example, the slave heritage and individual and institutional racism have produced the low self-esteem and self-hatred blacks have, according to social scientists, and if they are correct in saying these negative feelings are absorbed by the black family out of the national bloodstream and passed on to children in their early years—if all of this is accurate—then how a black parent reacts to his child's first questions about skin color and nappy hair and what "nigger" means is far more important than how much time that child spends in black studies programs. Yet even family influence is limited. Listen to a mother describe her son:[2]

> Although he has not yet attended kindergarten, he can both read and write, and can accurately identify colors and forms with an acuity beyond his years. He collects American flags and pictures and ceramics of our national emblem. . . . He learned from somewhere on his own initiative the Pledge of Allegiance, which he recites with deep fervor. . . . My precious, precocious Mark is very proud of his white, Anglo-Saxon heritage. But he's black: a beautifully carved and polished piece of black American earth.

Cynthia Shepard took Mark South and placed him in an all-black nursery school while she taught during the day.

> The first evening, when I brought him home, he was in tears, writhing and retching in painful confusion. "Why did you make me go to school with all those Negroes?"
> Then, just like NOW, I dig! Intellectuality had blocked my insight, creating of me a blind broad and of my black son a white racist. In his innocence—or highest sophistry, you see—he had intuitively perceived race not as a color but as an attitude that he did not exemplify. My arguments to the contrary were completely hushed by his own words: "You said I could be anything I choose, and I choose to be white; I am white."

And this happened before the public schools got Mark. Of course, none of this is new. Kenneth B. Clark, Mary Ellen Goodman, and other researchers documented the development of self-esteem and racial concepts in pre-schoolers as early as the 1940's and 1950's. Modifying such feelings is an enormous task requiring skilled, compassionate human beings and much interaction and individual attention as well as massive amounts of patience. And hope.

There is no substantial evidence now that courses, books, programs, or any such planned experience in public schools as they are presently organized results in meaningful changes in attitudes and values. The complex process of identity and attitude formation is very personal, seldom public; identity and values are not products that can be packaged and distributed to people out there who seemingly know not who they are.

While too much of ethnic education has been married to white instruction, this has not been a shotgun marriage; both bride and bridegroom marched down the aisle willingly. Proponents of ethnic studies eager to legitimize their efforts embraced the durable and familiar apparatus of course titles, approved book lists, lectures, tests, homework, and the like. Conservative forces in the schools, duly supportive of that apparatus, and anxious about the noise of curricular and instructional reformers, welcomed ethnic studies with surprising ardor. While as bedmates each may keep the other at arm's length, there is a clear recognition of similar interests. The process of establishing the legitimacy of ethnic studies, traditionalists recognize, will damp down efforts at reforming conventional practices because the current thrust of ethnic studies in the schools is disseminating a Message; messages need senders and receivers, a formula familiar and comfortable for those beating back innovative changes.

To put it more directly, since the advocates of ethnic studies are the "outs," getting "in," many have adopted, for various reasons, the forms of white instruction and knowingly or unknowingly have reinforced traditional instruction. In doing so, they threaten to kill off one of the few reform efforts mounted to change instruction, especially in the social sciences.

In the recent sweep of curricular and instructional reform, the accumulation of factual knowledge has been secondary. Primary emphasis has been placed upon students' developing the skills of comprehension, analysis, and evaluation. Most resistant to these changes have been the social sciences, particularly history. As tardy and slow as changes have been, still, some significant strides have been undertaken to introduce and sustain programs where children learn the skills of inquiry and apply them to new information. Certainly no panacea, nonetheless these reforms aimed at teaching children how to learn at least attempt to crack the traditional role of the teacher and student and replace it with one where students actively participate and question.

Ethnic education (where it focuses upon lifting self-esteem and catching up on omitted facts) and these infant reform efforts at a different learning process produce a dilemma. For the fact-oriented, information is intrinsically valuable and must be learned by the student; the product, i.e., knowledge, is crucial and must be distributed to the children. For the reformer, skills are critical, knowledge is instrumental; a process is to

"But most important, I see the raw power of ethnic content in charging the intellectual batteries of youngsters."

be learned and assimilated. For the one, coverage of information is essential; for the other, careful selectivity of concepts and information act as a vehicle to teach skills. Most proponents of ethnic studies fail to sense this dilemma and eagerly charge into the classroom, indiscriminately firing blast after blast of facts. A few, after discharging their load, dimly perceive that there is more to ethnic content than facts.

But the angry, choked-up emotions of past decades explosively locked into ethnic content will not permit knowledge to become secondary to skill development.

There are, fortunately, some teachers who resolve the dilemma by ignoring it. They see no rigid dichotomy, because in teaching through process, one must teach content. Moreover, they see that there is no such thing as a "true history" of, say, the black man or black literary truth. They see that "telling it like it is" is only a code phrase for passing along one's point of view, not rendering truth. They see that the only advocacy worth pursuing is advocacy of inquiry and analysis. But most important, I see the raw power of ethnic content in charging the intellectual batteries of youngsters. And it is here that I sense the enormous possibilities for invigorating curriculum and instruction.

Ethnic content, carefully selected, contains the conflicts and dilemmas of the human condition that inherently interest youngsters. From the question of why the black man was permanently enslaved and not the white or red man to the question of why so many black youths wear afros and dashikis, fundamental issues of power, identity, and values arise. A quick rebuttal would be that such issues can be found in any content. No doubt. But the point is that ethnic divisions and racism are critical domestic issues now and have been since the founding of this country. Their continuing irresolution gives ethnic content an emotional voltage that will last as long as this society tolerates injustice.

Ethnic content can vibrate with electric energy. It is an immensely effective tool to connect up with children if, and this is an enormous if, teachers know how to select the material and how to use it in class. Race, for example, is a controversial topic in both black and white classrooms. As with any controversial issue, teachers must be sensitive and skilled. A teacher who walks into a sex education class on the first day and asks students to discuss their feeling about intercourse is a fool; and a white teacher in a black class who is eager to talk about race and tries to start a discussion by using the word "nigger" is both insensitive and unskilled and, I should add, foolishly destructive.

Ethnic content can make contact with students. In the hands of a craftsman, it can get youngsters to explore knowledge, develop skills, and clarify values. Ethnic content can be used to create interaction between teachers and students and among students in sensitive areas often unexplored in class. Such things do happen occasionally in the public schools.

Where it does happen, teachers intuitively know how to channel the electrical charge of ethnic content into intellectual energy. What they know is that such content by itself is an inert body of knowledge. They know that there is nothing intrinsically magical about it. What brings it to life, and I shudder at saying the obvious, is the effective teacher.

How often the cliché about the effective teacher is shoved aside and forgotten! But the caliber of the teacher determines the success or failure of ethnic content. Those yawning students enrolled, for example, in a Swahili class have discovered the truth buried in that cliché.

And this is my final point. Ethnic content will be drained of its vitality by white instruction as long as the community of students and educators continues to formulate the problem of educational change upon the

"The caliber of the teacher determines the success or failure of ethnic content."

narrow base of curricular reform. We need teacher change, not so-called curricular change. Sharp teachers can change the real curriculum, and some were doing so long before alternative schools became fashionable.

If we focus upon the introduction of ethnic studies into the curriculum with only an afterthought to the teachers and teaching strategies used, the future is fairly predictable. My guess is that two decades from now ethnic studies will exist, but they will be a shell with all content sucked dry by a pedantic instruction more concerned with form than substance. Perhaps ethnic studies will go the way of Latin and Greek, given time and dull educational leadership.

Putting more emphasis upon the effectiveness of teachers than upon establishing new forms may be politically impossible, considering the vulnerability of public schools. Many educators have discovered that they can get more bang from the buck by investing in curricular changes and thereby creating the image of real reform. Consultants arrive, new materials appear, course titles change—reforms are under way. This may be politically wise, but it is educationally destructive.

Some educators realize curriculum reform is just tinkering. But few have the spine or support from superiors both to reorganize the school and revitalize instruction through retraining of teachers. Thus creating ethnic educational enclaves without introducing substantive changes elsewhere will ensure political survival for a school but little else. It is cheap. It projects the image of concern and modernity. But when ethnic content is married to white instruction, kids will fall asleep in class. Educators often forget that the first signs of student protest are not placards and sit-ins but yawns.

FOOTNOTES

[1] Andrew Greeley and Peter Rossi, *Education of Catholic Americans.* Chicago: Aldine, 1966.

[2] Cynthia Shepard, "The World Through Mark's Eyes," *Saturday Review,* January 18, 1969.

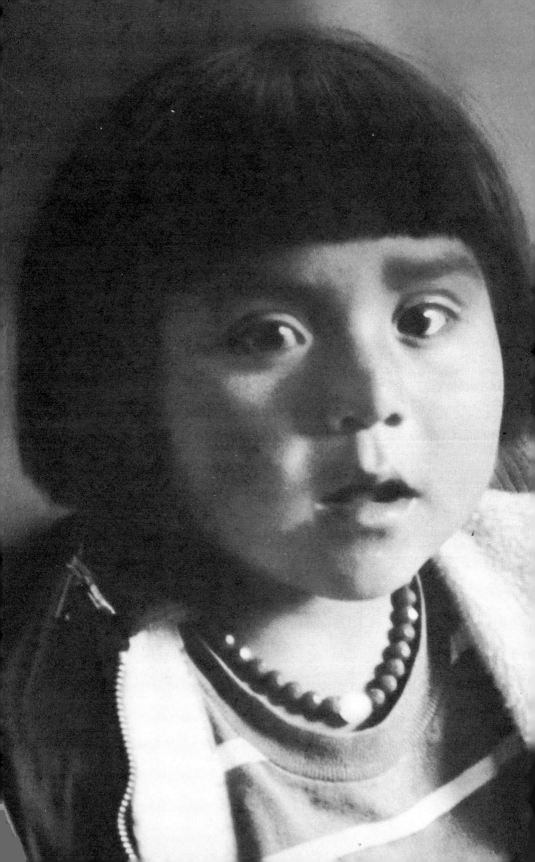

Part Two

TEACHING ABOUT ETHNIC MINORITY CULTURES

In Part One, the authors discuss some of the basic problems related to race and ethnicity in American society, and suggest factors which the teacher and his students must consider if meaningful ethnic studies programs are to be formulated and implemented. These include issues related to cultural pluralism, institutional racism, the melting pot myth, and the attitudes of teachers and students. It is absolutely imperative that serious attention be given to these factors in a sound ethnic studies program.

However, an ethnic studies program must also have a carefully planned knowledge component. Teachers must know basic facts, concepts, generalizations and theories about ethnic minority groups to teach about these cultures intelligently. They must also be able to view minority cultures from the points of view of the victims of oppression since prevailing conceptions of these groups reflect an Anglo-Saxon bias. Minority groups are often distorted, stereotyped and neglected in textbooks. The chapters in Part Two include basic information about different American ethnic minority groups and present novel ways to interpret their experiences. Strategies and materials for teaching about minority cultures are also suggested. An annotated bibliography is appended to each chapter.

In the opening chapter, Chun-Hoon argues that Asian-Americans are often seen in more positive ways than other ethnic minority groups because of the economic success which a few of them enjoy. He suggests that emphasis on the social mobility of a few has obscured the serious

115

problems of the bulk who are poor. Chun-Hoon attempts to bring the Asian-American experience into perspective. He sensitively describes the problems of poor Asian-Americans, and gives a vivid picture of the slums in which they live. He makes a plea for a comprehensive analysis of the Asian-American experience, and argues that it should be taught from a dual perspective: that of the American majority as well as that of the Asian-American minority.

Ethnic studies has suffered largely because its goals are confused, conflicting and ambiguous, contends Banks in the next chapter. He reviews a number of alternative goals, and suggests that the main goal of ethnic studies should be the same as the total social studies program: to help students develop the ability to make reflective decisions so that they can resolve personal problems, and through social action, influence public policy and develop a sense of political efficacy. He then illustrates, using elements from Black Studies, how ethnic content can become an integral part of an inquiry-oriented social studies curriculum that focuses on decision-making skills. The conceptual framework described by Banks can be used to study the other cultural groups discussed in Part Two.

A historical overview of the Chicano experience and some little known but fascinating facts about Mexican Americans are presented in the next chapter by Cortés. He describes the ways in which Chicanos have been culturally abused in textbooks and the stereotypic concepts that are often applied in studying them. Cortés proposes five alternative frames of reference which can be effectively used to analyze the Chicano experience. The teacher will find his descriptions of strategies and materials very helpful.

Our educational system, argues Forbes in the following chapter, has promoted a narrow and one-sided view of American history which is Anglo-Saxon dominated. He attempts to redefine the concept of *American*, which includes a full recognition of the significant role played by the first Americans in shaping our nation's past and present. Forbes makes a compassionate plea for the teacher to teach the very essence of Native American life—which is not material elements such as baskets and houses—but a system of basic values which he believes can help immensely to solve our intractable social problems.

The final chapter in Part Two focuses on a group of Americans who have been highly invisible in most discussions of the culturally different: Puerto Rican Americans. Cordasco and Castellanos vividly delineate some of the unique problems which these children experience in school and describe some ways in which they can be solved. Arguing that the melting pot theory has not and will not work with Puerto Rican Americans, the authors suggest that bilingual education programs are absolutely essential for Spanish-speaking children to succeed in school. They focus their discussion on bilingual education because of their strong conviction that Puerto Rican students will not succeed in any subject area—including the social studies—until programs are structured in languages which they can read and comprehend. Most of the conclusions which the authors derive can also be applied to Chicano students.

Suggested Teaching Strategies

Elizabeth O. Pearson is the author of "Suggested Teaching Strategies" which appear at the end of Chapters 6, 9, 10, 11, and 12.

Elizabeth O. Pearson

Elizabeth O. Pearson is a Lecturer in Social Studies Education and a Ph.D. candidate at the University of Washington, Seattle. She graduated from Northwestern University and received her M.Ed. from the University of Washington. Ms. Pearson taught social studies and language arts in the Glencoe (Illinois) Public Schools and was a Teacher Participant in the Tri-University Project at the University of Washington. She was a member of the History Education Project sponsored by the American Historical Association and has served as a Consultant to the Continental Can Company. Ms. Pearson has contributed to Professional Growth for Teachers *and teaching strategy exercises to* Teaching Strategies for the Social Studies: Inquiry, Valuing and Decision-Making.

Lowell K.Y. Chun-Hoon

LOWELL KOON YING CHUN-HOON is Editor-in-Chief of the Am-
erasia Journal, *which is published at the Asian-American Studies Center*
at the University of California, Los Angeles. Mr. Chun-Hoon is a gradu-
ate of Yale University, where he completed a thesis on "The Anomalous
and the Expected: Anson Burlingame and the Anti-Chinese Movement
in California, 1848-1902." Mr. Chun-Hoon has taught high school En-
glish to gifted inner-city youth and courses on Asian-American studies
at the University of California, Los Angeles. In 1971 he was a member
of the Pacific Rim Education Project and was appointed by the Califor-
nia State Department of Education to serve on an Ethnic Education
Task Force to evaluate social studies textbooks. His articles and book
reviews have appeared in the Amerasia Journal, Chinese Awareness *and*
The Honolulu Advertiser. *He contributed to a forthcoming book,* Asian
American: Psychological Perspectives.

LOWELL K. Y. CHUN-HOON

6

Teaching the Asian-American Experience

Learning from History

If one of the primary stereotypes of Asian persons in America has been that they are passive and docile, it is equally true that their historical experience has also been seen as compliant, flexible, and malleable. Non-Asian militants are always likely to be dumbfounded, for example, when one politely introduces the all-Nisei 442nd combat regiment, the most decorated unit of World War II, which fought heroically against fascism in Italy while 100,000 of their own people were interned in concentration camps in the United States, and only the most cantankerous of minority groups will not recoil in shame when reference is made to the 1960 census figures that reveal Chinese-American families with a higher average family income than the average American family. Indeed, there is literally something to please everyone in the varied history of Asians in the United States: images of slimy Filipino sensuality for the perverse; the enormous imbalance in the historical ratio of Chinese men to Chinese women for the misogynist; and riots, harassment, and lynchings too numerous to mention to satiate the appetite for violence of the most vindictive among us. Even the most jaded masochist will surely find refuge in the statement by Yung Wing, a Westernized Chinese official and the first Asian graduate of an American university (Yale, Class of 1854), that he would remain celibate because, "There is no Chinese woman I could marry, and no American lady who would marry me."[1]

Despite such versatility of content, Asian-American history nonetheless remains neglected in present secondary and intermediate school curricula. When Asians in America are discussed at all they are discussed illustratively or tangentially as examples of particular generalizations which textbook writers may wish to stress—the cultural diversity of American pluralism or the fundmental equity of a social system in which certain Asian minorities appear to have risen above discrimination to success.

Sometimes, however, textbook authors fail to reach even these paltry half-truths. *Voices of the Americas,* a 1971 Leswing publication, noted, for example, that "Immigration laws changed frequently," then adding, "In 1882, not only were the Chinese excluded, but also criminals, paupers, and the insane."[2] Another book, *The Human Adventure* by Capellutti and Grossman, found Asian society a useful means of reinforcing in students the traditional belief in the superiority of Western over Eastern civilization: "In 1853, the American Commander Perry visited Japan and introduced Western ways. Within twenty years new political systems, new educational methods, and new industrial plans brought the Japanese into the modern world."[3] Other books, however, have simply overestimated the strengths and capacities of the Republic itself: "Note how long ago unfavorable attitudes about America began to grow in China," suggests the teacher's manual to *The Social Sciences: Concepts and Values,* a fifth-grade text by Harcourt Brace and Jovanovich. "Why did the United States government let this happen?"[4]

Illustrations such as these are not intended to be overtly offensive or injurious. They are merely contrite statements of what the authors accept to be facts. The writers do not intend to denigrate Chinese people by lumping them with criminals, paupers, and the insane; they intend to mollify the existence of anti-Chinese legislative racism by presenting it in a broader social context. The comment that the Japanese rapidly adopted Western political systems, educational methods, and industrial plans hardly endeavors to insult traditional Japanese mores, but rather praises the flexible intelligence of a resourceful people capable of shedding the fetters of a medieval past for the resilient technology of the future. Lastly, the effort to understand why the United States government allowed hostility to grow in China towards this nation is an attempt to comprehend the defect in universal affection for America, not an attempt to swindle from the Chinese people their sacred right of emotional self-determination.

All of these statements, however, have something further in common beyond the innocence of their intentions. Consciously or unconsciously, they work to rationalize American behavior for the student. In the process, they foreclose any discussion of real historical content in a

"*Unless ... we can understand the relocation of Japanese-Americans during World War II both from the perspective of those who were interned as well as ... those who interned them, we achieve only a partial understanding of the event itself.*"

manner that is fundamentally unscholarly and irrational. The omission of Asian-Americans or a neglect for their sensitivies in these books can only inform the reader that this group of people is marginal and irrelevant, if not absolutely expendable. Thus, these books indoctrinate rather than educate the student, and by excluding Asian-Americans from serious consideration or by treating them insensitively, they can only lay the foundation for the growth and perpetuation of anti-Asian attitudes.

Such indoctrination, in turn, has two specific consequences. The first and most obvious of these is that such teaching works to suppress the history of almost 2,000,000 Chinese, Japanese, Koreans, and Filipinos in the United States. Second, and interrelated, such indoctrination precludes the possibility of Asian-American minorities defining their own experience, both for themselves and for the larger society of which they are a part.

In some ways the ability to define a group's experience in the prevailing channels of communication is the ability to control that group in mass society by regulating the perception of that group for society-as-a-whole. A group such as Asian-Americans, who constitute at best one percent of the American population, are particularly vulnerable to such forms of control, and education, as a primary agent of mass socializa-

121

tion, bears a large responsibility for ensuring that such minority groups are not intellectually misrepresented or colonized by the process of learning itself.

This in turn can only be assured when the experience of minority groups in the United States is taught both from a majority and a minority perspective. Unless, for example, we can understand the relocation of Japanese-Americans during World War II both from the perspective of those who were interned as well as from the perspective of those who interned them, we achieve only a partial understanding of the event itself. For in this instance, the fullness of the historical event is not measured by the inconsequential effects experienced by the overwhelming American majority, but the extreme effects experienced by the Japanese minority. History is not made or experienced impartially, and attempts to report it or teach it neutrally all too often merely neutralize the real significance of events themselves. Accordingly, the major imperative of teaching the Asian-American experience, or any minority's history, is the ability to represent these dual perspectives fairly and completely.

To be sure, an accurate representation of these dual perspectives is not always possible, for Asian-American history itself remains inadequately researched. Source materials in Asian languages are relatively sparse since many Asian immigrants were illiterate laborers and many of the writings that were authored are now deposited in Asia or in private collections that have not been accessible to scholars. One principal result of this lack of research in Asian language sources is the further difficulty that what Asian-American history there is, is primarily an analysis of what was done to Asians rather than what was done by Asians. The resultant impression of a passive and fatalistic acceptance of this treatment by Asian immigrants themselves may thus be wholly unjustified, although the impact of those materials now available would tend to create that idea.

In the present context, then, an adequate portrayal of the Asian-American experience would probably have to content itself with certain rudimentary and by no means definitive explorations of Asian-American history. While such surveys would not produce ultimate judgments about the Asian-American experience, they should raise instructive questions about American society and about the traditional stereotypes of the role of Asians in American history, simply by offering an alternative perspective to what is currently taught: an Asian-American perspective on Asian-American history. In establishing this perspective here, heavy emphasis will be placed on the history of Chinese in America because of the author's own nationality, the preponderance of recent scholarship in this area, and because, as the first Asian immigrants to

America, the Chinese established patterns that were largely duplicated by the other Asian immigrants who followed them later.

An Asian-American Perspective on Asian-American History

One simple prerequisite for teaching Asian-American history from an Asian-American perspective is an adequate representation of the contributions of Asian-Americans to American life. A survey of fifteen basic social studies texts recently adopted in grades five through eight in California reveals that none of the books even comprehends the basic extent to which Asians were instrumental and indispensable in developing the West. No book, for example, mentioned that Chinese revenues paid to the Foreign Miner's Tax of 1850 constituted the principal source of funding for the California state government from 1850-1870. Yet, during the period from 1850-1854, Chinese paid approximately 50 percent of the tax, and between 1855-1870, Chinese contributed 98 percent of the revenues, in effect financing the operation of the California state government during the latter sixteen years.

More directly, Chinese constituted 1/3 of the state's farm labor in 1884 and 1/2 of it by 1884. Fifty of sixty major vegetable peddlers and wholesalers in Los Angeles during the same period were also Chinese, and tule lands reclaimed through the efforts of Chinese workers were valued at $289,000,000 alone. Finally, and perhaps most important, as many as 10,000 Chinese labored to complete the transcontinental railroad during the peak years of employment, 1867-1868. Asked in congressional hearings to assess, "In your opinion, would those roads have been built without Chinese labor?", Mr. William Hollister replied:

> I do not see how they could have been built. They might have been built but at such expense that they would be almost worthless. I do not see how a bushel of wheat could have been carried over the land; it would have cost more than the wheat was worth to transport it.[5]

Although statistical quantification is less available for Japanese, Koreans, and Filipinos their own contributions to the growth of the Western agricultural economy has also been impressive. Japanese small farmers furthered the development begun by Chinese workers after their exclusion from the United States and Filipinos became the primary source of farm labor when the cry for Japanese exclusion arose.

However, these enormous contributions also raise disquieting social issues that should be explored in the classroom. Coupled with the indispensability of black slave labor in the development of Southern agriculture, the contributions of Asian immigrants radically question to what extent the agricultural development of this country must not fairly be attributed to the industry of underpaid Asian indentured laborers and colonized black peoples. In a larger sense the entire history of the recruitment and utilization of Asian workers in America during the nineteenth and twentieth centuries poses other pertinent questions about the general relationship between racism directed at exploited minority laborers and the economic development of this country. For example, it is often supposed that overt forms of colonial slavery were only practiced against African slaves prior to 1865. Yet very similiar attempts to enforce almost identical forms of absolute, though theoretically temporary, control over Asian laborers were also attempted from the very first arrival of Chinese immigrants sometime around 1850.

Although there was a distinctly favorable welcome accorded to early Chinese immigrants from certain quarters, in 1852 one direct effort at formalizing quasi-colonial control over them was attempted. A bill introduced by California State Senator Tingley, "An Act to Enforce Contracts and Obligations to Perform Work and Labor," proposed that Chinese workers be allowed to sell their services under contracts for periods up to a maximum of ten years' time, thus creating a legally enforceable variety of slave labor.[6]

This bill did fail, however, but the reasons for its failure are also instructive. A qualified humanitarian belief in the ideal of frontier individualism and personal freedom in one direction reinforced less noble desires by other segments of the population to keep the West white man's country by excluding any institutions of slavery, and therefore, slaves themselves. Another important reason was the belief of white workingmen, expressed by State Senator Philip Roach, that such a bill would give "to capital *the hand and heart of labor,*" while allowing the Chinese government itself, "if it be to their advantage" to unleash "every malefactor in the prisons ... here as contract laborers." A government "as skilled in tact as is that of the Celestial Empire," the Senator reasoned, "could not fail to perceive the advantages of permitting its criminal element to emigrate."[7] Thus, in this particular instance, the desire to preserve the racial purity of California combined with the class interests of white workingmen to defeat the interests of capital and the possibility of legalized slavery.

Such an attempt at overt colonization might be dismissed as an aberration if it were not for the fact that other parallel incidents are numerous. In 1868, an unsuccessful attempt was made to colonize 48,600 square miles of lower California through the importation of 10,000 Chinese who were to be required to work and develop the land for several years in exchange for passage to the United States, though no indication in the proposed plan gives any evidence that anything but steerage fare and supplies would be awarded to the Chinese.[8] Simultaneously, in Memphis, Tennessee, $260,000 was raised to import Chinese laborers by the Arkansas River Valley Immigration Company in an effort to replace newly-emancipated black slaves. "Small farms and white labor or large farms and coolie labor," the Franklin *St. Mary's Planters Journal* had speculated, "may save the land." With the coming of Chinese laborers, the *Lexington Observer and Reporter* had warned freedmen, "the tune ... will not be 'forty acres and a mule,' but 'work nigger or starve.' "[9]

While these many efforts to institute a formal and legitimate system of wage slavery failed with the Chinese, the indentured servitude that evolved informally was similar to slavery itself. Whether involuntarily deceived by ruse or voluntarily seeking to escape poverty, Chinese workers from Southern China signed thousands of individual contracts bringing them to American soil in return for several years' labor either for opportunistic fellow countrymen or white capitalists. Because most Chinese immigrants considered their stay in the United States a temporary sojourn and emigrated without their wives or family, the Chinese family and district associations to which they were indentured exerted enormous control over these immigrants through their ability to regulate, in cooperation with American steamship companies, return passage to China. The associations also controlled available outlets of recreation, such as gambling and prostitution, which were, for the overwhelmingly male population (twenty-seven men per female in 1890), the chief diversions from labor. In any event, this informal influx of cheap indentured labor which evaded formal constitutional provisions against slavery after 1865 proved ideal for the manpower needs of the developing frontier, at least from a purely economic standpoint. By 1860, 34,933 Chinese had arrived in California through this system and by 1880 this number had swelled to 75,132. Chinese also provided badly needed labor in the service sector of the economy—in laundries, restaurants, and occasionally in semi-skilled trades such as cigar making.

Similar systems of control were imposed on other Asian immigrants and attempts to use Japanese laborers in Hawaii on sugar plantations adhered more closely to the traditional colonial model. When the islands' sugar industry expanded in production from 4,286 lbs. in 1837 to 17,127,161 lbs. in 1868, the need to import cheap labor became acute. In 1868, 148 Japanese emigrated to Hawaii on three-year contracts which provided only four dollars a month in pay, half of which was usually withheld until completion of the contract. Conditions, quite similar to those experienced by blacks in the South, were so oppressive that three workers committed suicide, although some 30,000 Japanese ultimately arrived in Hawaii from 1885-1894.

Almost simultaneously, other attempts were made on the mainland United States to use the Japanese farmers' skill in intensive cultivation to transform other areas of California into productive agricultural lands. In 1869, Henry Schnell, a German, imported twenty-six Japanese colonists to cultivate tea and silk and to establish the Wakamatsu Colony near Coloma, California, but the experiment failed. Similar attempts were also made in 1886 near Santa Cruz and Vacaville-Winters in 1888. The former attempt ended in failure, but the limited use of eighty Japanese as laborers alongside the Chinese in the latter case met with more success. Thereafter, Japanese immigration to America continued, reaching a peak between 1901-1908 of some 127,000 people.

Korean and Filipino immigration followed a similar pattern and were also exploited as cheap labor. Both peoples were actively recruited by growers for Hawaii's sugar plantations, like the Japanese, and both became disillusioned with the low wages and harsh demands of their condition. Ninety-three Koreans arrived first in 1903 and their number rapidly increased to 6,647 in 1904, rising eventually to 11,000 in 1905, when the Korean government stopped emigration. Wages ran roughly 70¢ per ten-hour day in Honolulu, but railway labor on the mainland U.S. yielded $1.20-$1.50 per day, luring many workers away from the tyranny of the plantations to scattered settlements across the West Coast. Because of their small numbers Koreans remained a minority-minority, essentially indistinguishable from the Chinese and Japanese in California. Ironically, only in 1913 when eleven Korean farmworkers were mistaken by whites for Japanese in the Hemet Valley did they become a *cause célèbre,* provoking growers in the valley to pack them aboard a train and angrily send them back to Los Angeles. Sensitive relations between rapidly modernizing Japan and the United States brought prompt State Department pressure to bear in defense of the perceived insult to the Japanese and apologies were duly issued. Significantly, however, the Koreans—who had been annexed by Japan in 1910 and had always struggled to rid themselves of the yoke of foreign domination—resented this error and strenuously resisted attempts by the Japanese Consulate to file protests on their behalf.[10]

Filipino immigration, finally, was conceived to conform to an identical design. As the Gentleman's Agreement of 1908 and subsequent restrictions on Japanese immigration to America were formulated, new sources of labor were necessary to continue the harvest of sugar cane on Hawaiian plantations. Recently annexed in the Spanish-American War of 1898, the Philippines provided a fertile hunting ground for labor recruitment, and from 1907-1919 25,000 Filipinos were persuaded to migrate to the Hawaiian Islands to replace the diminishing numbers of Japanese and Chinese laborers. From there, Filipinos gradually migrated to the mainland and assumed roles in agriculture similar to those of the Chinese, Koreans, and Japanese before them.[11]

The significance of this exploitation does not lie in the mere fact that Asian immigrants were underpaid and abused, for early European immigrants often endured equal hardships and equal forms of oppression. What is significant is that all of these varied Asian groups, each representing a separate country and unique culture, encountered a similar or identical pattern of racial oppression and economic exploitation. Just as all groups were utilized as a supply of cheap labor for the demands of the rapidly expanding western economy, so were all of the groups effectively excluded from the United States by law.

The most important of these laws, however, were the prototype Chinese Exclusion Laws which barred Chinese laborers from entering the United States in 1882 in direct contravention of the Senate-ratified Burlingame Treaty of 1868 which guaranteed the rights of reciprocal travel between China and America for citizens of either country for purposes of travel, trade, or study. Other principal extensions and variations of the basic exclusion laws were passed in 1888, 1892, 1902, and

". . . all of these varied Asian groups, each representing a separate country and unique culture, encountered a similar or identical pattern of racial oppression and economic exploitation."

1924. These laws denied departing Chinese immigrants the right to return to America after they had already departed, despite constitutional provisions against the *ex post facto* nature of such legislation, and also prevented the creation of natural Chinese families in America by denying married sojourners the right to bring their spouses to America, while further passing anti-miscegenation statutes against marriage to white women.

With the Japanese, a similar series of laws were passed, aimed chiefly at reducing their substantial agricultural holdings, which in 1919 totaled sixty-seven million dollars in crop value alone, or about 10 percent of the total agricultural value of California's crops. The Alien Land Law of 1913, for example, forbade alien Japanese from owning property, and in 1924 they too were formally excluded from the United States. To complete the pattern, Filipinos, who could not be excluded because their homeland was technically a possession of the United States, were assigned an immigration quota of fifty Filipinos per year in 1935. In addition, President Roosevelt offered free provision for repatriation to the Philippines for any Filipinos who wished to return to their homeland.

The concomitant processes of labor exploitation and legal discrimination also took place within the context of an incredible array of illegal personal violence that was directed against Asian immigrants, chiefly, though not exclusively, the Chinese. At least as early as 1852, widespread agitation and harassment of the Chinese was occurring in the mining regions of Chinese Camp, North Forks, Horseshoe Bay, New Kanaka Camp, Tuolome Colony, Vallecito, Douglas Flat, Sacramento Bar, Coyote Flat, Sand Flat, Rock Creek, and Buckeye. By 1862, the California Legislature's Joint Select Committee on the Chinese population was itself reporting that

> Your committee were furnished with a list of eighty-eight Chinamen, who are known to have been murdered by Collectors of the Foreign Miner's License Tax—sworn officers of the law. But two of the murderers have been convicted and hanged. Generally, they have been allowed to escape with the slightest punishment.
>
> The above number of Chinese who have been robbed and murdered comprise, probably, a very small proportion of those who have been murdered but they are all which the records of the different societies or companies in the city show.[12]

More sensational outbursts followed in the 1870's and 1880's in such locales as Los Angeles, where nineteen Chinese were killed in an 1871 riot after the shooting of a white policeman, and in Rock Springs, Wyoming in 1885, where Chinese were rounded up and driven out of town and assaulted. At the conclusion of the massacre, twenty-eight Chinese were found dead and property damage assessed at $148,000 was recounted. Similar but less drastic riots occurred in Seattle, Tacoma, Snake River, San Francisco, and elsewhere throughout the West.

While the Japanese managed to escape incidents of extreme mass violence, to some degree because they emigrated as entire families and thus aroused less hostility, they received no less harassment or general maltreatment. Especially when Japanese socialists entered the United States in the 1890's and successfully organized workers' strikes in Fresno and Bakersfield against growers, they prompted angry physical reprisals from whites. Finally, in World War II collective wartime hysteria and the legacy of accumulated anti-Asian racism culminated in the incarceration of 100,000 Japanese-Americans, although throughout the war no case of sabotage against this country by Japanese was ever discovered. With Filipinos, riots in Exeter, California, in 1929 and the Watsonville Riots of 1930, where a Filipino was shot through the heart after white female entertainment was employed at a Filipino party in that city, bear ample testimony to shared hostility against Asians.

Although the comprehensive analysis of Asian-American history or the history of any of the particular Asian minorities has yet to be written, information like the above should not be obscured and deserves presentation as the very real and brutal heritage of some two million American citizens who directly or indirectly bear the scars of this legacy of hatred. Even more important, the cyclical nature of the successive exploitation and exclusion throughout the period from 1850 to 1935 demands further scrutiny.

In observing this pattern in conjunction with the development of modern racism in industrial America, one sociologist, Stanford Lyman, has argued in his book *The Asian in the West* that, "If American racism may be defined as the attempt to impose white Anglo-Saxon culture on the inhabitants of a continent, then two epochs may be distinguished." The first of these, he maintains, is the total exclusion of non-whites, characterized by "total institutionalization of the non-white population on plantations and reservations." This phase lasted from 1607 to roughly the twentieth century. The second phase from the turn of the twentieth century to the present substitutes "segmented, partial, institutionalized racism in a wide variety of arenas of action for the abandoned and moribund method of total incarceration." Thus, in this context, "the pivotal group for the study of this transition from total to partial institutionalized racism is the Asian and especially the Chinese."[13]

It is this challenging and controversial hypothesis which Lyman proposes that distinctly separates the consideration of European immigration and Asian immigration to America. The American response to

Asians needs to be considered within the framework Lyman suggests as well as the traditional arguments one finds in textbooks which characterize anti-Asian racism as an act of deviance fomented by frontier yahoos, or worse, the "unfair" labor competition and demeaning ability Asians possessed to survive "inhuman" and "debasing" conditions. These are dangerously reminiscent of the xenophobia AFL leader Samuel Gompers proffered in his famous anti-Chinese tract, "Asiatic Coolieism: Meat vs. Rice."

Even if one chooses to reject Lyman's thesis, one thing is abundantly clear: the history of anti-Asian legislation and expulsion in California and the United States constitutes a clear statement of the inability of the democratic process itself to prevent assaults against the rights of non-white persons in this country. As early as 1854, the California Supreme Court case of *People v. Hall* stipulated that Chinese fell under the purview of legislation that provided that "No Black, or Mulatto person, or Indian shall be allowed to give evidence in favor of, or against, a white man," thus effectively denying Chinese any, much less equal, protection under the law. Separate schools were authorized for Chinese, and later Japanese, children, and in San Francisco specific ordinances were passed to discourage Chinese immigration, such as forms of taxation on the entry of Chinese immigrants into American ports, as well as anti-queue legislation, cubic air ordinances applied only to overcrowded Chinese dwellings, and statutes that restricted the hours in which it was legally permissible to iron clothes.

Invisible Communities: Modern Asian Ghettoes

In more contemporary terms, what is or is not taught about the present status of Asians in America has a substantial impact on social conditions within Asian-American communities themselves. No textbooks, for example, even attempt to analyze the fate of remaining Asian ethnic enclaves, such as Chinatowns, Little Tokyos, or Manilatowns. Yet instructively, an examination of these communities reveals problems of drug addiction, overcrowding, deteriorating housing, unemployment, and political powerlessness that rival or exceed the problems of any barrio, reservation, or black ghetto in America.

San Francisco's Chinatown, for example, serves as one illuminating case study. The core area of Chinatown has a population density of 231 persons per acre, the second highest density in the country, as compared with 33 persons per acre in surrounding San Francisco. The tuberculosis rate in the community is also the highest in the city, and suicides are committed three times more frequently than the national average. Seventy-five percent of the families who live there earn less than $6000 a year, 13 percent of the adults are unemployed, and 45 percent of the population in Chinatown's core area never attended school, though in the greater Chinatown area the median level of education is 8.0 years as compared to 12.0 years in San Francisco at large.[14] 67 percent of the community's housing is substandard in the Chinatown core area, and 51 percent is substandard in the greater Chinatown region. A random sampling of immigrant employment by Lillian Sing of the Chinese Newcomers Service Center found under-employment to be striking. Ms. Sing found a Chinese doctor employed as a laundryman, a sweater-weaver as a cook, a factory owner as a janitor, another Chinese doctor as an errand boy, and a newspaper reporter, teacher, and accountant all employed as busboys. Testimony before the California Fair Employment Practice Commission also revealed that only 4.3 percent of the city's civil servants and 1.7 percent of the city's construction workers were Asian-Americans in a city that is 14 percent Chinese alone. Finally, the subject of police-community relations deserves special attention for an unforgettable remark by Sergeant Louis E. Colobro in response to a suggestion by District Court of Appeals Justice John Molinari that police-community relations could be improved by bringing minorities and police representatives closer together. Quipped Colobro: "I don't know what they mean, whether we have to date homosexuals or dance with Chinese."

These particular statistics about San Francisco are roughly matched by conditions in New York Chinatown, and Los Angeles or Boston Chinatowns do not fare substantially better, though, because of smaller size, their problems are less intense and potentially more manageable. What is of significance, though, is the invisibility of these problems in school textbooks which concentrate on paying homage to successful Asian-Americans instead. This is especially troublesome because harping on the model minority stereotype of Asian-Americans creates a resistance on the part of the wider society to respond to legitimate needs for change. Boston's Chinatown is an excellent, if depressing, example of this problem. Although its community of 8,000 has a median family income that is $530 less than that of the next lowest anti-poverty target area in the greater Boston area, Chinatown itself is not classified as an anti-poverty target area.[15]

Further, curricula that remain oblivious to these problems reinforce the entrenched conservatism of oligarchic community elites such as the Chinese Six Companies in San Francisco or the Chinese Benevolent Association in New York who continue to dominate the economic life of these communities only by resisting external pressures for change that would force increased wages, increased contact with external society, and an erosion of the carefully constructed networks of social and political control they have established over the decades. Significantly, assaults on their studiously cultivated image of community propriety and prosperity in the media of the wider society are one of the few forms of petitioning to which they have been forced to respond.

Despite such squalor in these communities, there are also many Asian-Americans who have been economically successful in the wider society. Exposure to these contradictions of extreme wealth and extreme poverty in a single ethnic group are in fact one of the best reasons for studying the Asian-American experience and contrasting it with other minority groups. Insights into the process and problems of acculturation are many, and students would do well to ponder the forces that motivated one successful Chinese person interviewed by Kit Louis in the 1930's to lament that, "I have not heard much about Chinatown. It seemed such a dingy, dirty place. I went there as little as possible and think I was rather ashamed of it." Something should be said, too, for recognizing the dilemmas and cultural conflicts of minority members as in the case of one woman discussed in the 1962 *Cattell Report* on New York Chinatown. Asked to describe the relationship between the first and second generations in the community, she replied:

> People like me are emotionally tired all the time. When we were children we gave to our parents; we followed their orders; we never asked for anything. Now, our children are Americanized; they make demands on us and don't give us anything so we feel like we have given emotionally all our lives and never received.[16]

Psychological Colonization: Imposed Identity and Its Consequences

Ultimately, it is this unexplored region of personal identity and individual personality that needs expression, and acceptance, on its own terms. Both in the American overseas record of neocolonial exploitation of Asia and the anti-Asian aggressions in nineteenth- and twentieth-century America, there runs a basic rejection of the humanity and equality of non-white races. The images of John Chinaman in the U.S.A. and the slope-headed Celestials abroad were similar and commonly debased.

Extraordinary vituperations were heard in the popular press against Chinese in the United States, such as the following statement from the *Annals of San Francisco* in 1855:

> The manners and habits of the Chinese are very repugnant to Americans in California. Of different language, blood, religion, and character, inferior in most mental and bodily qualities, the Chinaman is looked upon by others as somewhat inferior. It is needless to reason upon the matter. Those who have

"Ultimately, it is this unexplored region of personal identity and individual personality that needs expression, and acceptance, on its own terms."

mingled with "celestials" have commonly felt before long an uncontrollable sort of loathing against them. "John's" person does not smell very sweetly; his color and the features of his face are unusual; his penuriousness, his lying, knavery, and natural cowardice are proverbial; he dwells apart from white persons, herding only with countrymen, unable to communicate his ideas to such as are not of his nation, or to show the better part of his nature. He is poor and mean, somewhat slavish and crouching, and is despised by the whites, who would only laugh in derision if even a divine were to pretend to place the two races on an equality.[17]

Public officials also confirmed this image. San Francisco's Mayor Kelloch noted in 1880 that "the vital evil of Chinese cheap labor" was "not so much that it cheapens labor; it degrades it," and he added that Chinese places of residence "are absolutely without proper ventilation, and it seems unaccountable how human beings can live in them for a single night. The sickening stench arising from thousands of such foul places in the very heart of our city would breed a plague in a week, if Providence, in His mercy, did not open the Golden Gate and pour the cleansing breezes of the sea over us." Still, if Mayor Kelloch was simply guilty of exaggerating actual conditions, men such as Dr. H.H. Tolland marshalled the credentials of science to buttress their racist fantasies about Chinese prostitution. "I have seen boys eight and ten years old," he reported

> with diseases they told me they contracted on Jackson Street. It is astonishing how soon they commence indulging in that passion. Some of the worst cases of syphilis I have seen in my life occurred in children not more than ten or twelve years old. . . .

In answer to what extent these diseases come from prostitutes he said:

> I suppose *nine-tenths*. When these persons come to me, I ask them where they got the disease, and they generally tell me Chinese women. . . . I am satisfied that nearly all the boys in town, who have venereal diseases, contracted them in Chinatown. They have no difficulty there, for the prices are so low they can go whenever they please. The women do not care how old the boys are, whether five years old or more, so long as they have the money. . . . It is my opinion that the maintenance of this population, instead of advancing civilization, is a crime against it.[18]

Such images, combined with the image of Chinese overseas, led Robert McClellan to conclude in his recent study *The Heathen Chinee: A Study of American Attitudes Towards China, 1890-1905* that

> The keystone to American policy in the Far East was the myth of Chinese inferiority. The myth was developed by Americans to shield themselves from the apparent threat to America's superiority offered by China's civilization. The Far Eastern policy of the United States was designed to fit the American image of China, not the actual conditions of the Orient.[19]

Even at the height of paternalistic American benevolence a constant attempt at restructuring and reshaping Asian identity has been evident. The indemnity scholarships to China made after the anti-foreign Boxer Rebellion of 1900, as one instance, have often been hailed as a prime example of American generosity towards conquered peoples. In reality though, it was only a partially benign attempt to educate and Americanize a young student elite in China that would return sympathetic to the views of American society and its entrepreneurial class. Similarly, the reformist efforts of such educational institutions as Yale-in-China were publicly proclaimed as humanitarian endeavors to save China through the light of Western learning. As Henry Luce, father of the later editor of *Time Magazine*, had expressed the hope, "We may work together for God, for China, and for Yale." Yet, in reality, such programs, taught as they were, revealed more sophisticated means of expressing the basic sense of superiority felt by Americans towards Chinese. Wrote Jerry

Israel in an astute book on *Progressivism and the Open Door: America and China, 1905-1921:*

> China was to be a market for all types of early twentieth century progressive American reform. It was this idea of China as a *tabula rasa* for American interests that provided a most revealing link between domestic and diplomatic attitudes. Canton, like Chicago, was to be cleansed of crime and corruption. China was to be remade in the American image.[21]

Sadly, even the many missionaries who earnestly and sincerely worked for reform, bringing their foreign gospel and zeal to Chinese soil, were seen by key American decision-makers as part of this cultural onslaught. Said Charles Denby, then American minister to China in 1895, "Missionaries are the pioneers of trade and commerce . . . Civilization, learning, and instruction breed new wants which commerce supplies. . . . The missionary, inspired by holy zeal, goes everywhere, and by decrees foreign commerce and trade follow."[22]

In this fashion, the reshaping of Chinese cultural identity and civilization in the early twentieth century was seen by some Americans as a means to increased commercial expansion. If only the 400 million Chinese would each add 1/2 inch length to their undershirts, the argument ran, the mills of England and cotton growers of America could be occupied for a lifetime with profitable employment. Instead of conquering China barbarously and elbowing Great Britain, France, and Germany aside, American diplomats devised the Open Door Policy—a means to allow the superior agencies of American acculturation and enterprise to win the Chinese Empire with *McGuffey's Reader* and *The Bible,* rather than the military field manual. The exertion of war and empire could be avoided without sacrificing the profits of commercial enterprise. As John Hay, the American Secretary of State, once phrased it elegantly, "the ideal policy . . . is to do nothing but be around when the watermelon is cut. Not that we want any watermelon, but it is always fashionable to be seen in smart colored circles on occasions of great festivity."[23]

In a larger and more contemporary context it is not difficult to see parallels between the acculturation of China into American cultural-economic mores and the dangers of blind assimilation into American society today. If one primary reason for reforming China was to create an appropriate market demand for the products of American industry, it is logical to view the Americanization of Asian-American history and Asian-American identity with caution and suspicion, not for the sake of Asians who may freely choose to disappear into the American mainstream but for the sake of overseas Asian nations who are entitled to their own economic independence and self-determination. Indistinguishable to the American eye, the Asian national and the Asian-American remain united in a common perception, for better or for worse. The attempt to refashion or distort the identity of either group has had tragic consequences whether we consider the hysterical fear of China during the McCarthy Era that led to the Cold War and Arms Race, the images of backward and diseased China that colored the perception of Asian immigrants to America and provoked the anti-Chinese movement in the nineteenth century, the transference of aggression from Imperial Japan to Japanese-Americans in World War II, or the problems of the solitary Asian-American child whose psyche and sense of self is irreparably warped by the internalization of an education that degrades and maligns his cultural identity.

There needs, instead, to be a recognition of Asian-American personalities in the teaching of the Asian-American experience so that there can be some discovery of the common human dimension shared by Asians and Americans alike. Teaching the Asian-American experience demands some confrontation with the emotional significance of that history for Asian-Americans themselves. This is not an easy task but the growing literature of Asian-American expression makes accessible this buried human dimension of historical experience. Recently translated poems from the *Ti-Chih-Mei-Kuo (Boycott of the United States)*, to cite one possibility, recount the feelings of Chinese laborers when they were blamed in the contemporary press for an epidemic in Honolulu:

> I remember
> When Hawaii was plagued by an epidemic
> And the blame fell upon us
> For spreading the disease.
> With our homes burned to the ground,
> We fled like clusters of frightened crabs.
> There were old men and tender babes,
> And other helpless beings
> Being burned to death.
> The tormented feelings
> Of these tragedies,
> Bitter to the ear,
> Excruciating for the eyes,
> Cannot be repeated
> By paper and pen.
> Such events,
> Sad to say,
> Are consequences of our silent indifference
> To foreign oppression,
> And our own
> Not-so-silent disunity.[24]

"There needs ... to be a recognition of Asian-American personalities in the teaching of the Asian-American experience so that there can be some discovery of the common human dimension shared by Asians and Americans alike."

Neither need the personal dimension of Asian-American history emerge quite so dramatically. A moving opportunity for sensing the quiet side of historical turmoil is found in Shizuye Takashima's *A Child in Prison Camp*, the narrative of the Japanese internment experience in Canada, in which the author describes her own girlish reactions on the morning of relocation itself:

> We rise early, very early, the morning we are to leave.
> The city still sleeps. The fresh autumn air feels nice.
> We have orders to be at the Exhibition grounds.
> The train will leave from there, not from the station
> where we said good-bye to father and to David.
> We wait for the train in small groups scattered
> alongside the track. There is no platform.
> It is September 16. School has started. I think
> of my school friends and wonder if I shall ever see
> them again. The familiar mountains, all purple and
> splendid, watch us from afar. The yellowy-orangey
> sun slowly appears. We have been standing
> for over an hour. The sun's warm rays reach us,
> touch a child still sleeping in its
> mother's arms, touch a tree, blades of grass.
> All seems magical. I study the thin yellow rays
> of the sun. I imagine a handsome prince will come and
> carry us all away in a shining, gold carriage with
> white horses. I daydream, and feel nice as long as I don't
> think about leaving this city where I was born. . . .
>
> I see the black, dull colored train. It looks
> quite old. Somehow I expected a shiny new one.
> Yuki remarks, "I hope it moves. You never know
> with the government." Mother looks, smiles,
> "Never mind, as long as we get there. We aren't
> going on a vacation; we are being evacuated."
>
> Bang . . . bang . . . psst . . . the old train gurgles,
> makes funny noises. I, seated by the window,
> feel the wheels move, stop, move, stop.
> Finally, I hear them begin to move in an
> even rhythm slowly.
>
> I look out the dusty window.
> A number of people still wait their turn.
> We wave. Children run after the train.
> Gradually, it picks up speed. We pass the gray
> granaries, tall and thin against the blue Vancouver sky.
> The far mountains, tall pines, follow us
> for a long time, until finally they are gone.

"We aren't going on a vacation; we are being evacuated."

Mother sits opposite; she has her eyes closed,
her hands are on her lap. Yuki stares out the window.
A woman across the aisle quietly dabs her
tears with a white cloth. No one speaks.[25]

The greatest danger to an open society is an education that homogenizes its people into limited and fixed conformity; the greatest danger to a small minority like Asian-Americans is that they will be imprisoned in the images created for them by mass society and that their own personal reality will not be able to transcend the imposed psychological colonization of society-as-a-whole. In a like fashion, Hannah Arendt has suggested that intellectual freedom can exist only in the context of psychic space, while psychic space can be created only between distinct and contrasting points of view. Teaching the Asian-American experience from an Asian-American perspective is one way of attempting to ensure these freedoms, personally and intellectually.

Suggested Teaching Strategies

by Elizabeth O. Pearson*

Main Idea

A. Asian-Americans were victims of labor exploitation in America.

1. Although attempts at enslavement of Asians were unsuccessful in the U.S., indentured servitude provided the means for many Asians to come to the U.S. Ask students to compare the characteristics of slavery with indentured servitude. Then apply those characteristics to the conditions under which Asians and Blacks lived and worked. Ask students to consider for Blacks and Asians:

   a. the amount of money offered for emigrating to America.
   b. the kinds of jobs offered.
   c. the wages.
   d. the working conditions.
   e. the reasons for emigrating.

2. So that students can see the difference in conditions under which Asians lived when they arrived in the U.S. compared to conditions for many Asian-Americans in the 1970's, ask students to develop a data retrieval chart. They can determine the categories they want to include for Chinese, Japanese, Koreans and Filipinos. Some possibilities are illustrated below.

	Reasons for Immigration	Average Income	Kind of Work	Years of Greatest Immigration	Area of Pop. Concentration
Japanese					
Chinese					
Filipino					
Korean					

* See page 117 for biographical sketch. Suggested Teaching Strategies by Ms. Pearson also accompany Chapters 9, 10, 11, and 12.

Another chart to indicate the conditions for Asian-Americans today might include the following categories:

	Average Income	Kind of Work	Immigration Since 1950	Area of Pop. Concentration
Japanese				
Chinese				
Filipino				
Korean				

An intermediate stage should be included which would focus upon the hardships Asian-Americans encountered, including the Chinese Exclusion Act of 1882 and the Japanese internment during World War II.

3. A study of anti-Chinese and anti-Japanese agitation, particularly in California and Washington, illuminates the problem of labor exploitation. Labor elements began pushing for more employment of whites, eventually phasing out Chinese workers in the Puget Sound area in 1885. Agitation continued in 1886. Other agitation against Chinese and later Japanese occurred in California. Students can do research into the circumstances of these events by referring to histories of Chinese and Japanese Americans. Documentary evidence also would be useful. The relationship between labor unrest and the large number of laundries and restaurants run by Chinese and the sizable number of Asian farmers should be determined.

Main Idea

B. The personal reality of being an Asian-American allows a focus different from the view the mass society maintains of Asian-Americans.
   1. Understanding the way Asian-Americans see themselves can be facilitated by studying China or Japan at the peak of immigration. Ask students to determine what aspects of each civilization should be studied. They might choose to familiarize themselves with aspects of everyday life, governmental structure and religion. Comparisons can be drawn with the Chinese or Japanese way of life in the U.S., primarily California, after the immigrants settled into their jobs. Here again, a data retrieval chart would be useful.

2. It is difficult for anyone to truly feel the experiences others have gone through unless he has been through similar situations. However, it is important for students to feel history as well as know it. For example, students can study the circumstances under which Japanese were removed from cities and encamped in isolation during part of World War II. The chapter entitled "From the Orient to the Golden Gate" in *From Many Lands* by Albert Eiseman provides some information on this subject. *A Child in Prison Camp* by Shizuye Takashima provides a personal portrait of Japanese internment.

Ask students to consider the following questions:
a. What did adults have to do upon leaving their homes?
b. What were some occupations in which Japanese were involved?
c. How do you think they felt about having to leave?
d. How do you think they felt toward the American government?

Now set up a role-playing situation in which two Japanese families learn about the internment and prepare to leave their homes. Ask each family member to identify his or her age and role. Then ask the group to role play the situation which would occur when they were informed that they would be placed in concentration camps. Ask also how they would feel as they left their homes.

After one group has participated in a role-playing session, ask another group to participate.

At the completion of two or more role-playing sessions, discuss what happened in each with the whole class. Focus upon the feelings of each participant as he or she verbalizes them. Then ask for reactions from the class.

a. Did they empathize with the characters?
b. Can they think of situations which exist today that might in some ways be parallel to what the Japanese experienced?

3. Recent Filipino and Chinese immigrants encounter a variety of cultural differences upon their arrival in the United States. So that students may become more aware of the problems Asian immigrants experience, have them role play a recent Filipino immigrant on his first day of classes in an American city high school. Find a speaker who can report to the class the cultural traditions and ways of life from which Asian immigrants, particularly Chinese and Filipino, are severed in their move to the United States. Ask students to find out the rate of employment for Filipinos and Chinese in cities such as San Francisco, Los Angeles and Seattle which have sizable groups of Asian immigrants. Then have them role play a situation in which a Chinese immigrant with specific skills is interviewed by a counselor for an employment agency.

"It is difficult for anyone to truly feel the experiences others have gone through unless he has been through similar situations."

Main Idea

C. The power of pressure groups in the U.S. has been an effective means of discriminating against Asian-Americans.

1. Dennis Kearney
   Chinese Exclusion Act 1882
   White gold miners in California
   Pacific Coast Anti-Coolie Association
   1879 California State Constitution
   Asiatic Exclusion League 1905
   Anti-Japanese Laundry League
   California newspapers, World War II

   The above persons and groups acted in some way to pressure for exclusion of Japanese and Chinese from the U.S. After students determine the purpose and methods of these persons and groups, all operating in California between 1860 and 1945, have them try to generalize about the methods of these persons and groups and their goals to determine just why they were so effective in limiting the activities of Asian-Americans.

2. For the individual citizen's recollection of pressure groups, ask students to interview adults who remember World War II. Questions should focus upon remembered statements by public officials and groups about the necessity, or lack of, for internment of the Japanese after Pearl Harbor. Questions also could probe an individual's recollection of others' views of Japanese-Americans and the necessity for internment.

3. In the decade of the sixties, attempts to cease discrimination against minorities resulted in a variety of pressure groups organized for that purpose. To develop student awareness of these groups, ask students to find out what groups function as spokesmen for Asian-Americans, both in their state and nationally. The goals, methods of attaining them, and kinds of membership should be discussed for each group. Inviting a speaker from each group along with examining the group's literature are useful ways of informing students. Some students may choose to join the organization or establish a chapter in their town.

FOOTNOTES

¹ Thomas E. La Fargue, *China's First Hundred* (Pullman, Washington: State College of Washington, 1942), p. 42. Also quoted in Bill Lann Lee, "Yung Wing and the Americanization of China," *Amerasia Journal,* Volume I, No. 1, March 1971, p. 30.
² *Voices of the Americans* (San Francisco: Leswing Publications, 1971), p. 76.
³ Frank Capellutti and Ruth Grossman, *The Human Adventure* (New York: Field Educational Publications, 1971), p. 463.
⁴ *The Social Sciences, Concepts and Values* (Level Five, Purple) (New York: Harcourt Brace and Jovanovich, 1970), p. 333 (Teacher's Manual Edition).
⁵ William Hollister testifying before the *Joint Special Committee to Investigate Chinese Immigration,* November 16, 1876, p. 777. The hearings of this committee were reproduced in a massive thousand-page volume, copies of which are available in select libraries such as those of Yale University and the University of California at Los Angeles and Berkeley.
⁶ See Gunther Barth, *Bitter Strength: A History of the Chinese in the United States, 1850-1870* (Cambridge, Massachusetts: Harvard University Press, 1964), p. 139.
⁷ Philip A. Roach, "Minority Report of the Select Committee on Senate Bill No. 63, 'an act to enforce contracts and obligations to perform work and labor'," *California Senate Journal,* 3rd session, 1852, appendix pp. 669-674, in Barth, p. 140.
⁸ Mention of this attempt is found in the letter from George Wilkes, President of the Lower California Company, to J. Ross Browne, then American minister to China, in communications dated July 24, 1868 between Browne and Secretary of State William Seward in *U. S. Diplomatic Correspondence, 1868,* part I, pp. 528-529. The letter between Browne and Wilkes itself is dated June 7, 1868.
⁹ Franklin *St. Mary's Planters Journal* quoted in *New Orleans Commercial Bulletin,* January 16, 1867, in Barth, p. 187, and the *Lexington Observer and Reporter,* July 12, 1869, in Barth, p. 187.
¹⁰ For a concise history of Korean labor in America see Linda Shin, "Koreans in America, 1903-1945" in *Amerasia Journal,* Volume I, No. 3, November 1971, pp. 32-39.
¹¹ A general discussion of Filipino immigration to the United States can be found in "Filipino Immigration: the Creation of a New Social Problem" in *Roots: An Asian American Reader* (Los Angeles: UCLA Asian American Studies Center, 1971), pp. 188-201.
¹² California Legislature, "Report of the Joint Select Committee Relative to the Chinese Population of the State of California" (Sacramento: 1862), p. 7 in Thomas Chinn, H. Mark Lai, and Philip P. Choy (editors), *A History of the Chinese in California, A Syllabus* (San Francisco: Lawton and Kennedy by the Chinese Historical Society of America, 1969), p. 32.
¹³ Stanford M. Lyman, "The Significance of Asians in American Society" in *The Asian in the West* (Reno: University of Nevada, 1970), pp. 3-8.
¹⁴ Mary Ellen Leary, "San Francisco's Chinatown" in *Atlantic Monthly,* Volume 225, March 1970, pp. 32-42.
¹⁵ Action for Boston Community Development, Inc., Planning and Evaluation Department, "The Chinese in Boston," pp. ii-iii. Monograph reproduced for limited use, apparently by the authors themselves.
¹⁶ Stuart Cattell, *Health, Welfare, and Social Organization in Chinatown, New York City,* a report prepared for Chinatown Public Health Nursing Demonstration Department of Public Affairs (New York: Community Service Society, 1962), p. 59. Limited reproduction.
¹⁷ Frank Soule, John H. Gihon, and James Nisbet, *The Annals of San Francisco, 1855.* (Palo Alto: Lewis Osborne, reprinted 1966), pp. 411-412.
¹⁸ Dr. H. H. Tolland before the Special Committee to Investigate Chinese Immigration 1877-1878 in "Chinatown Declared a Nuisance," by The Committee (of the Workingman's Party), pp. 4-5. Pamphlet on file in the Special Collections on Chinese Immigration in the UCLA Research Library.

[19] Robert McClellan, *The Heathen Chinee, A Study of American Attitudes Towards China, 1890-1905* (Ohio State University Press, 1971), p. 253.

[20] Henry Luce to Prof. Reed, May 10, 1904, Yale-in-China Archives, Henry Luce file, reprinted from *Progressivism and the Open Door, America and China, 1905-1921* by Jerry Israel (by permission of the University of Pittsburgh Press, ©1971) by the University of Pittsburgh Press.

[21] Israel, p. xi.

[22] *China Dispatches*, 98, No. 2172, Denby to Gresham, March 22, 1895; 100, No. 2341, Denby to Olney, November 14, 1895 in Thomas McCormick, *China Market, America's Quest for Informal Empire, 1893-1901* (Chicago: Quadrangle Books, 1967), p. 66.

[23] John Hay to Henry Adams, July 8, 1900, Hay Papers, Library of Congress, in Marilyn B. Young, *The Rhetoric of Empire, American China Policy, 1895-1901* (Cambridge: Harvard University Press, 1968), p. 102.

[24] *Ti-Chih-Mei-Kuo (Boycott of the United States)* quoted in "Chinese in the United States: A View From Peking," translated by Odoric Wou in *Bridge Magazine*, Volume I, No. 4, March/April 1972, p. 23. Reprinted with permission.

[25] Shizuye Takashima, *A Child in Prison Camp* (Plattsburgh, N.Y.: Tundra Books, 1971), no pagination, section entitled "An End to Waiting." Reprinted with permission of the publisher.

BIBLIOGRAPHY

Books Dealing with the Asian-American Experience from a Multi-Ethnic Perspective:

Jacobs, Paul and Saul Landau with Eve Pell, *To Serve the Devil, Volume 2, Colonials and Sojourners* (New York: Random House, Vintage Books, 1971). A collection of primary source materials, carefully edited to present a documentary history of minorities in America.

Kitano, Harry and Roger Daniels, *American Racism* (New York: Prentice-Hall, 1970). An interesting sociological and historical introduction to anti-Asian racism.

Lyman, Stanford, *The Asian in the West* (Reno: Desert Research Institute of the University of Nevada, 1970). A series of meticulously researched essays on Japanese and Chinese in the Western United States, concentrating on the nineteenth century, but including some valuable research on contemporary developments in Asian communities.

Odo, Franklin, Amy Tachiki, and Eddie Wong, *Roots: An Asian American Reader* (Los Angeles: UCLA Asian American Studies Center, 1971). A documentary collection of recent works on Asian Americans that reflects the tensions and aspirations of emerging generations. *Roots'* diversity in style, content, and regional representation make it as broadly representative as any current publication in the field.

Books on the Chinese-American Experience:

Barth, Gunther, *Bitter Strength: A History of the Chinese in the United States, 1850-1870* (Cambridge: Harvard University Press, 1964). The first comprehensive recent study of early Chinese immigrant history in the United States. Barth's book abounds in constructive details about the 1850-1870 period but has a dangerous tendency to generalize without substantiation about the acculturation of Chinese into California life.

Isaacs, Harold, *Scratches on Our Minds* (also published as *Images of Asia*) (New York: John Day, 1958). An analysis of the shifting image of China and the Chinese throughout American history.

Miller, Stuart C., *The Unwelcomed Immigrant: The American Image of the Chinese, 1785-1882* (Berkeley and Los Angeles: University of California Press, 1969). A path-breaking study of the American image of the Chinese prior to the Chinese Exclusion Act of 1882. By analyzing the writings and reports of American traders, diplomats, and missionaries, and their transference into the contemporary nineteenth-century media, Miller argues that the causes of Chinese exclusion were national as well as regional.

Saxton, Alexander, *The Indispensable Enemy: Labor and the Anti-Chinese Movement in California* (Berkeley and Los Angeles: University of California Press, 1971). A compellingly reasoned and marvelously thorough study of the roots of anti-Chinese agitation in California's developing labor movement and Democratic Party. An advanced work for the reader who wishes to pinpoint the details of the origins of the anti-Chinese movement.

Books on the Japanese-American Experience:

Bosworth, Alan, *America's Concentration Camps* (New York: W. W. Norton, 1967). A popular treatment of Japanese-American relocation in World War II.

ten Broek, Jacobus, Edward N. Barnhart, and Floyd Matson, *Prejudice, War, and the Constitution* (Berkeley: University of California Press, 1954). An erudite and exhaustively researched study of Japanese-American relocation.

Daniels, Roger, *The Politics of Prejudice* (Gloucester, Massachusetts: Peter Smith, 1966). A concise and highly readable account of the development of anti-Japanese sentiment in California prior to World War II.

Ichihashi, Yamato, *Japanese in the United States* (New York: Arno Press and the *New York Times,* 1969, originally published in 1932). The most rigorous and detailed treatment of Japanese immigration to America.

Books on the Filipino-American Experience:

Bulosan, Carlos, *America Is in the Heart* (New York: Harcourt, Brace, and World, 1943). One immigrant's personal account of his life in the United States.

Lasker, Bruno, *Filipino Immigration to the Continental United States and Hawaii* (Chicago: University of Chicago Press, 1931). The seminal scholarly work on Filipinos in the United States.

James A. Banks

JAMES A. BANKS is Associate Professor of Education at the University of Washington, Seattle. He received his bachelor's degree from Chicago State University, and the M.A. and Ph.D. degrees from Michigan State University. Professor Banks taught in the public schools of Joliet, Illinois, and at the Francis W. Parker School in Chicago. He is a member of the National Advisory Board, ERIC Clearinghouse for Education and Social Science, the Social Science Education Consortium Publications Task Force, and the United States Office of Education Leadership Training Institute on Teacher Education. His articles have appeared in such journals as Social Education, The Instructor, School Review, and Educational Leadership. *He has served as guest editor of a special issue of the* Phi Delta Kappan *which focused on ethnic education.*

Professor Banks is the author of March Toward Freedom: A History of Black Americans, Teaching the Black Experience: Methods and Materials, Teaching Strategies for the Social Studies: Inquiry, Valuing and Decision-Making, *and the forthcoming* Teaching Strategies for Ethnic Studies. *He coedited and contributed to* Teaching Social Studies: Strategies of Teaching to Culturally Different Children, Teaching the Language Arts to Culturally Different Children, *and* Black Self-Concept: Implications for Education and Social Science. *He contributed to the 1972 NCSS Yearbook, the 1974 ASCD Yearbook, and to the books* Racial Crisis in American Education, Black Image: Education Copes with Color, *and* Teaching Social Studies in the Urban Classroom.

JAMES A. BANKS

7

Teaching Black Studies
for Social Change

With the emergence of the Black revolt of the sixties, Black people began to shape and perpetuate a new identity. "Black Power" and "Black Is Beautiful" were rallying cries of this identity search. Blacks rejected many of the components of the dominant white culture, and searched for elements out of which a new identity could be formed. Such elements include intensified racial pride and cohesiveness, a search for power, and an attempt to identify cultural roots in Africa. African dashikis, tikis, Afro hair styles, and Swahilian phrases emerged as new cultural components.

Written history is an important part of a people's heritage. As the Black revolt gained momentum, Blacks demanded that history be re-written so that the role played by them in shaping America's destiny would be more favorably and realistically portrayed. Organized interest groups pressured school districts to ban lily-white history books from the schools. When the pressure on school districts mounted, they encouraged publishers to include more Blacks in schoolbooks.

In response to Black demands for Black history and Black studies, educational institutions at all levels have made some attempts to institute Black studies programs. Publishers, seeking quick profits, have responded to the Black history movement by producing a flood of

Parts of this chapter are based upon the author's "Teaching Black History with a Focus on Decision-Making," *Social Education,* Vol. 35, November, 1971, pp. 740-745, 820-21. A more extended discussion of the ideas contained in this chapter are in the author's text, *Teaching Strategies for the Social Studies* (Reading, Mass.: Addison-Wesley Publishing Company, 1973).

textbooks, tradebooks, and multi-media "kits," many of dubious value. Most of the "integrated" materials now on the market are little more than old wine in new bottles, and contain white characters painted brown, and the success stories of "safe" Blacks such as Crispus Attucks and Booker T. Washington. The problems which powerless ethnic groups experience in America are de-emphasized or ignored.[1]

Despite the recent attempts to implement Black history programs, few of them are sound because the goals of Black studies remain confused, ambiguous, and conflicting. Many Black studies programs have been structured without careful planning and clear rationales. Divergent goals for Black history programs are often voiced by experts of many different persuasions and ideologies. Larry Cuban, a leader in ethnic education, argues that "the only legitimate goals for ethnic content [in the public schools] ... are to offer a *balanced* view of the American past and present ..."[2] (emphasis added). Nathan Hare, another innovator in ethnic studies, believes that Black history should be taught from a *Black perspective* and emphasize the struggles and aspirations of Black people.[3]

Many young Black activists feel that the main goal of Black history should be to equip Black students with an *ideology* which is imperative for their liberation. Some Blacks who belong to the over-thirty generation, such as Martin Kilson and Bayard Rustin, think that education which is designed to develop a commitment to a fixed ideology is antithetical to sound scholarship and has no place in public institutions. Writes Kilson, "... I don't believe it is the proper or most useful function of a [school] to train ideological or political organizers of whatever persuasion. A [school's] primary function is to impart skills, techniques, and special habits of learning to its students. The student must be free to decide himself on the ideological application of his training."[4] The disagreement over the proper goals for Black studies reflects the widespread racial tension and polarization within American society.

Classroom teachers are puzzled about strategies to use in teaching Black history and have serious questions about *who* can teach Black studies because of the disagreement over goals among curriculum experts and social scientists. Effective teaching strategies and sound criteria for judging materials cannot be formulated until goals are identified and explicitly stated. In the past, most social studies teachers emphasized the mastery of factual information, and tried to develop a blind commitment to "democracy" as practiced in the United States. Unless a sound rationale for Black studies programs can be stated and new approaches to the teaching of Black history implemented, students will get just as sick and tired of Black history as they have become with white chauvinistic schoolbook history. Some students already feel that Black history has been "oversold." Many teachers who teach Black history use new materials but traditional strategies because multi-ethnic materials, although necessary for sound social studies programs, do not in themselves solve the classroom teacher's pedagogical problems.

Without *both* new goals and novel strategies, Black history will become just another fleeting fad. Isolated facts about Crispus Attucks don't stimulate the intellect any more than isolated facts about Abraham Lincoln. In this chapter, the author offers a rationale for Black studies programs for the reader's consideration, attempts to resolve the question, "Black history for what?", and illustrates how Black history can be taught as an *integral* part of a modern social studies curriculum which is spiral, conceptual, and interdisciplinary, and which emphasizes decision-making and social action skills.

The Purpose of Black History Instruction

The goal of Black history should be to help students develop *the ability to make reflective decisions so that they can resolve personal problems and, through social action, influence public policy and develop a sense of political efficacy.* To help liberate Black Americans from physical and psychological captivity, we must help them to attain effective decision-making and social action skills which can be used to solve personal problems and to influence the making of public policy. Thus, the ultimate goal of social studies for Black students should be to make them effective *political activists.* While social action skills are needed by *all* students, they are especially needed by Black students because most of them are still physically and psychologically victimized by institutional racism. When an individual develops the ability to make reflective decisions, he can act effectively to free himself from oppression and colonialism. Poverty, political powerlessness, low self-esteem, consumer exploitation, institutional racism, and political alienation are the kinds of problems which the social studies must help Black youths to resolve through effective political action.

We must radicalize Black and other colonialized students so that they will continually challenge the position of those in power. We should also train them so that they will develop the skills and knowledge to obtain power and use it to build institutions which they will control. Until oppressed people obtain power and independent institutions, they will be victims of the whims of the ruling elite because policy made by those in power is made primarily to enhance, legitimize and to reinforce their power. I will illustrate in this chapter how Black history, as an integral part of an inquiry-oriented social studies curriculum, can help students to develop skills in decision-making and social action. First, however, I will state the *assumptions* of my theory of social education.

Assumptions

My beliefs about the proper goal of the social studies are based on the assumption that man will always face personal and social problems, and that all citizens should participate in the making of public policy in an open society. The focus for the social studies which I recommend is not only grounded in a cultural pluralistic ideology, but one of its basic assumptions is that maximum participation of all citizens in the making of public policy is essential for the creation and perpetuation of a society in which each ethnic minority group can maintain its unique cultural identity, and yet fully participate in all social and political institutions. The theory advocates cultural diversity rather than assimilation. It rejects the notion that elitists, ruling and powerful groups or academic specialists should determine the *goals* of social and political institutions. The proper role of the academic specialist is to facilitate the realization of the goals and values shaped by all groups within a society.

I am also assuming that individuals are not born with the ability to make *reflective* decisions, but that decision-making consists of a set of skills which can be identified and systematically taught. Further, I am assuming that man can both identify and clarify his *values*, and that he can be trained to reflect upon problems before acting on them.

I have suggested that students should not only become decision-makers, but that they should develop the ability to make *reflective* decisions. An important question which I have a responsibility to answer is: "How do I distinguish between a *reflective* and a *non-reflective* decision?" or "What criteria do I use to evaluate the effectiveness of a decision?" In this chapter, I am going to delineate a *process* with definite steps and attributes which a decision-maker must satisfy before I am willing to call his decisions and actions *reflective*. It is extremely important for the reader to realize that I am primarily concerned with a *process* of decision-making, and not with specific *products* of decisions.

The careful reader may raise several legitimate questions about my position and wonder about the consequences for a society in which individuals are free to make uncoerced decisions. Such individuals may, for example, violate norms which are essential for the survival of his group. In principle, a *social actor** who reached a decision using the

---

* *Social actor* refers to an individual who makes a deliberate effort to influence his social environment and persons within it, including societal laws, public policy, norms, values and the distribution of wealth. The activities in which he participates are *social action*. Social action may be effective or ineffective.

process which I will spell out below may decide to murder all of his perceived enemies. This possibility forces me to make explicit other assumptions on which my theory of social studies education is based. I am assuming that social actors who make decisions using the *process* which I advocate will act in ways that will perpetuate the cultural identity and integrity of their group, and the creation of a humane and just society. I believe that most persons who habitually violate humane values do so primarily because they are the victims of a society which perpetuates myths about the inferiority and superiority of different groups, have confused values, and act before rationally reflecting upon the possible consequences of their actions. Most such actions, I believe, are impetuous, impulsive and non-reflective.

While my position assumes that *reflective* decision-makers will act in ways consistent with humane values, it is not a theory which does not advocate *social change*. It also assumes that if the social actors within a society use the process which I will describe to reach decisions, societal goals, values and mores will be changed by intelligent social action when they no longer contribute to the satisfaction of human needs and aspirations, or when they no longer meet the current needs of society. When goals and values become obsolete and dysfunctional, the public, through massive and effective social action, will construct new goals and values which are more consistent with current needs, purposes, and beliefs. Thus, while the theory is not necessarily a revolutionary one, it opens up the *possibility* for revolution in values and in social and political institutions.

The social studies curriculum which I advocate could possibly prevent chaos and destructive instability within our society, while at the same time providing means and methods whereby oppressed groups and new generations can shape their own destinies, use those aspects of traditional society which are consistent with their needs, and create new, legitimate life-styles and values when it is necessary to do so. *What is legitimate, normative and valued is subject to reconstruction in each new generation.* Each generation, however, can use those aspects of the past which are functional for current needs and purposes. Thus our theory advocates both stability and change within a society.

Essential Components of Decision-Making

Knowledge is one essential component of the decision-making process. There are many kinds of knowledge and ways of attaining it. To make a reflective decision, the decision-maker must use the *scientific method* to attain knowledge. The knowledge on which reflective decisions are made must also be *powerful and widely applicable so that it*

"What is legitimate, normative and valued is subject to reconstruction in each new generation."

will enable the decision-maker to make the most accurate predictions possible. There are several *categories* of knowledge and they vary in their predictive capacity and in their ability to help us to organize our observations, and thus to make decisions.

Factual knowledge, which consists of specific empirical statements about limited phenomena, is the lowest level of knowledge, and has the least predictive capacity. *Concepts* are words or phrases which enable us to categorize or classify a large class of observations, and thus to reduce the complexity of our social environment. Because of their structure and function, concepts in and of themselves do not possess predictive value. However, *generalizations,* which state the relationship between concepts or variables, enable us to predict behavior; the predictive capacity of generalizations varies directly with their degree of applicability and amount of empirical support. Generalizations which describe a large class of behavior and which have been widely verified are the most useful for making predictions and thus decisions. *Theory* is the highest form of knowledge, *and is the most useful for making predictions.* A theory consists of a deductive system of logically interrelated generalizations. Although no grand or all-inclusive theories exist in the social sciences as in the physical sciences, numerous partial or middle range social science theories exist, such as Durkheim's theory of suicide and Allport's theory of prejudice.

To make reflective decisions, the student must be able to use the *scientific method** to derive higher level generalizations and theories, since these forms of knowledge will enable him to make the most accurate *predictions.* The most predictive generalizations and theories are those which are related to the key or *organizing* concepts in the social sciences. The identification of *key* concepts within the social sciences enables the decision-maker to use the most powerful generalizations which constitute the behavioral sciences, and which can make the greatest contribution to the resolution of personal and social problems, and facilitate the influencing of public policy.

Students must not only master higher levels of knowledge in order to make reflective decisions, they must also learn to view human behavior from the perspectives of all of the social and behavioral sciences. A social studies curriculum which focuses on decision-making and the Black experience must be *interdisciplinary;* it should incorporate *key* (or

---

* The *basic* steps of this method include problem formulation, formulation of hypotheses, definition of terms (conceptualization), data collection, evaluation and analysis of data, testing hypotheses: deriving generalizations and theories, and beginning inquiry anew. Social inquiry is cyclic rather than linear and fixed. Generalizations and theories in social science are continually tested and are never regarded as absolute. For a useful reference, see Abraham Kaplan, *The Conduct of Inquiry* (San Francisco: Chandler Publishing Company, 1964).

organizing) concepts from all of the social sciences. Knowledge from any one discipline is insufficient to help us make decisions on complex issues such as poverty, institutionalized racism and oppression. To take effective social action on a social issue such as poverty, students must view it from the perspectives of geography, history, sociology, economics, political science, psychology, and anthropology. (See Figure 1.)

FIGURE 1

UNDERSTANDING A SOCIAL ISSUE
WITH SOCIAL SCIENCE CONCEPTS AND THEORIES

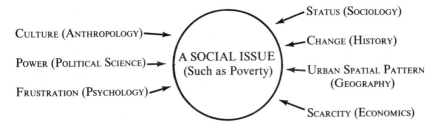

This figure illustrates how a social issue such as poverty can be sufficiently understood and therefore reflectively acted upon only after the social actor has viewed it with the concepts and theories from a number of social science disciplines. Any one discipline gives only a partial understanding of a social problem or issue. Thus, the social studies programs must be *interdisciplinary*.

While higher-level, interdisciplinary knowledge is necessary to make sound decisions, it is not sufficient. Students must also be able to identify, clarify, and analyze their values. *Value inquiry* and *clarification* are essential components of a sound social studies curriculum which incorporates the Black experience. Students should also be taught how to relate the concepts and generalizations which they derive to their values, and thus to make decisions. *Decision-making* consists essentially of affirming a course of action after synthesizing knowledge and clarified values. Students should also be provided opportunities whereby they can *act* on some of the decisions which they make. It would be neither possible nor desirable for children to act on all of the decisions which they make in social studies classes. However, "... under no circumstances should the school, deliberately or by default, continue to maintain the barriers between itself and the other elements of society."[5] Social action and participation activities are necessary components of a conceptually-oriented, decision-making social studies curriculum which incorporates the Black experience.

The Structure of History

We must identify the key concepts within the disciplines and their related generalizations to plan a curriculum which focuses on decision-making and incorporates the Black experience. Identifying the key concepts within history poses special problems. While the behavioral sciences use unique conceptual frameworks to view human behavior, history's uniqueness stems from the fact that it views behavior which has taken place in the *past*, is interested in the *totality* of man's past, and uses a modified mode of scientific inquiry. While the sociologist and the political scientist are primarily interested in *socialization* and *power* respectively, the historian may be and sometimes is interested in how each of these concepts is exemplified in man's past behavior. History, then, is an interdisciplinary field since historians, in principle, are interested in all aspects of man's past. It is difficult to speak about unique historical concepts. Every discipline makes use of the *historical perspective,* and has historical components. When a sociologist studies *norms* and *sanctions* during the period of slavery, and the economist describes how the slaves produced *goods* and *services,* they are both studying history.

While history, in principle, is concerned with the totality of man's past, in practice history is largely *political* because most of the concepts which it uses, such as *revolution, government, war,* and *nationalism,* belong to political science. History as it is usually written focuses on great political events and leaders, and largely ignores the experiences of the common man, non-Western man, ethnic groups, and key concepts from most of the other social sciences, except geography. *However, since history, in principle, is concerned with the totality of man's past, it is potentially the most interdisciplinary of all of the social disciplines and for that reason can serve as an excellent framework for incorporating the Black experience into the curriculum from an interdisciplinary perspective,* as illustrated in Figure 2.

Although historians have largely ignored concepts from most of the behavioral sciences, and the struggles and aspirations of the common and Third World man, a modern program in historical studies *can* and should incorporate these knowledge components. In recent years, historians have become acutely aware of how limited and parochial written history is, and have taken steps, but still inadequate ones, to include both the contributions and struggles of ethnic groups in their accounts and to use more concepts from the behavioral sciences. Stanley M. Elkins, in his classic study of slavery, uses a number of psychological concepts and theories to explain the behavior of the slave and master.[6]

FIGURE 2

STUDYING THE BLACK EXPERIENCE FROM AN INTERDISCIPLINARY PERSPECTIVE
WITHIN A HISTORICAL FRAMEWORK

Discipline	Analytical Concepts	Key Questions
Sociology	*Values, Norms*	What unique values and norms have emerged within the Black community?
Political Science	*Power*	What power relationships have existed within the Black community?
Anthropology	*Acculturation*	What kind of culture exchange has taken place between Blacks and whites in the United States?
Psychology	*Self-Concept*	How has the Black experience affected the Black man's feelings and perceptions of himself?
Geography	*Region*	Where have Blacks usually lived within our cities and why?
Economics	*Goods, Services, Production*	What goods and services have been produced in the Black community? Why?
History	*Change*	How has the Black community changed in recent years?

The trend toward more highly interdisciplinary history will undoubtedly continue as historians become more familiar with behavioral science concepts.

Incorporating the Black Experience into a Conceptual Curriculum

To illustrate how a program in historical studies can be both *interdisciplinary* and *incorporate* the experiences of Black Americans, we have identified seven key concepts from the various disciplines which can be taught within a historical framework, related organizing generalizations, and sub-generalizations related to Black History. While the sub-generalizations in our examples relate exclusively to the Black experience, a sound social studies program should include content samples that are related to man's total past, including the experiences of Native Americans, Puerto Rican Americans, Chicanos, and Asian-Americans.

Key Concept: CONFLICT (History)

Organizing Generalization: Throughout history, conflict has developed between various racial and ethnic groups.

Sub-Generalizations:
1. Violence and conflict occurred on the slave ships.
2. Several Black leaders led slave revolts during slavery in which Blacks and whites were killed.
3. When Blacks began their migration to Northern cities near the turn of the century, violent racial confrontations occurred in major urban areas.
4. During the Black Revolt of the 1960's, racial rebellions took place in a number of United States cities which resulted in the murder of many Black citizens.

Key Concept: CULTURE (Anthropology)

Organizing Generalization: Many different racial and ethnic groups have contributed to and enriched American culture.

Sub-Generalizations:
1. Skilled Black slaves helped to construct and decorate the Southern mansions.
2. The slave songs made a significant impact on American music.
3. The blues and jazz forms of music created by Black Americans constitute America's most unique musical heritage.
4. The literature written by Black Americans during the Harlem Renaissance contributed greatly to American culture.
5. Black American art expresses the poignant experiences of Black people in highly creative ways.

Key Concept: RACISM (Sociology)

Organizing Generalization: All non-white groups have been the victims of racism and discrimination in America.

Sub-Generalizations:

1. During slavery Blacks were not permitted to learn to read, to form groups without a white being present, or to testify in court against a white person.
2. The "Black Codes" that were established after the Emancipation Proclamation was issued created, in many ways, a new kind of "slavery" in the South.
3. For many years, legal segregation in the South forced Blacks to attend inferior schools, denied them the ballot, and sanctioned segregation in public accommodation and transportation facilities.
4. Blacks still experience discrimination in all phases of American life, including education, the administration of justice, and employment.

Key Concept: CAPITALISM (Economics)

Organizing Generalization: In a capitalistic society, powerless groups are unable to compete equally for jobs and rewards.

Sub-Generalizations:

1. During slavery, Blacks were forced to work without wages so that whites could make large profits from Southern crops.
2. After the Emancipation Proclamation was issued, "freed" Blacks were forced to work in a sharecropping system which cheated and exploited them.
3. When Blacks migrated to Northern and Western cities, they were the last hired and the first fired.
4. Today, many Blacks are unable to find steady and meaningful employment because they control few production industries.

Key Concept: POWER (Political Science)

Organizing Generalization: Individuals are more likely to influence public policy and to bring about social change when working in groups than when working alone.

Sub-Generalizations:

1. During slavery Blacks, by working cooperatively, were able to help many slaves escape with a system known as the "Underground Railroad."
2. By gaining group support, civil rights organizations such as the NAACP and CORE were able to end lynchings, and to reduce legal discrimination in such areas as employment, education and transportation.

3. The Black Revolt of the 1960's was able to reduce legal discrimination in such areas as employment, law, education and transportation.
4. The Nation of Islam has been able to provide many Blacks educational and job opportunities.

Key Concept: SELF-CONCEPT (Psychology)

Organizing Generalization: Self-Concept highly influences an individual's perceptions of the world and affects his behavior.

Sub-Generalizations:

1. The slave masters were able to convince many Blacks that they were less than human; the success of the slave masters in this task helped to reduce Black resistance to slavery.
2. Many slaves never accepted the views of themselves which were perpetuated by the slave masters and ran away or participated in slave revolts.
3. The movement led by Marcus Garvey in the 1920's enabled many Blacks to think more highly of their race and to develop group pride.
4. The Black Revolt of the 1960's caused many Blacks to feel more positively toward their race and to protest vigorously for their rights.

Key Concept: REGION (Geography)

Organizing Generalization: Every region is unique in its own way.

Sub-Generalizations:

1. The central area of the city where most Blacks live is usually characterized by substandard housing, higher prices, and public officials who are largely unaccountable to their constituents.
2. Prices for goods and services are usually higher in the central area of the city where most live than in outlying areas.
3. Police protection, city services, and public schools are usually inferior in the areas of a city where Black populations are concentrated.
4. Culture elements which are unique to the Black community can usually be found within a designated area of a city; often these culture elements do not diffuse outward to other metropolitan regions.

Once a teacher or curriculum committee has identified the key concepts and generalizations which can serve as a framework for a social studies curriculum or unit, and stated sub-generalizations that relate to the Black experience, he (or the committee) can then identify the materials and teaching strategies which are necessary to help the students derive the concepts and their related generalizations. The seven key concepts and generalizations stated above can be taught at every level within a spiral conceptual curriculum and developed at increasing levels of complexity with different content samples. At each level materials related to the Black experience, as well as content related to other groups, should be used to teach the key concepts and generalizations. Figure 3 illustrates how the seven key concepts can be spiralled within a

FIGURE 3

This diagram illustrates how information related to the Black experience can be organized around key concepts and taught at successive levels at an increasing degree of complexity.

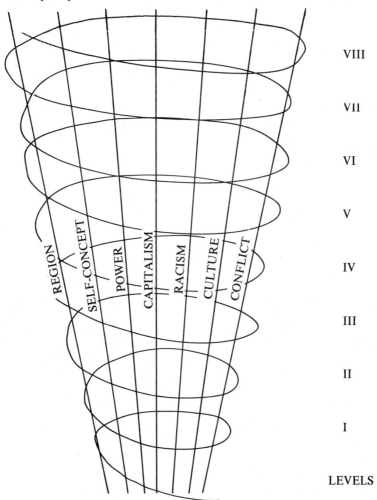

conceptual curriculum at eight different levels. Ideally, however, a conceptual curriculum should constitute the social studies program from kindergarten to grade 12.

To assure that every sub-generalization identified in the initial stages of planning is adequately developed within a unit, the teacher can divide a sheet of paper in half and list the concepts and sub-generalizations on one side of it and the strategies and materials needed to teach the ideas on the other half, as illustrated in Figures 4 and 5.

FIGURE 4

KEY IDEAS AND TEACHING STRATEGIES

Key Ideas	Activities
RACISM *Key Generalization:* All non-white groups have been the victims of institutionalized racism in America. *Sub-Generalization:* Blacks have experienced discrimination in all phases of American life, including education, the administration of justice, and employment.	1. Reading selections from *South Town, North Town,* and *Whose Town?* by Lorenz Graham. 2. Discussing the discrimination which the Williams family experienced in this story and how they coped with it. 3. Discussing the discrimination which David Williams experienced in school and how he reacted to it. 4. Viewing a filmstrip on Black slavery and listing ways in which it was a form of discrimination. 5. Finding copies of such documents as the *Slave Codes* and the *Grandfather Clause* and role-playing how they affected the lives of Blacks. 6. Compiling statistics on the number of Blacks who were lynched during the early years of the 1900's. 7. Reading and discussing accounts of the *discrimination* which Blacks experience in employment, education, and in the administration of justice today.

FIGURE 5

KEY IDEAS AND TEACHING STRATEGIES

Key Ideas	Activities
CULTURE *Key Generalization:* Many different racial and ethnic groups have contributed to and enriched American culture. *Sub-Generalization:* The literature written by Black Americans during the Harlem Renaissance contributed greatly to American culture.	1. Reading "Montage of a Dream Deferred" by Langston Hughes. 2. Discussing what the author means by "deferred dream." 3. Discussing the dreams of Black people which have been deferred and why. 4. Reading "If We Must Die" by Claude McKay. 5. Discussing the racial rebellions which took place near the turn of the century and the ways in which the two poems are social commentaries about racial conflict. 6. Reading "Incident" by Countee Cullen. 7. Discussing how the child felt when he first came to Baltimore and why. 8. Discussing why and how his feelings changed. 9. Discussing ways in which the Harlem Renaissance poets expressed their feelings, emotions, and aspirations in their writings, and how they contributed to American literature and culture.

Teaching the Historical Method (History as Process)

Because the historian's method is much more unique than his substantive concepts and generalizations, it is important to teach students the historical method (process), as well as concepts related to historical conclusions (products). History is a *process* as well as a body of knowledge. A historian's view of the past is influenced by the availability of evidence, his personal biases, purposes for writing, and the society and times in which he lives and writes. Although history reflects the biases of the writer, it is often taught in school as a body of truth not to be questioned, criticized, or modified. Such a parochial approach to the teaching of history stems largely from classroom teachers' confusion about the nature of history, and the widely held belief that history contributes to the development of patriotism.

Much confusion about the nature of history would be eliminated if teachers distinguished *historical statements* from *past events*. The historical statement, often referred to as the historical fact, is quite different from the actual event. The event itself has disappeared, never to occur again. An infinite number of statements can be made about any past event. Historical data related to the Black experience constitute a gold mine of information which can be used to teach students about the nature and writing of history.[7] This kind of knowledge will not only help them to become more adept decision-makers, but more intelligent consumers of history. Conflicting accounts of slavery, the Civil War, and the rebellions which took place in our cities in the sixties can be used to teach the concept of *historical bias*. To help students see the regional influences on written history, the teacher can have them compare the treatment of slavery in different textbooks as illustrated in the two accounts below, one of which is from a state history of Mississippi and the other from a junior high school Black history text:

Account 1

Slave Treatment. While there were some incidents involving the abusing of slaves, public opinion and state law generally assured the slaves of good treatment. Plantation owners usually cautioned their overseers against using brutal practices. Naturally, there were some abuses on large plantations ... Most people, however, favored kind treatment of slaves. . . .[8]

Account 2

Under the slave codes, blacks were not allowed to own property or weapons. They could not form groups without a white person present. They could not buy or sell goods, or leave the plantation without permission of their master. In towns and cities, blacks were required to be off the streets by a specified hour each night. A slave could not testify in court against a white person. A slave who was charged with a crime against a white person was therefore unable to defend himself. Any slave who violated the laws was likely to be severely punished, perhaps by death.[9]

Questions

1. How are these two accounts alike?
2. How are they different?
3. Why do you think that they are different?

4. Who do you think wrote the first account? The second account? Why?
5. Which account do you think is more accurate? Why?
6. Which author supports his statements with facts? Give specific examples.
7. Read other accounts on the treatment of slaves and write in your own words about how the slaves were treated. How do your conclusions compare with the accounts written by the two authors above?

The Value Component of Decision-Making

While higher level, scientific knowledge is necessary for reflective decision-making, it is not sufficient. To make a reflective decision, the social actor must also identify and clarify his *values,* and relate them to the knowledge which he has derived through the process of social inquiry.

Because of the immense racial problems within our society that are rooted in value confusion, the school should play a significant role in helping students to identify and clarify their values, and in making value choices intelligently. While the school has a tremendous responsibility to help students to make moral choices reflectively, there is abundant evidence that educators have largely failed to help students to deal with moral issues intelligently.

Some teachers treat value problems like the invisible man; i.e., they deny their existence. They assume that if students get all of the "facts" straight, they can resolve racial problems. Such teachers may be said to practice the cult of false objectivity. Other teachers use an evasion strategy; when value problems arise in the classroom, they try to change the subject to a more safe topic. Probably the most frequently used approach to value education in the elementary and high school is the inculcation of values which are considered "right" by adults, or the indoctrination of these values. Teachers who use this method assume that adults know what the "correct" values are for all times and for children from all cultural groups. Such values as justice, truth, freedom, honesty, equality and love are taught with legendary heroes, stories, rituals and patriot songs. This approach to value education is unsound for several reasons. It assumes that most value conflicts and problems result because children are unable to distinguish "good" from "bad" values. However, this is not the case. Children can rather easily distinguish the good from the bad. Most value problems result because students must often choose between two goods.[10] When teachers use didactic methods to teach children contradictory but equally "good" values, their conflicts are intensified when they must choose between two goods.

Didactic inculcation of values also denies students free choice and does not help them to develop a *method* for deriving and clarifying their

"Each generation should have a right to determine its own values."

values. *Each generation should have the right to determine its own values.* Children should be taught a *process* by which they can derive their own values because we have no reliable way to predict the values which a child will find functional in the future.[11] Didactic strategies are also unsound because there is no general agreement among adults about what values should be inculcated or about their meanings. Diverse goals and meanings have been proposed by various writers on moral education. Didactic strategies are also invalid because we cannot expect standards to guide a person's life unless those standards have been *freely* chosen from alternatives, and after thoughtful consideration of the consequences of the alternatives. Michael Scriven argues that it is *immoral* for teachers and other adults to force our cultural values upon our youth.[12] He suggests that such values may not be worth passing on, and that students should be taught how to decide on their own values. The wider culture does an excellent job of indoctrinating its values; the school, argues Scriven, should teach *resistance* to them.

Teachers should help students to develop a *method* (or process) for deriving and clarifying their values rather than teach them a set of predetermined values. *This is the only approach to value education*

168

which is consistent with a cultural pluralistic ideology and that is educationally sound. Perhaps no more serious value questions and problems are raised in the classroom than during a study of the Black experience. Black students have important questions about the value of Blackness, their identity, and about effective strategies to use to release themselves from institutionalized racism and colonization. I have developed a value inquiry model that is presented in detail in my social studies methods book which teachers can use while teaching the Black experience to help students *to identify, clarify and to reflectively derive their values.*[13] Space prevents me from elaborating on the steps of this model here. However, I will present it in outline form, and a sample exercise illustrating how parts of it can be used during a study of the Black experience.

VALUE INQUIRY MODEL

    a. Recognizing Value Problems
    b. Describing Value Relevant Behavior
    c. Naming Values Exemplified by Behavior
    d. Determining Value Conflicts
    e. Hypothesizing About Sources of Values
    f. Naming Value Alternatives
    g. Hypothesizing About the Consequences of Values
    h. Choosing (Declaring Value Preferences)
    i. Stating Reasons, Sources and Consequences of Personal Value Choice(s)

For value inquiry lessons, the teacher may use case studies clipped from the daily newspaper, such as incidents involving police attacks on the Black Panthers, or cases related to the current "busing" controversy. Children's literature, photographs, role-playing activities, and open-ended stories related to these kinds of incidents can also be effectively used. In using a case study related to the Black Revolt of the sixties, for example, the teacher can ask the students these kinds of questions:

1. What was the problem in this case?
2. What does the behavior of the persons involved tell us about what was important to them?
3. How do you think that the values of the demonstrators differed from those who were in power?
4. What are other values that the persons in the case could have endorsed?

5. What were the possible consequences of the values held by the demonstrators?
6. What would you have done if your life experience had been similar to the experiences of the persons who protested?
7. What might have been the consequences of your beliefs?
8. Could you have lived with those consequences?

During value inquiry lessons, the teacher should be careful *not to* condemn values which are inconsistent with his beliefs. This is not to suggest that the teacher should remain neutral on value issues, but rather that he should not declare a value preference until the students have expressed their value choices. Unless the teacher creates a classroom atmosphere which will allow and encourage students to express their true beliefs, value inquiry will simply become a game in which students will try to guess what responses the teacher wants them to make. Even the bigoted white student or the psychologically captivated Black student should be able to express his beliefs freely and openly in the classroom. Beliefs which are unexpressed cannot be rationally examined. While we must eliminate racism in America in order to survive the challenges of the twenty-first century, students must be able to reflectively analyze racism and its effects before they can develop a commitment to eliminate it. It should be stressed that this commitment must come from the student; *it cannot be imposed by the teacher.*

Providing Opportunities for Social Action

Black people throughout the United States are victims of colonialism, institutional racism, poverty and political powerlessness. *When the teacher identifies concepts and generalizations from the social sciences, he should select those which will help students to make decisions and to take actions to help eliminate these problems.* This is absolutely imperative if the social studies curriculum is going to help to liberate Black people and other oppressed groups. After they have mastered higher level knowledge related to these problems, and analyzed and clarified their values, the teacher can ask the students to list the possible actions which they can take regarding these problems in their school and community, and to predict the possible consequences of each alternative course of action. Alternatives and consequences which the students state should be realistic and based on knowledge which they have mastered during the earlier phase of the unit. They should be intelligent predictive statements and not ignorant guesses or wishful thinking. Students should state *data* and *reasons* to support the alternatives and consequences which they identify.

Students will be unable to *solve* the racial problems in their communities. However, they may be able to take some effective actions which can improve the racial atmosphere in their classroom and school, or contribute to the resolution of the racial problems in the wider community through some types of meaningful and effective social action or participation projects. Students should participate in social action projects only after they have studied the related issues from the perspectives of the social sciences, analyzed and clarified their values regarding them, identified the possible consequences of their actions, and expressed a willingness to accept them. Since the school is an institution with racial problems which mirror those of the larger society, students can be provided practice in shaping public policy by working to eliminate racism in their classroom, school or school system.

Racism, drug abuse, forced bussing, the closing of Black schools, class stratification, theft and arson are the kinds of problems which schools have on which students can take concerted action. Other social action projects, especially for more mature students, can take place in the wider community. Social action may take the form of observation, participation or leadership. The school can work with civil rights groups and political organizations to involve students in meaningful and purposeful social action activities. The levels of involvement in such activities can be diverse. *The primary purpose of such activities should be to provide students with opportunities to develop a sense of political efficacy and not to provide community services,* although both goals can be attained in the most effective types of projects.

Student participation in social action activities within our society is not without precedence. However, the most dramatic and effective social action by American students has usually been undertaken by college students. During the Black Revolt of the 1960's, students comprised one of the most cogent and effective components. The Black Revolt of the 1960's was signaled when four Black college students sat down at an "all white" lunch counter at a Woolworth's store in Greensboro, North Carolina on February 1, 1960. Throughout the Black Revolt of the 1960's, students remained active and influential. They helped to desegregate restaurants, interstate transportation, schools and swimming pools with such tactics as sit-ins, freedom-rides, and swim-ins. Student effectiveness in the Black Revolt of the sixties is one of the most dramatic indications of the potential of student power in America. Protests by students in the sixties also resulted in enlightened curriculum reform in public schools and colleges.

In discussing ways in which students have participated in social action and protest, we do not mean to suggest that all or even most of their actions were maximumly effective and undertaken after reflective thought. However, we must stress the fact that students will become involved in important social issues in the community and nation whether the school facilitates that involvement or not. Schools did little, if anything, to facilitate the involvement of students in the actions which are reviewed above. *The involvement of students in social action must become institutionalized within the social studies curriculum so that their actions can become both more effective and thoughtfully directed.* Some of the student action which occurred on our college campuses was irresponsible and irrational. A social action focused social studies curriculum *may* have made such actions more effective and significant. In a 1971 publication, the National Council for the Social Studies stresses the need for educators to involve students in social action projects:

> Extensive involvement by students of all ages in the activities of their community is . . . essential. Many of these activities may be in problem areas held, at least by some, to be controversial; many will not be. The involvement may take the form of observation or information-seeking; such as field trips, attending meetings, and interviews. It may take the form of political campaigning, community service or improvement, or even responsible demonstration. The school should not only provide channels for such activities but build them into the design of its social studies program, kindergarten through grade twelve.[14]

Conclusion

We have argued that effective Black studies programs must be based on a sound and clearly articulated rationale in order to result in effective student learning. A rationale has been suggested for the reader's consideration. We stated that the main goal of Black history should be to help students develop the ability to make reflective decisions so that they can resolve personal problems and shape public policy by participating in intelligent social action. In other words, we suggested that the goal of Black history should be *to help students become effective change agents.* Higher level, interdisciplinary knowledge, social science inquiry, and value inquiry are necessary for sound decision-making and reflective social action. History can be used both as a framework to help students master decision-making skills and to become familiar with the Black experience since it is concerned with the totality of man's past. Historical data can also evoke many value questions. Since the present is intimately related to the past, history can provide students with insights which are essential for making decisions related to the urgent social problems which are polarizing our society.

The most important variable for the successful implementation of the kind of Black studies program proposed in this essay is the classroom

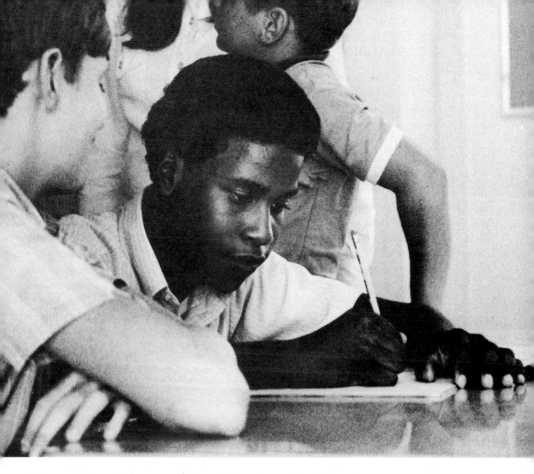

"We can help students to attain humanistic values only within a classroom atmosphere which tolerates differences and where students are free to express their feelings."

teacher. For teachers to help Black students to develop effective social action skills, they must learn how social science reflects the norms, values and goals of the ruling and powerful groups in society, and how it validates those belief systems which are functional for groups in power and dysfunctional for oppressed and powerless groups. Many teachers perpetuate the historical and social science myths which they learned in school and that are pervasive in textbooks because they are unaware of the racist assumptions on which social science research is often based. Much information in textbooks is designed to support the status quo and to keep powerless ethnic groups at the lower rungs of the social ladder.

To help students derive higher levels of knowledge using the Black experience, and to make sound decisions about race relations, the teacher must accept the *scientific method* as the most valuable way to attain knowledge. He must be willing to allow students to examine and derive their own beliefs. He cannot be a demagogue who tries to force his beliefs on students. We can help students to attain humanistic values only within a classroom atmosphere which tolerates differences and where students are free to express their feelings. Beliefs which are unexpressed cannot be rationally examined. While we must eliminate racism in America in order to survive the challenges of the twenty-first century, students must be able to analyze racism rationally before they can develop a commitment to eliminate it.

No school can truly educate its citizens unless it teaches about the aspirations and struggles of Third World man. His experience is part of the human drama, and education should deal with man's total experience. To base a curriculum only on the experiences of part of mankind will not only inculcate a false sense of superiority in white students and make Black students feel inferior, but it will make whites think that they are separate and apart from the rest of mankind, and believe, as many do today, that they are the only *humans* on earth. The modern world cannot survive this kind of insidious ethnocentrism.

FOOTNOTES

[1] James A. Banks, "A Content Analysis of the Black American in Textbooks," *Social Education,* Vol. 33 (December, 1969), pp. 954-957, 963.

[2] Larry Cuban, "Black History, Negro History, and White Folk," in James A. Banks and Willian W. Joyce (Editors), *Teaching Social Studies to Culturally Different Children* (Reading, Mass.: Addison-Wesley Publishing Company, 1971), p. 318.

[3] Nathan Hare, "The Teaching of Black History and Culture in the Secondary Schools," *Social Education,* Vol. 33 (April, 1969), p. 388.

[4] Martin Kilson, "Black Studies: A Plea for Perspective," reprinted from *The Crisis* (October, 1969), with the permission of The Crisis Publishing Company, Inc.

[5] NCSS Task Force (Gary Manson, Gerald Marker, Anna Ochoa, and Jan Tucker), "Social Studies Curriculum Guidelines" (Washington, D.C.: National Council for the Social Studies), unpublished second draft, p. 17.

[6] Stanley M. Elkins, *Slavery: A Problem in American Institutional and Intellectual Life* (New York: Grosset and Dunlap, 1963).

[7] For other examples see James A. Banks, *Teaching the Black Experience: Methods and Materials* (Belmont, California: Fearon Publishers, 1970).

[8] John K. Bettersworth, *Mississippi Yesterday and Today* (Austin, Texas: Steck-Vaughn, 1964), p. 143. This book is currently used in the state of Mississippi.

[9] James A. Banks, *March Toward Freedom: A History of Black Americans* (Belmont, Calif.: Fearon Publishers, 1970), p. 16.

[10] For a further discussion of this point see Maurice P. Hunt and Lawrence E. Metcalf, *Teaching High School Social Studies: Second Edition* (New York: Harper and Row, 1968), Chapter 6.

[11] Louis E. Raths, Merrill Harmin, and Sidney B. Simon, *Values and Teaching: Working with Values in the Classroom* (Columbus, Ohio: Charles E. Merrill Publishing Company, 1966), p. 28.

[12] Michael Scriven, "The Social Studies in the 21st Century: What is Needed?" A paper presented at the 50th Annual Meeting of the National Council for the Social Studies, New York, New York, November 24, 1970.

[13] James A. Banks (With Contributions by Ambrose A. Clegg, Jr.), *Teaching Strategies for the Social Studies: Inquiry, Valuing and Decision-Making* (Reading, Mass.: Addison-Wesley Publishing Company, 1973), Chapter 12, "Valuing: Inquiry Modes and Strategies."

[14] NCSS Task Force on Curriculum Guidelines (Gary Manson, Anna Ochoa, Gerald Marker and Jan Tucker), *Social Studies Curriculum Guidelines* (Washington, D.C.: National Council for the Social Studies, 1971), p. 15.

BIBLIOGRAPHY

Herbert Aptheker (Ed.), *A Documentary History of the Negro People in the United States* (New York: The Citadel Press), Two Volumes. Although these two volumes treat Black history only through 1910, it is still one of the best collections of Black history documents available for the periods from colonial times up to the turn of the century.

Houston A. Baker, Jr., *Black Literature in America* (New York: McGraw-Hill, 1971). A gold mine of Black literature, from Black folklore to contemporary writers such as LeRoi Jones, Hoyt Fuller and Don Lee, is contained in this comprehensive anthology which teachers can use to vitalize their social studies programs.

James Baldwin, *The Fire Next Time* (New York: Dell Publishing Co., 1963). This book contains a collection of perceptive, courageous and widely acclaimed essays by one of the most distinguished writers of this century. The teacher should also examine his *Notes of A Native Son* (Dell), and *Nobody Knows My Name* (Dell).

James A. Banks, *March Toward Freedom: A History of Black Americans* (Belmont: Fearon, 1970). An illustrated history of Black Americans written especially for teenagers.

James A. Banks (With Contributions by Ambrose A. Clegg, Jr.), *Teaching Strategies For The Social Studies: Inquiry, Valuing and Decision-Making* (Reading: Addison-Wesley, 1973). This general methods text provides a conceptual framework, with illustrations throughout, that will help the teacher to integrate ethnic content into the regular social studies curriculum. The book is designed for use by teachers in the elementary and junior high school grades.

James A. Banks, *Teaching The Black Experience: Methods and Materials* (Belmont: Fearon, 1970). This book deals with ways to teach units in Black Studies and how to integrate ethnic content into the regular social studies and language arts curricula. The major portion of the book is concerned with a description of promising teaching strategies. An extensive bibliography constitutes the final chapter.

James A. Banks & Jean D. Grambs (Eds.), *Black Self-Concept: Implications for Education and Social Science* (New York: McGraw-Hill, 1972). This book contains a series of original papers by educators and social scientists that explore effective ways to help Black children attain more positive self-images and academic success in school. The divergent points of view presented should stimulate a continuing dialogue.

Andrew Billingsley, *Black Families in White America* (Englewood Cliffs: Prentice-Hall, 1968). A noted Black social scientist challenges many popular myths which have been perpetuated by white social scientists about the Black family in this seminal and compassionate book.

Arna Bontemps, *American Negro Poetry* (New York: Hill and Wang, 1963). "The Negro Speaks of Rivers," "Mother to Son," and many other immortal poems by Langston Hughes and other gifted Black poets are found in this immensely popular book. The newer Black poets, such as Niki Giovanni and Don Lee, are absent, but the Harlem Renaissance group is well represented.

B. A. Botkin (Ed.), *Lay My Burden Down: A Folk History of Slavery* (Chicago: University of Chicago Press, 1945). This book contains a fine collection of documents written by former slaves which the social studies teacher will find very useful when he structures inquiry lessons using primary resources. It is one of the most comprehensive collections of slave documents that is available in book form.

Ruth Kearney Carlson, *Emerging Humanity: Multi-Ethnic Literature For Children and Adolescents* (Dubuque: William C. Brown, 1972). Although this book is occasionally flawed by white bias, it contains many useful suggestions and resources which the teacher can use to enrich his social studies program with ethnic literature.

Bradford Chambers (Ed.), *Chronicles of Black Protest* (New York: Mentor Books, 1968). This book contains an excellent collection of documents on the Black experience, with extensive commentaries by the editor preceding each document.

Abraham Chapman (Ed.), *Black Voices: An Anthology of Afro-American Literature* (New York: Mentor Books, 1968). Fiction, autobiography, poetry and literary criticism by eminent Black writers are included in this thoughtful anthology. Arna Bontemps, Langston Hughes, Richard Wright, Claude McKay, Countee Cullen and W.E.B. DuBois are among the brilliant writers represented in this book. It is available in an inexpensive paperback edition.

Kenneth B. Clark, *Dark Ghetto: Dilemmas of Social Power* (New York: Harper and Row, 1965). In one of the most widely acclaimed books of recent times, Professor Clark poignantly and sensitively describes the devastating effects which the Black ghetto has on its victims. This book is an excellent introduction to lower class Black life in the city.

Angela Y. Davis (and Other Political Prisoners), *If They Come in the Morning* (New York: Signet Books, 1971). A powerful and perceptive book about race and political prisoners in the United States. This book would be an excellent supplement to a unit on our judicial system.

Melvin Drimmer (Ed.), *Black History* (Garden City, N.Y.: Doubleday, 1969). This deservedly popular documentary history of the Black American contains excellent and informative commentaries by the editor. The teacher can use many of these documents with older students.

Editors of Ebony, *Ebony Pictorial History of Black History* (Chicago: Johnson Publishing Company, 1971), Three Volumes. A beautifully illustrated and well written, detailed history of Black Americans in three volumes which can be profitably read by young readers, as well as by adults.

Russell Endo and William Strawbridge (Eds.), *Perspectives on Black America* (Englewood Cliffs: Prentice-Hall, 1970). Both scholarly and popular writings make up this useful collection of papers which provides perceptive sociological perspectives on the Black experience in America. Contributors include Claude Brown, St. Clair Drake, C. Eric Lincoln and Jonathan Kozol.

Charlotte Epstein, *Affective Subjects in the Classroom: Exploring Race, Sex, and Drugs* (Scranton: International Textbook Company, 1972). A number of ingenious techniques which teachers can use to stimulate thinking about race-related topics are contained in this useful book.

Lillian Faderman & Barbara Bradshaw (Eds.), *American Ethnic Writing: Speaking For Ourselves* (Glenview: Scott Foresman, 1969). Exciting selections from literature written by many ethnic groups are contained in this carefully compiled anthology. The teacher will find it useful for both literature and social studies classes.

Jack D. Forbes, *Afro-Americans in The West: A Handbook for Educators* (Berkeley: Far West Laboratory for Educational Research and Development, 1967). This book includes an excellent historical and sociological overview of the Black man in the West, suggestions for teachers and administrators, and a comprehensive bibliography on the Black man in the United States.

John Hope Franklin and Isidore Starr (Eds.), *The Negro in 20th Century America* (New York: Vintage Books, 1967). A thoughtful anthology which explores various aspects of Black life and culture in the 20th century which has been, unfortunately, neglected. High school students will find this book informative. Contributors range from Malcolm X to Gunnar Myrdal.

Robert Goldston, *The Negro Revolution* (New York: Macmillan, 1968). This is an extremely well written history for young people, although the vocabulary is difficult. The illustrations are sparse and dull.

Milton M. Gordon, *Assimilation in American Life* (New York: Oxford University Press, 1964). In this widely acclaimed and award-winning book, the author sets forth a number of theories about cultural and structural assimilation that the teacher will find helpful in understanding ethnic minority groups in America.

Robert L. Green (Ed.), *Racial Crisis in American Education* (Chicago: Follett Educational Corporation, 1969). A brilliant and hard-hitting collection of papers which explores various dimensions of educating Black children in both integrated and segregated settings. The book is distinguished by the large number of Black contributors.

George Henderson, *To Live in Freedom: Human Relations Today* (Norman: University of Oklahoma Press, 1972). This lucidly written book by an expert in human relations contains valuable ideas and suggestions which social studies teachers can use to clarify their racial attitudes and perceptions, and to create a more humane atmosphere in their classrooms.

Florence Jackson, *The Black Man in America 1791-1861* (New York: Franklin Watts, 1971). One in a series of books by Mrs. Jackson, this volume is well written, accurate and contains good drawings and photographs. It is designed for younger readers.

George Jackson, *Soledad Brother: The Prison Letters of George Jackson* (New York: Bantam Books, 1970). These brilliant and cogent letters reveal a young imprisoned Black man's attempt to understand an oppressive and dehumanized world. This is a courageous and touching book.

Stephen M. Joseph (Ed.), *The Me Nobody Knows: Children's Voices from the Ghetto* (New York: Avon Books, 1969). This book contains an unusual collection of beautiful, poignant, and revealing poems by children in the Black ghetto which tells much about their limited but eventful world.

William W. Joyce and James A. Banks (Eds.), *Teaching the Language Arts to Culturally Different Children* (Reading: Addison-Wesley, 1971). A collection of articles and original papers designed to help teachers plan effective language and literature programs for children from diverse cultural groups. Ways to use ethnic literature to enrich the social studies curriculum are explored.

Julius Lester, *To Be A Slave* (New York: Dell, 1968). A poignant collection of documents written by former slaves which will evoke deep feelings in the reader. The book was written for young readers. It was a Newberry Medal runner-up.

August Meier and Elliott M. Rudwick, *From Plantation to Ghetto: An Interpretive History of American Negroes* (New York: Hill and Wang, 1966). This book is an excellent history of Black Americans that contains perceptive interpretations of ideologies and protest movements which have emerged within Black communities in America.

Milton Meltzer (Ed.), *In Their Own Words: A History of the American Negro* (New York: Thomas Y. Crowell, 1964, 1965, 1967), Three volumes. This is one of the few collections of documents which are designed especially for the middle grade student. The books are illustrated and the size of the print is ideal for the young reader.

Louise Meriwether, *Daddy Was a Number Runner* (New York: Pyramid Books, 1970). The author's heroine, Francie Coffin, takes the reader into her Harlem world. The reader experiences the joys and sorrows of being Black, poor and powerless. This is a powerful and significant book.

Gertrude Noar, *Sensitizing Teachers to Ethnic Groups* (Boston: Allyn and Bacon, 1972). This short book by a veteran in intergroup education provides important hints as to how the teacher can become more sensitive to ethnic groups within his classroom and the larger society. This book is in the Anti-Defamation League of B'nai B'rith series on minority groups. The entire series is recommended.

Gilbert Osofsky, *The Burden of Race: A Documentary History of Negro-White Relations in America* (New York: Harper and Row, 1967). This is an excellent history of Black-white relations in America vividly revealed by the men who were the stars in our racial drama.

Talcott Parsons and Kenneth B. Clark (Eds.), *The Negro American* (Boston: Beacon Press, 1965). The essays in this book, which originally appeared in two issues of *Daedalus*, form one of the most scholarly and thorough books which treats diverse aspects of Black life in America. Daniel P. Moynihan, Lee Rainwater, Oscar Handlin, and Thomas F. Pettigrew are among the distinguished contributors.

Vincent R. Rogers and Thomas P. Weinland (Eds.), *Teaching Social Studies in The Urban Classroom* (Reading: Addison-Wesley, 1972). The teachers who contributed to this book describe promising strategies that they used to teach about the experiences of ethnic groups in both inner-city and suburban classrooms. Some of the chapters contain useful bibliographies.

Karel Rose, *A Gift of the Spirit: Readings in Black Literature for Teachers* (New York: Holt, 1971). Helpful teaching hints as well as exciting and involving selections from Black literature are contained in this book. Many social science concepts and generalizations can be taught with the resources in this volume.

Peter I. Rose, *They And We: Racial and Ethnic Relations in the United States* (New York: Random House, 1964). A good introduction to race, ethnicity and social status in America which can be read with understanding by high school students. The author's distinction between *prejudice* and *discrimination* is especially useful.

Kenneth M. Stampp, *The Peculiar Institution* (New York: Vintage Books, 1956). An extremely scholarly and deeply moving book which shatters many pervasive stereotypes about slavery. This book well deserves the acclaim which it has received.

Dorothy Sterling, *Tear Down the Walls! A History of the Black Revolution in the United States* (New York: Signet Books, 1968). A deeply moving and extremely well written history of Black Americans designed especially for young readers. The book contains good illustrations and reads more like a popular book than a schoolbook.

Piri Thomas, *Down These Mean Streets* (New York: The New American Library, 1967). This is a powerful and touching autobiography about the problems which haunted a Puerto Rican American whose skin happened to be dark. The book reveals the pain which our society inflicts upon those who are members of stigmatized groups.

Staten W. Webster (Ed.), *Knowing and Understanding the Socially Disadvantaged: Ethnic Minority Groups* (Scranton: International Textbook Company, 1972). The teacher will find articles in this anthology which deal with all of America's major ethnic minority groups. It is a useful book for general information for the teacher.

Frederick Williams (Ed.), *Language and Poverty: Perspectives on a Theme* (Chicago: Markham Publishing Co., 1970). This scholarly and sensitive book of essays will help the teacher to understand the variety of languages spoken by America's ethnic minority groups and other poor children. Joan C. Baratz, William Labov and Roger Shuy are among the notable contributors.

John A. Williams, *The Man Who Cried I Am* (New York: New American Library, 1967). The author unfolds a frightening but credible tale of a master plot designed to eliminate Blacks in America. The story centers around the protagonist's discovery of the plot and his attempt to disclose it.

Walter Wilson (Ed.), *The Selected Writings of W. E. B. DuBois* (New York: Mentor Books, 1970). This is a fine collection of the writings of the brilliant Black leader and sociologist. Selections are included from the classic, *The Philadelphia Negro,* as well as from DuBois' creative writings and policy statements.

Richard Wright, *Black Boy* (New York: Harper and Row, 1937). This is the gripping story of what it meant to be Black and insightful in the South in an earlier era by one of America's most distinguished and gifted writers.

Samuel F. Yette, *The Choice: The Issue of Black Survival in America* (New York: Berkeley Publishing Corporation, 1971). In this alarming and disturbing book, Yette argues that the extermination of the Black man in America is a genuine possibility. His argument is cogent and thought-provoking.

Carlos E. Cortés

CARLOS E. CORTÉS is Associate Professor of History and Chairman of the Mexican American Studies Program at the University of California, Riverside. Professor Cortés was graduated from the University of California, Berkeley (Phi Beta Kappa). He holds graduate degrees in journalism and foreign trade from Columbia University and the American Institute for Foreign Trade. He received his M. A. in Portuguese and Ph. D. in history at the University of New Mexico. He was formerly Chairman of the Latin American Studies Program and Assistant to the Vice Chancellor for Academic Affairs at the University of California, Riverside. Professor Cortés has served as a consultant to a wide variety of institutions and agencies, including the United States Commission on Civil Rights and the Ford Foundation. In 1971, he was appointed by the California State Department of Education to serve on an Ethnic Education Task Force to evaluate social studies textbooks. He is a contributing editor for Aztlán, Chicano Journal of the Social Sciences and the Arts. *He has written for* Aztlán and the Journal of Church and State, *and has edited* Mexican Americans and Educational Change *and* Bibliografia da História do Rio Grande do Sul (Período Republicano). *Forthcoming works include* Blacks, Chicanos, Native Americans, Puerto Ricans: History and Self-Expression, Struggle for Aztlán: A History of Mexican-American Resistance, The Bent Cross: A History of the Mexican American in the San Bernardino Valley, *and* Gaúcho Politics in Brazil: Rio Grande do Sul in Brazilian Politics, 1930-1964.

CARLOS E. CORTÉS

8

Teaching
the Chicano Experience

The Mexican American was born in December, 1845, when the United States annexed the Lone Star Republic into the union as the state of Texas, thereby transforming 5,000 Mexican Texans (Texans of Mexican descent) into Mexican Americans.[1] The following year, as part of United States war operations against Mexico, United States military forces invaded and occupied the Mexican Northwest (today the U.S. Southwest). Through the ensuing 1848 Treaty of Guadalupe Hidalgo, the United States obtained official sanction for this gigantic land grab (one third of Mexico's territory) and, at the same time, added to the Chicano[2] population by proffering United States citizenship to the 75,000 Mexicans living in the dismembered territory.[3]

Since those mid-nineteenth-century events, the Mexican-American population has grown until Chicanos now form the nation's second largest ethnic minority (some six to ten million)[4] and make their homes in every state in the union.[5] Yet despite their long, rich history, their growing population, and their increasing geographical dispersal, not until the Chicano Movement of the 1960's and 1970's did Mexican Americans truly begin to penetrate the American[6] consciousness. And only in the last few years have significant numbers of American educators become interested in incorporating the study of the Chicano experience into our educational system.

Unfortunately, this long-overdue educational reform has met with uneven success. In part this has resulted from continued lack of knowledge and awareness by many educators, lack of reformist concern by others, and even outright resistance to change by some. Even those interested in making the study of the Chicano experience an intrinsic part of our educational system have encountered difficulty in transforming commitment into effective pedagogy. To a degree this difficulty stems from the short time during which educators have dealt seriously with teaching the Chicano experience. But this difficulty also stems from the very nature of our society and our educational process.

Within the social studies, three basic elements are necessary for the effective teaching of the Chicano experience—awareness of the major obstacles to understanding the Chicano experience, development of new exploratory concepts for analyzing the Chicano experience, and use of innovative teaching strategies for exploring the Chicano experience. In the following pages, I will devote myself to these three basic issues.

Obstacles to Effective Teaching

Four major obstacles impede the effective teaching of the Chicano experience. These are: (1) the persistence of societal stereotypes of the Mexican American, (2) the inadequacy of existent social studies textbooks, (3) the general lack of knowledge about the Mexican-American past and present, and (4) the rigidity of traditional frames of reference for examining the Chicano experience.

Our educational system does not operate in a vacuum. It reflects the society around it and deals with students produced by that society. Unfortunately, the teaching of the Chicano experience is severely limited by the fact that students come to school pre-conditioned in their perceptions of the Mexican American.

In both historical and contemporary terms, U. S. society has been pervaded subtly and sometimes not too subtly by anti-Mexican prejudice. The roots of this prejudice stretch back over the centuries to the European power struggle for New World domination. Since Spain had arrived first from Europe and had claimed most of the New World, it became the prime target for other European contenders. Through its own vigorous internal debate over the treatment of Indians, Spain unwittingly furnished fuel for its antagonists' propaganda machines. Using Spanish cruelty toward Indians as the base and blending in other anti-Spanish themes, these contending nations propagated a collection of anti-Spanish stereotypes which became known as the Black Legend (*leyenda negra*). English colonists carried this Hispanophobia to the New World. Here their constant conflict with Spaniards and residents of Spanish possessions reinforced anti-Spanish attitudes and made anti-Hispanism an intrinsic, if sometimes unrecognized or unadmitted, part of the national psyche.[7]

Paralleling anti-Hispanic prejudice in the Anglo mentality was a feeling of Anglo superiority over non-whites, including Native Americans.[8] Moreover, Englishmen and Anglo Americans took a particularly scornful view of the genetic and cultural offspring of Hispanic-Indian fusion—the mestizo—whom they considered a "mongrelized" product of two inferior peoples.[9]

As the United States expanded westward during the early nineteenth century, it found this Mexican mestizo in its way. Texas Revolution and Mexican War propaganda emotionally supercharged the already existent anti-Mexican attitudes, as did such other anti-Mexican prose as nineteenth-century travelers' accounts and the popular dime novel, which commonly used the theme of the triumph of the good Anglo-American cowboy over the degenerate Mexican mestizo.[10] The dime novel, with its blatant racism, has disappeared. However, it is clear that its prejudice-producing role has been taken over by more subtle image purveyors.

From the time he is born, an American is bombarded by anti-Mexican impulses, including those spread by the mass media. Let us take a few examples. Frito Bandito and his serape-clad, sombrero-wearing, mañana-saying Mexican brothers in the U.S. advertising menagerie leap to mind as obvious perpetrators of anti-Mexican stereotypes.[11] Comic strips, such as "Gordo," the living Mexican stereotype, help to reinforce these negative Mexican images. Whether intentionally, uncaringly, or unwittingly, the motion picture industry has produced a long series of prejudice-building movies. For example, in the "my-bad-guy-is-better-than-yours" movie genre, such films as "The Magnificent Seven," "The Professionals," and "The Wild Bunch" celebrate the victory of tiny bands of Anglo gunmen over whole armies of Mexicans—the reassertion of Anglo superiority even at the bad-guy-to-bad-guy level.[12]

In short, the classical anti-Spanish Black Legend has given way to a Modern Black Legend: anti-mestizo, anti-Mexican, and anti-Chicano. As I have defined it elsewhere, this Modern Black Legend is "a negative attitude toward, stereotype of, or prejudice against the Mexican American created by the steady bombardment of the American mind by anti-Mexican sensory impulses, made more effective by the absence of any significant institutionalized defense or counter-attack against these impulses."[13]

In teaching the Chicano experience, therefore, the social studies teacher must confront the Modern Black Legend's pervasive effects on his students. But the problem does not end here. Not only must the teacher contend with anti-Chicano prejudice-creating and stereotype-building aspects of society, he must also come to grips in the classroom with text materials which, in relation to the Chicano, are almost always inadequate and often clearly destructive.

Inadequate Textbooks

The Mexican American has always suffered in social studies text-books.[14] For the past four years I have been deeply involved in analyzing elementary and secondary school social studies textbooks and have found little in them which would specifically contribute to the pride of the young Mexican American, but much that could assault his ego and reinforce a concept of Anglo-American superiority over the Mexican American. Social studies texts usually either ignore or distort the Mexi-can-American experience (as well as the experiences of other ethnic minorities). Relatively few texts specifically discuss the Mexican Ameri-can, and those which do devote at most a few inadequate (and often inaccurate) pages to this topic. Therefore, the student's image of the Chicano experience is derived tangentially—from depictions of his In-dian, Spanish, and Mexican ancestors—and the image is a defeatist one.

U.S. history texts generally say little about the Mexican American's Indian heritage, except for an occasional line or so on Aztec and Mayan civilization. The long, rich history of the Mexican Indians—including their many scientific, educational, cultural, societal, governmental, and economic accomplishments—remains missing from these books. The major impression of the pre-Columbian Indians is one of defeat at the hands of the Spanish conqueror.

Then what about Spain, the conqueror? Usually these books contain a few more lines about Spain, but these too are suffused with negativism. The student gets no sense of Spain's brilliant culture or contributions to world civilization, but merely receives a unidimensional Black Legend image of Spaniards as oppressors of New World Indians. However, when faced with an English rival, the Spaniard, too, turns out a loser, usually dramatized by a lengthy, culturally chauvinistic depiction of England's victory over the Spanish Armada in 1588.

Independent Mexico receives somewhat more attention than Spain or pre-Columbian Mexico, but the emphasis on defeat remains. Mexico seldom appears in U.S. history texts except when being defeated or invaded by the U.S. or by those of Anglo-American descent, as in the 1835-1836 war for Texas independence, the 1846-1848 U.S.-Mexican War, and the 1914 U.S. occupation of Vera Cruz. By selecting Anglo victories over Mexico as the principal means of portraying the latter, textbook authors, whether intentionally or unintentionally, reinforce feelings of Anglo superiority and Mexican-American inferiority.

So much for traditional U.S. history texts. But what about the modern inquiry method social studies textbooks? Although their framework is often altered from chronological historical narrative to topical treatment of various aspects of life, society, and culture, the traditional cultural biases generally remain when these books deal with matters directly pertinent to or tangentially relevant to the Chicano experience.

Ironically, the Mexican American suffers from tokenism even in exposés of textbook treatment of minorities and in so-called multi-ethnic syllabi. In Michael B. Kane's recent 148-page *Minorities in Textbooks: A Study of Their Treatment in Social Studies Texts,* Mexican Americans receive only one page as part of a six-page section on the "Spanish Speaking."[15] And in Warren J. Halliburton and William Loren Katz's recent *American Majorities and Minorities: A Syllabus of United States History for Secondary Schools,* Chicanos receive limited, sporadic, and inaccurate treatment.[16]

Knowledge and Frames of Reference

To societal stereotypes and inadequate textbooks must be added two other basic pedagogical obstacles—limited knowledge about and rigid traditional frames of reference concerning the Chicano experience. Our knowledge is limited not only by the relatively modest amount of research done on the Chicano past, but also because most of that research has been concentrated on a small number of topics.[17] Most major areas of the Chicano experience have been barely touched upon or entirely ignored by researchers. We have only begun to illuminate the totality of the Chicano experience. Our current knowledge, which only hints at that vibrant past, must be used sensitively with this limitation in mind.[18]

Similarly, the teacher must also contend with invalid traditional frames of reference, whose persistence in society and education has hindered the study of the Chicano experience. Let me mention merely five of these frames of reference:

(1) the idea that U.S. history is an essentially unidirectional east-to-west phenomenon,

(2) the attempt to explain the Chicano experience by labeling it "just like" the experiences of Blacks, Native Americans, or various immigrant groups,

(3) the view of the Chicano experience as essentially homogeneous, with most Mexican Americans following a single stereotyped historical pattern,

(4) the concept of the "awakening Mexican American," arising from a century-long siesta,

(5) the attempt to explain the Chicano experience by presenting a parade of Mexican heroes and individual Mexican-American success stories.

In their place, I would like to suggest and briefly discuss the following five alternative frames of reference, which I call exploratory concepts for analyzing the Chicano experience:

Traditional Frames of Reference	*Suggested Alternative Exploratory Concepts*
(1) U.S. history as an east-to-west phenomenon	(1) Greater America concept
(2) "just like" explanations	(2) comparative ethnic experiences
(3) Chicano homogeneity	(3) Chicano diversity
(4) "awakening Mexican American"	(4) history of activity
(5) heroes and success stories	(5) the Chicano people

The Greater America Concept

One of the basic structural concepts of U.S. social studies has been the culturally distorted idea that the United States is strictly an Anglo product which began on the east coast and flowed west. At best, most books on U.S. history and society give only token recognition to the fact that cultures existed in the West prior to the coming of the European, that explorers and settlers came north from Mexico into that area during the sixteenth, seventeenth, eighteenth, and early nineteenth centuries, and that Mexicans were living in the Southwest when the U.S. invaded the area in 1846. Little substantive attention is paid to the northward flow of culture and society from central Mexico or its impact on the pre-1846 American Southwest.

In order to create true intercultural understanding, the social studies must be reoriented on the basis that the Greater American heritage developed from the dual advance of societies from the Atlantic coast west and from Mexico City north, as well as from the fusions and conflict between these advancing cultures and the already existent Southwestern civilizations.[19] For students to understand the Greater America in all of its cultural and ethnic dimensions, the study of the Mexican heritage of the U.S. must become an intrinsic part of the social studies process, beginning with the first year of school. The teaching of social studies must include, from grade one on, the continuous, parallel study of Anglo and Mexican cultural and societal patterns, their contributions, their conflict, and the process or failure of fusion or coexistence.

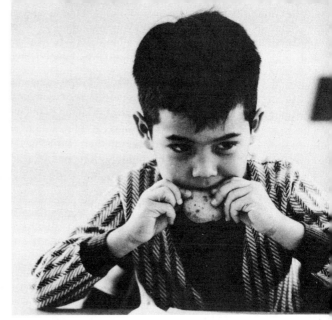

". . . the study of the Mexican heritage of the U.S. must become an intrinsic part of the social studies process, beginning with the first year of school."

In this manner, the social studies would begin operating on the reality of this dual heritage by examining such bicultural topics as:

(1) explorers and settlers of both the Mexican Southwest and the Atlantic colonies,
(2) Native American civilizations and their relations with expanding U.S. society from the east and expanding Mexican society from the south,
(3) types of economic systems that developed in the western and eastern sections of our country,
(4) various concepts of law, land, and water rights which became implanted throughout the country within different cultural settings,
(5) Mexican and U.S. political systems,
(6) Mexican and U.S. class and caste structures, and
(7) ethnic relations in the U.S. and Mexico.

This continuous Greater America approach can reduce the inherent ethnocentrism which has always plagued U.S. social studies and place in proper perspective the bicultural heritage and multi-ethnic reality of the United States.

Comparative Ethnic Experiences

The teaching of the Chicano experience has also suffered from misguided attempts to describe Chicanos by explaining them in terms of superficially similar experiences of other U.S. ethnic groups. This means simplistic depictions of the Chicano experience as "just like" those of Blacks, Native Americans, or various immigrant groups.

The Chicano experience does have certain similarities with the experience of each of these groups. However, social studies teachers must

187

avoid the comfort of easy generalizations, for just as there are similarities, there are salient differences which invalidate a simple "just like" approach. For example, like Blacks, Native Americans, and Asian Americans (but unlike European immigrant groups), Chicanos can rightfully attribute part of their sufferings to racial prejudice. Like Native Americans (but unlike Blacks, Asian Americans, or European immigrants), Chicanos were one of the two major ethnic groups which established large-scale societies *prior* to the coming of Anglos and, through military conquest, became aliens in their own land. Like European and Asian immigrants (but unlike Blacks or Native Americans), Chicanos have seen their numbers increased in the nineteenth and twentieth centuries by a major flow of free immigration.

These few examples demonstrate that the Chicano experience has parallel aspects in other ethnic experiences, but that as a unique composite, it contrasts with any other individual ethnic experience. Moreover, just as these three factors—racial prejudice, conquest and alienation in their own land, and flow of free immigration—are useful analytical tools for comparing ethnic experiences, any number of such categories can be devised for ethnic comparative analysis. This conceptual frame of reference should help the student in developing logical analytical thinking, help sensitize him to cultural nuances, and help eradicate the distorting tendency to explain the Chicano (or other ethnic) experience in simplistic "just like" terms.

Chicano Diversity

In examining the Chicano experience, the social studies teacher must avoid not only simplistic "just like" depictions. He must also reject another equally convenient, but equally distorting traditional frame of reference—the view of the Chicano experience as essentially homogeneous, with most Mexican Americans following a single stereotyped historical pattern. Instead, the teacher should adopt a third exploratory concept—the great internal diversity of the Chicano experience and the Chicano people.

In applying this concept, an almost unlimited number of questions can be devised. Let me suggest a few which could prove useful in probing Chicano diversity. For example, what aspects of the Chicano experience are essentially Spanish, Mexican Indian, Native American, Black, American (U.S.), or simply variations of universal human experience (for when we go beyond ethnic categories, all people have co-participated in such universal experiences as fear, love, hunger, cold, heat, and hope)? What have been the geographical variations in the Chicano experience—between regions, states, sections of states, cities, or

"What have been the differences in experience of different generations . . . ?"

barrios? What have been the comparative experiences of various Mexican immigration waves? What have been the differences in experience of different generations of Chicanos? What have been the varieties of urban and rural experience? What have been the experience differences of various Chicano social classes, economic groups, political groupings, etc.? What have been the experience differences of Mexican-American men and women? For that matter, what differences in the Chicano experience have spawned such diverse appellations as *Chicano, Mexican American, Latin American, Spanish American, Hispano, Latino, Tejano, Californio,* or *American of Mexican descent?*

These are only a few of the questions which may help in examining the diversity of the Chicano experience. Not only will this line of exploration lead to an awareness of the variety in the Chicano past and present, but it will also provide an antidote to textbook and societal stereotyping of the Mexican American.

History of Activity

Ironically, some of these stereotypes have developed as byproducts of the Chicano Movement. Scholars and journalists, in jazzing up their treatment of the Movement, have come up with such catchy but pernicious phrases as "the awakening Mexican American" and "the siesta is over." These invalid, ahistorical concepts imply that, prior to the Movement, the Mexican American had been taking a century-long siesta and is now just emerging from more than a century of somnolence and passivity. Nothing could be further from the truth.

There are many sources for this misconception. For one thing, even more than the Black and Native American, the Chicano has lacked national visibility. As America's true "invisible man," he has failed to gain admission into traditional narratives of the U.S. past. Therefore, when the Chicano Movement forced the nation to notice its second largest ethnic minority, many writers treated the Movement as a deviancy in Mexican-American history—a sudden shift from passivity to activity.

In part, too, the historical myth of Chicano passivity has been reinforced by the recent flood of scholarly and journalistic accounts of Anglo prejudice against, discrimination against, and exploitation of ethnic minority groups. These are certainly major verities of U.S. history. However, the preponderance of books and articles about Anglo activity toward (usually against) Chicanos as contrasted with the few studies of Chicano activity itself has unfortunately produced the distorted impression of the Chicano experience as an essentially passive one, with the Chicano merely the passive recipient of Anglo discrimination and exploitation.

But the reality of Chicano-Anglo relations belies this. Since the 1846 conquest, Chicanos have established a long activist heritage of resistance against Anglo discrimination and exploitation.[20] Therefore, in examining Chicano-Anglo relations (and they should be examined in social studies classes), the teacher must avoid the trap of using a simple active Anglo (exploiter-discriminator) and passive Chicano (exploited-discriminated against) model.

Moreover, although discrimination, exploitation, and resistance are essential aspects of the Chicano experience, they comprise only part of it. These themes should not be permitted to monopolize the study of the Mexican-American past. The Chicano experience is a unique composite of a vast variety of human activities. By using the "history of activity" exploratory concept, teachers can help eradicate the distortions produced by the purveyors of "the awakening Mexican American" and "the siesta is over" image.

The Chicano People

Finally, while applying the "history of activity" concept, the social studies teacher must avoid the limitations of still another commonly used but distorting frame of reference—the attempt to explain the Chicano experience simply by presenting a parade of Mexican heroes and individual Mexican-American success stories. Certainly heroes and success stories comprise *part* of the Chicano experience. Chicanos can develop greater pride and non-Chicanos can develop greater respect by learning of Chicano lawyers, doctors, educators, athletes, musicians, artists, writers, businessmen, etc., as well as Mexican and Chicano heroes (heroes either to their own culture or to the nation at large). However, the teaching of the Chicano experience often becomes little more than the display of Emiliano Zapata, Pancho Villa, Benito Juárez, and Miguel Hidalgo posters or an extended exercise in "me too-ism"— the listing of Mexican Americans who have "made it" according to Anglo standards.

In falling into these educational clichés, the very essence of the Chicano experience is overlooked. For this essence is neither heroes nor "me too" success stories, but rather the masses of Mexican-American people. The social studies teacher should focus on these Chicanos, their way of life, their activities, their culture, their joys and sufferings, their conflicts, and their adaptation to an often hostile societal environment. Such an examination of the lives of Mexican Americans—not Chicano heroes or "successes"—can provide new dimensions for the understanding of and sensitivity to this important part of our nation's heritage.

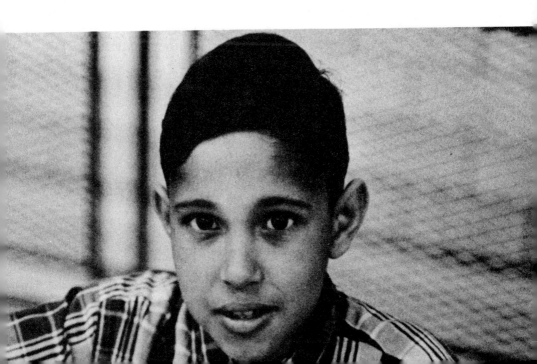

Teaching Strategies

So much for exploratory concepts. But what of specific teaching strategies for implementing these concepts? Many of the strategies already developed in social studies education are applicable or adaptable to the Mexican American. However, in view of the obstacles and exploratory concepts I have discussed, let me suggest three teaching strategies which are particularly useful for studying the Chicano experience:

(1) the critical analysis, from a Chicano perspective, of social studies textbooks and other image-creating (often stereotype- or prejudice-creating) elements of our society,
(2) the selective use of Mexican-American supplementary materials, and
(3) the constant use of local community resources, with a strong emphasis on oral investigation.

Critical Analysis

As I discussed earlier, the ethnocentrism of our social studies textbooks is a major obstacle to understanding the Chicano experience. However, the teacher can mitigate the negative impact of these textbooks and even make effective use of their cultural biases and distortions.

Young students cannot be expected to have the knowledge or critical facility to analyze fully or erect effective defenses against the inherent cultural deficiencies and biases in our social studies textbooks. Teachers provide the main and possibly only line of defense between these distortions and students' developing minds. After carefully analyzing books to be used in the classroom, teachers should present them to their students in proper perspective, indicating the ethnic biases—including how the book may reaffirm Anglo superiority and neglect or distort the role or image of the Mexican American. Going one step further, teachers should help students learn to identify and analyze cultural distortions in textbooks and encourage them to use this critical thinking with all text materials, including such supposedly objective supplementary works as almanacs, atlases, encyclopedias, and dictionaries.[21]

Moving beyond these standard materials, teachers should have students apply a Chicano perspective (as part of a multi-ethnic perspective) in analyzing other societal elements which create images (including stereotypes) and ideas (including prejudice). Motion pictures, comic strips, advertisements, speeches, newspaper and magazine articles, official government publications, and all types of books provide fine raw material for students to use in studying anti-Chicano biases which pervade society. In short, the teaching of critical analysis, particularly involving the development of sensitivity to ethnic and cultural nuances, should become an intrinsic part of social studies education.

Chicano Supplementary Materials

Considering the deficiencies of social studies textbooks in relation to the Mexican American, the teacher must also adopt a second teaching strategy—the selective use of Chicano supplementary materials. The current Chicano Renaissance has produced a sudden affluence in Chicano poetry, short stories, essays, novels, art, manifestoes, and plans.[22] Chicano magazines and newspapers—many cooperating through the Chicano Press Association—have increased rapidly in number and geographical distribution. Chicano scholarly journals now provide a forum for research results and intellectual debate over subjects vital to the Mexican-American people.[23] A small number of Movement films[24] and movies treating history from a Chicano perspective[25] are now available. When used effectively by the social studies teacher, these varied materials should prove stimulating and enlightening in the examination of the Chicano experience.

In addition, teachers can select from a number of recently published elementary and secondary school supplementary works on the Mexican American. The prolific and imaginative Rodolfo Acuña has written three fine books: *The Story of the Mexican Americans: The Men and the Land* (lower elementary), *Cultures in Conflict* (advanced elementary), and *A Mexican American Chronicle* (secondary).[26] Also available for elementary grades are *South by Southwest: The Mexican-American and His Heritage* by John Tebbel and Ramón Eduardo Ruiz, *Mexican Americans: Past, Present, and Future* by Julian Nava, and *The Mexican American: His Life Across Four Centuries* by Gilbert Martínez and Jane Edwards.[27] Despite its title, the Tebbel-Ruiz book is more "His Heritage" (105 pages on Mexican history and Mexican-U.S. relations) than "The Mexican American" (15 pages). Nava's book suffers from factual errors, an overemphasis on the Spanish aspects of the Mexican-American heritage (to the detriment of Indian, Mexican, mestizo, and African elements of the Chicano experience), and a failure to discuss the Chicano Movement.[28] For the advanced elementary or secondary level, *The Mexican-American in the United States* by Charles J. and Patricia L. Bustamante is a useful alternative to *A Mexican American Chronicle*,[29] which has proven too difficult for some high school students.

Use of Local Community Resources

But these supplementary materials notwithstanding, effective teaching of the Chicano experience requires expanding the classroom beyond four walls. The use of general Chicano books, magazines, journals, articles, films, art, and ephemera must be complemented by student discovery of Mexican-American heritage at the local level. Particularly in the Southwest, but increasingly in other sections of the country, potential materials are all around, including the richest resource of all— the Mexican-American people.

Students can explore their local communities to obtain information on the Chicano experience. Newspapers, city council and school board minutes, and records of such organizations as local clubs, churches, Mexican-American chambers of commerce, benevolent societies, and community settlement houses are all potential sources. However, since the Mexican American generally has been neglected in local books, newspapers, and other written sources, only the fringe of his experience can be discovered through reading. This study process must be supplemented by oral investigation if students are to develop a true knowledge and understanding of local Mexican-American society, culture, and history.[30]

Every Mexican American is a potentially valuable source of knowledge. There are no class, caste, educational, or linguistic qualifications for being a part of history, having a culture or society, having family or barrio traditions, perceiving the surrounding community, or relating one's experiences. Ideally, every Mexican American should have the opportunity to tell and record his own story and that of his family and friends—his personal contribution to the documenting of the Chicano experience.

The teacher can use various means to involve the student in the process of oral exploration. For example, each student may be assigned to write the biography of a local Mexican-American individual or family, including his own. The assignment may provide some non-Chicano students with their first personal contact with Mexican-American life. By hearing history and obtaining a perspective on society as viewed, recalled, and repeated by Mexican Americans, non-Chicano students should obtain a new outlook on the American past and the community around them. For Mexican-American students, the assignment can have a double payoff. First, it can help them discover a personal sense of historicity based on their own families' past, as contrasted to the generalized experience presented in books. Second, it can contribute to family pride. As parents and other relatives relate their stories to students, they should become increasingly aware that they are a meaningful part of our nation's heritage, a part worth being studied and recorded.

Or the teacher may bring local Mexican-American residents into the classroom. Here they can share their experiences and views with the students, relate their oral traditions, answer questions, give new outlooks on society and history, and open doors of investigation for students.

Using these family biographies and classroom interviews as basic data, students can test hypotheses, reevaluate previous conceptions (or

"Every Mexican American is a potentially valuable source of knowledge."

misconceptions), and develop new generalizations on the Chicano experience. Moreover, this process of oral investigation can give students of all ethnic backgrounds a firsthand, localized awareness of and sensitivity to the varieties of cultures in our country. It can open intellectual doors for them, stimulate within them a desire to continue their study of the local community, and, by revealing the community's past and present problems and possibilities, create the commitment to resolve these problems and fulfill the possibilities. Finally, it can "humanize" the study of the Chicano experience by revealing on a personal and affective level what students might never be able to discover in books.

The study of the Chicano experience offers both challenge and opportunity to the social studies teacher. Obstacles may be frustrating, new concepts may be demanding, and innovation may be difficult. But more difficult, yet, have been the lives of Mexican Americans for the past 125 years. America is finally recognizing the Chicano presence, and educators are finally recognizing that the study of the Chicano experience is a vital part of becoming aware of our nation's multi-ethnic and culturally pluralistic heritage. It is up to the social studies teacher to turn this overdue societal recognition into educational reality and thereby help create an open society of the future.

FOOTNOTES

[1] Prior to the admission of Texas, the Mexican-American population consisted of a handful of Mexican immigrants into the U.S.

[2] In this chapter, I use the words "Chicano" and "Mexican American" interchangeably, except when referring to the Chicano Movement.

[3] The Treaty of Guadalupe Hidalgo is *must* reading for anyone interested in the Chicano experience. The most useful edition of the treaty is the annotated version published by the Tate Gallery in Truchas, New Mexico.

[4] Not until 1970 did the Census Bureau include Mexican Americans as a population category. The Chicano population prior to 1970 can only be "guesstimated" on the basis of such occasionally used census categories as persons of Mexican birth, persons of the Mexican "race," persons of Spanish mother tongue, and white persons of Spanish surname. These categories were further limited in value by not being applied nationally, but only to selected states, particularly in the Southwest. Even the 1970 census has come under severe criticism because the Chicano and Puerto Rican categories were not included on the short form which went to everybody, but only on the long form which went to a 5 per cent random sample. A discussion of Chicano "census history" can be found in the Census Bureau's publication, *Persons of Spanish Surname.*

[5] Although Chicanos are most numerous in the Southwest, they are rapidly increasing in number throughout the rest of the country. For example, Michigan now has the nation's fourth largest Chicano population, while a quarter-of-a-million Mexican Americans live in Chicago alone.

⁶ For convenience, I use the term "American" in referring to the United States. However, it should be remembered that, strictly speaking, this term applies to all nations and inhabitants of the Western hemisphere.

⁷ For a history of the development of the Black Legend, see Philip Wayne Powell, *Tree of Hate: Propaganda and Prejudices Affecting United States Relations with the Hispanic World* (New York: Basic Books, 1971). In particular, pages 131-44 contain a discussion of the Black Legend's impact on U.S. education.

⁸ For an analysis of English and Colonial U.S. attitudes toward Native Americans, see Roy Harvey Pearce, *The Savages of America: A Study of the Indian and the Idea of Civilization* (Baltimore: Johns Hopkins Press, 1953). The classic study of English-Anglo attitudes toward people of color is Winthrop Jordan, *White Over Black: American Attitudes toward the Negro, 1550-1817* (Chapel Hill: University of North Carolina Press, [1968]). Although Jordan focuses on White-Black attitudinal relations, his book has serious implications for the history of Anglo-Chicano relations.

⁹ Américo Paredes presents a slight variation on this theme. In summarizing one of the elements of the Anglo-Texas anti-Mexican legend, Paredes writes that Anglo-Texans traditionally assumed that "The degeneracy of the Mexican is due to his mixed blood, though the elements in the mixture were inferior to begin with. He is descended from the Spaniard, a second-rate type of European, and from the equally substandard Indian of Mexico, who must not be confused with the noble savages of North America." See Américo Paredes, *"With His Pistol in His Hand:" A Border Ballad and Its Hero* (Austin: University of Texas Press [1958]), p. 16.

¹⁰ Cecil Robinson, *With the Ears of Strangers. The Mexican in American Literature* (Tucson: University of Arizona Press, 1963), pp. 15-30.

¹¹ Thomas M. Martínez, "Advertising and Racism: The Case of the Mexican-American," *El Grito*, II (Summer, 1969), 3-13.

¹² For a more complete discussion of the Mexican image in the mass media, see Carlos E. Cortés, "Revising the 'All-American Soul Course': A Bicultural Avenue to Educational Reform" in Alfredo Castañeda, Manuel Ramírez III, Carlos E. Cortés, and Mario Barrera (eds.), *Mexican Americans and Educational Change* (Riverside: Mexican-American Studies Program, University of California, 1971), pp. 319-22.

¹³ *Ibid.*, pp. 318-19.

¹⁴ The most intensive multi-ethnic analyses of current social studies textbooks are *Report and Recommendations of the Task Force to Reevaluate Social Science Textbooks Grades Five Through Eight* (Sacramento: Bureau of Textbooks, California State Department of Education, 1971), and *A Study of Elementary & Secondary Social Studies Textbooks* (Lansing: Michigan Department of Education, 1973).

¹⁵ Michael B. Kane, *Minorities in Textbooks: A Study of Their Treatment in Social Studies Texts* (Chicago: Quadrangle Books, 1970).

¹⁶ Warren J. Halliburton and William Loren Katz, *American Majorities and Minorities: A Syllabus of United States History for Secondary Schools* (New York: Arno Press, 1970).

¹⁷ Among these relatively well-researched topics are Hispano-Mexican Colonial Southwestern institutions, the Texas Revolution, the U.S.-Mexican War, the Hispano-Mexican land grant question, the Mexican Revolution, and the contemporary Mexican-American scene.

¹⁸ Among the more useful bibliographies on the Chicano experience are Luis G. Nogales (ed.), *The Mexican American: A Selected and Annotated Bibliography* (2d ed. rev.; Stanford, Calif.: Center for Latin American Studies, Stanford University, 1971); Ernie Barrios (ed.), *Bibliografía a de Aztlán: An Annotated Chicano Bibliography* (San Diego: Centro de Estudios Chicanos, San Diego State College, 1971); Ruben Cortez and Joseph Navarro (eds.), *Mexican-American History: A Critical Selective Bibliography* (Santa Barbara, Calif.: Mexican-American Historical Society, 1969).

¹⁹ The classical champion of studying the American past on a two-directional basis was Herbert Eugene Bolton. A discussion of the Bolton Theory can be found in Lewis Hanke (ed.), *Do the Americas Have a Common History? A Critique of the Bolton Theory* (New York: Alfred A. Knopf, 1964).

²⁰ Two books which explore aspects of this resistance heritage are Rodolfo Acuña,

Occupied America: The Chicano's Struggle for Liberation (San Francisco: Canfield Press, 1972) and Carlos E. Cortés, *Struggle for Aztlán: A History of Chicano Resistance* (Boston: Houghton Mifflin Co.). Forthcoming.

[21] The California Task Force Report and Michigan Department of Education Study (see footnote 14) should prove most useful in developing this teaching strategy.

[22] In Mexican and Chicano tradition, a plan is a manifesto of goals and grievances, issued by groups or individuals upon initiating a social or political movement.

[23] Among the more important Chicano scholarly journals are *Aztlán: Chicano Journal of the Social Sciences and the Arts* (Chicano Cultural Center, University of California, Los Angeles); *El Grito: A Journal of Contemporary Mexican-American Thought* (Quinto Sol Publications, Berkeley, Calif.); *The Journal of Mexican American History* (Santa Barbara, Calif.); *The Journal of Mexican American Studies* (Anaheim, Calif.).

[24] Such as *I am Joaquín* and *Tijerina*.

[25] Such as *North from Mexico: Exploration and Heritage* and *Northwest from Tumacácori*.

[26] Rudolph Acuña, *The Story of the Mexican American: The Men and the Land* (New York: American Book Company, 1969), *Cultures in Conflict* (with Peggy Shackelton) (Los Angeles: Charter School Books, 1970), and *A Mexican American Chronicle* (New York: American Book Company, 1971).

[27] John Tebbel and Ramón Eduardo Ruiz, *South by Southwest: The Mexican-American and His Heritage* (Garden City, N.Y.: Doubleday & Company, 1969), Julian Nava, *Mexican Americans: Past, Present, and Future* (New York: American Book Company, 1969), and Gilbert Martínez and Jane Edwards, *The Mexican American: His Life Across Four Centuries* (Boston: Houghton Mifflin, 1973).

[28] The author has indicated to me that he hopes to revise and update the book.

[29] Charles J. Bustamante and Patricia L. Bustamante, *The Mexican-American in the United States* (Mountain View, Calif.: PATTY-LAR Publications, 1969).

[30] For a more extensive discussion of the use of community resources, see Carlos E. Cortés, "CHICOP: A Response to the Challenge of Local Chicano History," *Aztlán. Chicano Journal of the Social Sciences and the Arts*, I (Fall, 1970), 1-14. An example of comparative Chicano community history is the forthcoming Carlos E. Cortés (editor and coordinator), John Faragher, Donald Miller, Robert Pinger, Susan Pinger, Lorenza Calvillo Schmidt, Carolyn Symonds, and Paul Viafora, *The Bent Cross: A History of the Mexican American in the San Bernardino Valley*.

BIBLIOGRAPHY

Acuña, Rodolfo. *Occupied America: The Chicano's Struggle toward Liberation.* San Francisco: Canfield Press, 1972. Strongly-worded interpretation of the Chicano experience employing a framework of historical internal colonialism.

Burma, John H. (ed.). *Mexican-Americans in the United States.* Cambridge, Mass.: Schenkman Publishing Company, 1970. Motley collection of articles on the recent Chicano experience.

Carter, Thomas P. *Mexican Americans in School: A History of Educational Neglect.* New York: College Entrance Examination Board, 1970. Pioneering study of the failure of the U.S. educational system in relation to Chicanos.

Castañeda, Alfredo; Ramírez, Manuel, III; Cortés, Carlos E.; and Barrera, Mario (eds.). *Mexican Americans and Educational Change.* Riverside: Mexican-American Studies Program, University of California, 1971. Major collection of articles on bilingual-bicultural education and the history and politics of educational change.

Gamio, Manuel. *Mexican Immigration to the United States.* Chicago: University of Chicago Press, 1930. Dated but basic study of Mexican immigration.

Grebler, Leo; Moore, Joan W.; and Guzmán, Ralph C. *The Mexican-American People: The Nation's Second Largest Minority.* New York: The Free Press, 1970. Massive compilation of information and statistics on the Mexican American, presented from an assimilationist perspective.

Ludwig, Ed and Santibañez, James (eds.). *The Chicanos: Mexican American Voices.* Baltimore: Penguin Books, 1971. Interesting collection of essays, fiction, and poetry by Chicanos about Chicanos.

McWilliams, Carey. *North from Mexico: The Spanish-Speaking People of the United States.* Philadelphia: J. B. Lippincott Co., 1949. Sensitive, poetic, although occasionally inaccurate history of the Mexican American, which *must* be read by all persons interested in the Chicano experience.

Meier, Matt S. and Rivera, Feliciano. *The Chicanos: A History of Mexican Americans.* New York: Hill and Wang, 1972. Pedestrian, uneven, but useful general history of the Mexican American.

Meinig, D.W. *Southwest: Three Peoples in Geographical Change. 1600-1970.* New York: Oxford University Press, 1971. Perceptive study of Chicano, Mexican, Native American, and Anglo interaction in New Mexico and Arizona.

Moore, Joan W., with Cuellar, Alfredo. *Mexican Americans.* Englewood Cliffs, N.J.: Prentice-Hall, 1970. Good short introductory work on the Mexican American.

Moquin, Wayne, with Van Doren, Charles (eds.). *A Documentary History of the Mexican Americans.* New York: Praeger Publishers, 1971. Useful collection of primary and secondary source materials on the Chicano experience.

Pitt, Leonard. *Decline of the Californios: A Social History of the Spanish-Speaking Californians, 1846-1890.* Berkeley: University of California Press, 1966. Study of the tribulations suffered by Mexican Americans following the U.S.-Mexican War.

Rendon, Armando B. *Chicano Manifesto.* New York: The Macmillan Company, 1971. Rhetorical but important expression of the content and spirit of the Chicano Movement.

Robinson, Cecil. *With the Ears of Strangers: The Mexican in American Literature.* Tucson: University of Arizona Press, 1963. Revealing analysis of American portrayals of the Mexican, with an emphasis on the nineteenth century.

Romano-V, Octavio I. (ed.). *El Espejo—The Mirror: Selected Mexican-American Literature.* Berkeley, Calif.: Quinto Sol Publications, 1969. Good examples of poetry, essays, and short stories produced by the Chicano Renaissance.

Samora, Julian (ed.). *La Raza: Forgotten Americans.* Notre Dame, Ind.: University of Notre Dame Press, 1966. Uneven but informative collection of articles on various aspects of the Chicano experience.

Steiner, Stan. *La Raza: The Mexican Americans.* New York: Harper & Row, 1969. Panoramic view of the Chicano Movement and the contemporary Mexican-American scene.

Jack D. Forbes

JACK D. FORBES is Professor of Native American Studies at the University of California, Davis and an Instructor at D-Q University. He has taught at the University of Southern California, Citrus College, San Fernando Valley State College, the University of Nevada, and has held research fellowships from the Social Science Research Council and the John Simon Guggenheim Memorial Foundation. Dr. Forbes has written extensively on Native American Studies, ethnohistory, and interethnic relations and is himself of Powhatan Indian descent. His articles have appeared in such journals as Phylon, Southwest Journal of Anthropology, American West, Journal of the West, Journal of Human Relations *and* Ethnohistory. *His books include* Apache, Navaho and Spaniard, The Indian in America's Past, Warriors of the Colorado: The Yumas of the Quechan Nation and Their Neighbors, Mexican-Americans: A Handbook for Educators, Nevada Indians Speak, Education of the Culturally Different: A Multi-Cultural Approach, Native Americans of California and Nevada: A Handbook for Educators *and* Afro-Americans in the Far West: A Handbook for Educators.

9

Teaching Native American Values and Cultures

No school can be truly "American" (having a character which is relevant to the history of this land) unless a rather significant part of its curriculum focuses on the Native American (American Indian) heritage. For at least 20,000 years the development and maintenance of this land was entirely in the hands of Native Americans. For the past 500 years Europeans, Africans, and Asians have also become a part of the American scene, but the Native has remained an important factor everywhere, especially in the Western half of the country. Only in the past century or so have people of the white race become a majority anywhere in the West.

Our schools, by and large, are not "American." Because of the political power of the Anglo (English-speaking white) ethnic group, the schools have assumed a European character, focusing entirely or predominantly upon the culture and legacy of Anglo-Americans. Of course, that culture has been greatly influenced by non-European peoples (including Indians) but the "mestizo" (hybrid) character of Anglo-American culture is seldom recognized, especially in the school curriculum. The fact that white heroes such as Daniel Boone, Davy Crockett, and Kit Carson were highly Indianized persons in terms of dress, life-style, and, to some degree, values, is overlooked. Instead, all of their Indian attributes simply are "appropriated" into white culture so that the pupil has no knowledge of the culturally "mestizo" status of such persons. The whole subject of cultural *mestisaje* (mixture), so widely discussed in South America, is not even acknowledged in Anglo schools. It, along with its companion subject, racial mixture, seems to be a "taboo" topic.

In order for our schools to be "American" they must become "Americanized." They must be consciously shorn of their alien European quality and must come to reflect the realities of this land's past. But it is not enough to say that little bits and pieces of Native American life and culture should be integrated into the curriculum. On the contrary, *we must be sure that the essence, the deepest meaning, of Indian life-ways are dealt with.* All too often curriculum-builders have felt that by looking at a few baskets in the third grade, or by having children examine different housing-styles, they could adequately dispose of Native culture. It should be borne in mind, however, that the essence of Indianness has next to nothing to do with canoes, moccasins or other material objects. A modern-day Native American can drive a pickup truck and fly in a jet airplane and still be a full participant in the central "core" of Native culture.

The meaning or significance of the Native American way of life basically revolves around *values* and it is this subject-area which should dominate curriculum-building. This is not to say that Native American cooking, dancing, music, and art should be ignored, but rather that stress should be placed upon the central dynamic *élan* of Native cultures. It is because of this *élan* that Native peoples are able to produce the arts, crafts, music, and poetry so admired by outsiders. Not only is the study of the basic values of Native American life important as a means of understanding Native cultures themselves, but these values (and the socio-cultural, religio-philosophical, and political behavior-styles resulting therefrom) are significant because they provide a means for solving many of the significant problems faced by modern man.

It is a tragedy that modern United States society seems to be tearing itself apart over such issues as protecting the environment, crime, drugs, dishonesty in government, poverty, unrepresentative government, over-population, uncontrolled technology, exploitation of other human beings, overseas imperialism, and growing militarism. The tragic nature of this situation is accentuated by the fact that Native American philosophy and culture possesses solutions for all of these problems, or at least has systems of behavior which would have prevented them from ever arising. One of the reasons why the white society is proceeding so rapidly in the direction of its own destruction is that the accumulated wisdom of 20,000 years of living on this land called America has been consciously excluded from the schools and colleges.

There are many reasons why the schools have excluded any discussion of the basic values of Native cultures: first, because of a white racist superiority complex which asserts that non-white cultures have nothing worthwhile to offer; second, because the ruling classes of the United States have sought to encourage an aggressive, exploitative approach to

"... we must be sure that the essence, the deepest meaning, of Indian life-ways are dealt with."

"Education should emphasize the perfection of individual character, that is, the development of a person functioning in a harmonious way with nature and with people . . ."

life (which is directly contradicted by Native values); and, third, because Native economic, social, and political democracy and respect for all living creatures is antithetical to the industrial capitalistic system as developed in the United States. What are these Native values? As an introduction, let us look at the subject from the perspective of a set of *goals of education* written from the Native American viewpoint.

(1) The survival and development of the people (the tribe or nation) is generally a paramount goal. Educational programs must contribute to the continued existence of the nation.

(2) An individual is "successful" in life insofar as he acquires the respect and esteem of his people. Educational programs must emphasize the acquisition of skills and development of personality characteristics valued by the particular Indian society.

(3) Education should emphasize the perfection of individual character, that is, the development of a person functioning in a harmonious way with nature and with people and one who seeks to perfect his own potential to the highest degree possible in the various spheres of life (in art, music, bodily development, crafts, the acquisition of knowledge, religious experience, or whatever). The emphasis is on life-long development and on attitude, and not merely on the acquisition of certain marketable skills coupled with a little random exposure to "general education" or the "humanities."

(4) The individual should be educated for personal strength and survival, that is, the ability to be alone for long periods of time, if necessary, without being either bored or fearful. In other words, the individual should be able to turn inward without being frightened by internal nothingness, should be able to be apart from other people without becoming "insane" or "queer," should possess the basic skills for functioning alone so as to know that survival is possible. (This does not mean that individuals are to be trained to be self-centered, but rather that they are able to relate equally well to the human and non-human worlds.)

(5) The individual should develop a profound conception of the unity of life, from the fact of his belonging to a community of related people to which he owes his existence and definition of being, to the total web of natural life, to which he and his people also owe their existence. The brotherhood of all living creatures must be existentially comprehended, along with the realization of one's origin from the earth and so-called non-living elements.

(6) The individual should develop a realization that "success" in life stems from being able to contribute to the well-being of one's people and all life. This means that the individual seeks to perfect behavior and skills which will add "beauty" to the world. To create "beauty" in actions, words, and objects is the overall objective of human beings in this world.

(7) The educational process must emphasize the development of an attitude of profound respect for the individuality and right to self-realization of all living creatures. What this means is that Indian people do not impose their wills on other Indians, do not interrupt other people when they are speaking, do not try to change other people's behavior except by example or indirect ways, do not attempt to use other people as "means," do not take advantage of, or exploit, other people, and do not try to impose any collective decisions on individuals except where the survival of the whole people is at stake. Even then, the dissenting individuals are subject to no more severe coercion than schism, i.e., going their own way.

(8) The individual should be encouraged to share with others and to show hospitality. The hoarding of possessions is an antisocial trait which is counter-productive since it initiates a vicious circle of hoarding. Also, hoarding is based upon an erroneous belief in the ultimate value of material possessions and a perverted conception of man's relationship to the universe.

(9) The individual must be helped to understand that material possessions are valuable primarily for the joy derived from sharing them with others, and that spiritual and character development are what is important. Likewise, a truly creative person (i.e., a craftsman) can continually create beauty and does not need to "own" it. In fact, the craftsman must realize that his skill and "talent" are derived from others (his "teachers") or from the nature of the creative process from which he originated and that he only gives concrete expression to that process.

(10) The individual should be helped to realize that the world of sense perception is not the only level of existence and that the eternal nature of the universe must be considered. Such Indian viewpoints such as that the empirical world is a place for giving expression to the self-realization process of the Great Mystery (the core of reality), but is not of intrinsic value when considered by itself, need to be understood.[1]

The above goals are, of course, general and do not relate specifically to any single Indian group. They do, however, probably reflect the basic values of Native societies. Quite obviously, persons raised according to traditional Native values would (and do) behave differently from many people in the dominant society. Generally speaking, a Native American community will be (1) extremely democratic, (2) very tolerant of individual differences, (3) very equalitarian, (4) typified by an absence of wealth concentrated in any particular family, (5) uninterested in technology if the latter threatens any basic values or offers no significant improvement in the quality of life, (6) typified by giving a low value to the possession of most material goods, (7) typified by a deep commitment to the spiritual life, (8) opposed to the unnecessary destruction of any living creature, (9) opposed to the unnecessary alteration or destruction of the earth or any part of the earth, (10) uninterested in warfare or scheming related to acquiring control over another group (i.e., imperialism), and (11) extremely oriented towards bringing forth "beauty" by means of arts, crafts, music, prayer, ceremony, and proper living.

It should be crystal clear that such a community represents a radical alternative to existing white cities and towns. In spite of rhetoric, the usual white town is typified by gross inequality of wealth, political dominance by wealthy elites and corporations, an absence of significant sharing and hospitality, very little concern for spirituality, little concern for the earth and non-human living creatures, noticeable intolerance directed towards non-conformists, laws or rules designed to punish people for matters of a purely individual nature (such as the length of hair of a teen-age boy), and, of course, by a great deal of aggressive, violent behavior. People tend to be concerned with the acquisition of wealth and power rather than with character-development and radiating "beauty."

The environmental-social crisis faced by the United States stems directly from the "logic" of the values and goals of white society. Therefore, it is crucial that alternative value systems be studied so as to provide the youth of today with options for the future. The advantage of studying Native American values stems from the fact that they are neither "utopian" nor theoretical. They have been, and are, the actual values of living peoples who have tested and perfected them over thousands of years. Let us now take a brief look at specific evidence of Indian values and how they relate to behavior.

Many centuries ago White Buffalo Woman gave to the Lakota (Sioux) people a sacred pipe and a small round stone. She said:

> With this sacred pipe you will walk upon the Earth; for the Earth is your Grandmother and Mother, and She is sacred. Every step that is taken upon Her should be as a prayer. The bowl of this pipe is of red stone; it is the Earth. Carved in the stone and facing the center is this buffalo calf who represents all the four-leggeds who live upon your Mother. The stem of the pipe is of wood, and this represents all that grows upon the Earth. And those twelve feathers which hang here where the stem fits into the bowl are from Wanbli Galeshka, the Spotted Eagle, and they represent the eagle and all the winged of the air. All these peoples, and all the things of the universe, are joined to you who smoke the pipe—all send their voices to *Wakan-Tanka*, the Great Spirit. When you pray with this pipe, you pray for and with everything.
> With this pipe you will be bound to all your relatives: your Grandfather and Father, your Grandmother and Mother. This round rock, which is made of the same red stone as the bowl of the pipe, your Father *Wakan-Tanka* has also given to you. It is the Earth, your Grandmother and Mother, and it is where you will live and increase. This Earth which He has given to you is red,

". . . all forms of life are our brothers and sisters and have to be respected."

and the two-leggeds who live upon the Earth are red; and the Great Spirit has also given to you a red day, and a red road [the good, straight road of purity and life]. All of this is sacred and so do not forget! Every dawn as it comes is a holy event, and every day is holy, for the light comes from your Father *Wakan-Tanka;* and also you must always remember that the two-leggeds and all other peoples who stand upon the Earth are sacred and should be treated as such.[2]

Black Elk, the great Sioux teacher, tells us also: "peace ... comes within the souls of men when they realize their relationship, their one-ness, with the universe and all its powers, and when they realize that at the center of the Universe dwells Wakan-Tanka, and that this center is really everywhere, it is within each of us."[3]

Some of the implications of the above religious beliefs (which are shared by most Indians) should be obvious. First, the Earth our Mother is holy and should be treated as such. Second, all forms of life are our brothers and sisters and have to be respected. Third, Life itself is a holy, sacred experience. Fourth, we must live our lives *as religion,* that is, with constant concern for spiritual relationships and values. Fifth, we must live lives that bring forth both physical and spiritual "beauty." All life has the potentiality of bringing forth Beauty and Harmony, but man in particular has also the ability to bring forth ugliness and disharmony. The true testing of man is, however, to overcome sickness and evil by giving voice to thoughts of Beauty, as in this Navajo prayer:

Tsegihi.
House made of dawn.
House made of evening light.
House made of the dark cloud.
House made of male rain.
House made of dark mist.
House made of female rain.
House made of pollen.
House made of grasshoppers.
Dark cloud is at the door.
The trail out of it is dark cloud.
The zigzag lightning stands high upon it.
Male deity!
Your offering I make.
I have prepared a smoke for you.
Restore my feet for me.
Restore my legs for me.
Restore my body for me.
Restore my mind for me.
This very day take out your spell for me.
Your spell remove for me.
You have taken it away for me.
Far off it has gone.
Happily I go forth.
My interior feeling cool, may I walk.
No longer sore, may I walk.
Impervious to pain, may I walk.
With lively feelings may I walk.
As it used to be long ago, may I walk.
Happily may I walk.
Happily, with abundant dark clouds, may I walk.
Happily, with abundant showers, may I walk.
Happily, on the trail of pollen, may I walk.
Happily may I walk.
Being as it used to be long ago, may I walk.
May it be beautiful behind me.
May it be beautiful before me.
May it be beautiful below me.
May it be beautiful above me.
May it be beautiful all around me.
In beauty it is finished.[4]

From the Native viewpoint, every blade of grass, every four-legged brother, every two-legged brother, every element of the Earth, and of the Air, and of the Water—all living things—*seek to realize their fullest potential.* An acorn seeks to explode and send forth roots and a stem, to grow into as mighty an oak as it can be. An acorn has "power," the only real "power," the *ability* to grow into what it should be. The Universe, the Creator, is like an acorn. It is "power exploding forth," it is "power yet unborn," it is "power going back into itself." A human being is like an acorn, except that a human not only has the "power" to grow in body but also has the "power" to develop other potentiality, such as in creating beauty, in doing great things, in learning about the Unseen World, and in many other ways. All life, but especially humans, have the ability to serve as the means whereby the Creator's dynamic potentiality is given expression.

A person must learn how to express the potential of the Great Creative Power. To do this a person should learn skills, and learn them well: skills that bring forth beauty, that bring forth knowledge, that bring forth harmonious living, that bring forth things which are useful. All these skills and others are important. A person without any skills, without any way to give expression to the Great Spirit, is an unhappy person, a person who is unrealized. To learn ways of doing things, and to strive for excellence, is necessary. Here is what the Mexicans (Aztecs) of the 1540's had to say about the attitude of the artist and craftsman (which applies to all persons in whatever field of endeavor):

The good painter is a Toltec, an artist;
he creates with red and black ink,
with black. . . . . .

The good painter is wise,
God is in his heart.
He puts divinity into things;
he converses with his own heart.

He knows the colors, he applies them and shades them;
he draws feet and faces,
he puts in the shadows, he achieves perfection.
He paints the colors of all the flowers,
as if he were a Toltec.

*   *   *

He who gives life to clay:
his eye is keen, he molds
and kneads the clay.

The good potter:
he takes great pains with his work;
he teaches the clay to lie;
he converses with his heart;
he makes things live, he creates them;
he knows all, as though he were a Toltec;
he trains his hands to be skillful.

The bad potter:
careless and weak,
crippled in his art.*

Juan, the Yaqui teacher, has said: "A man goes to knowledge as he goes to war, wide awake, with fear, with respect, and with absolute assurance.... For me there is only the traveling on paths that have heart, on any path that may have heart. There I travel, and the only worthwhile challenge is to travel its full length. And there I travel looking, looking, breathlessly.... Try it as many times as you think necessary. Then ask yourself, and yourself alone, one question.... Does this path have a heart? If it does, the path is good, if it doesn't it is of no use. Both paths lead nowhere; but one has a heart, the other doesn't."[5]

And so, from the Mexican and Yaqui viewpoint, one has to seek one's own paths of knowledge, of wisdom, of creativeness, and seek them diligently, ever mindful of the necessity of complete dedication to realizing all of the ultimate potentiality of what is being done. Many people have come to believe that work is something to be avoided, and especially working with one's hands. This is, of course, a product of the influence of the decadent white "leisure classes" with their notions of "upward mobility." The Mexicans had a different view, as expressed in this Huehuetlatolli (speech of the elders):

Act! Cut wood, work the land,
plant cactus, sow maguey;
you shall have drink, food, clothing.
With this you will stand straight.
With this you shall live.
For this you shall be spoken of, praised;
in this manner you will show yourself to your parents and relatives.

Some day you shall tie yourself to a skirt and blouse.
What will she drink? What will she eat?
Is she going to live off of the air?
You are the support, the remedy;
you are the eagle, the tiger.

---

* From *Aztec Thought and Culture: A Study of the Ancient Nahuatl Mind,* by Miguel León-Portilla. Copyright 1963 by the University of Oklahoma Press. Used with permission.

The Mexican not only valued work, but also devotion to diligent creativeness.

The artist—disciple, abundant, multiple, restless.
The true artist, capable, practicing, skillful,
maintains dialogue with his heart, meets things with his mind.

The true artist draws out all from his heart;
works with delight, makes things with calm, with sagacity;
works like a true Toltec; composes his objects; works dexterously, invents;
arranges materials; adorns them; makes them adjust.

The carrion artist works at random; sneers at the people;
makes things opaque; brushes across the surface of the face of things;
works without care; defrauds people, is a thief.

What was sought after was greatness of purpose, dedication to the full realization of one's potentiality, and humility.

Those of the white hair and wrinkled faces,
our ancestors. . . .
They did not come here to be arrogant;
they were not seeking;
they were not greedy.
They were such
that they were highly esteemed on earth;
they came to be eagles and tigers.*

To work at something, and to work at it well, to contribute to the Beauty of the world without seeking a material reward, that is the supreme "secular" goal of Native life. To be a true Mexican! To be a true Toltec, an artist, in whatever one does!

A society where billions must be spent each year to keep men in prison is not free. A society where a woman cannot walk alone without being in danger of attack is not free. A society where a man is murdered across the street from the White House is not free. A society where "Law and Order" comes from the barrel of a gun possesses neither "law" nor "order" but only a balance of terror. To discover true democracy and real freedom one must turn to traditional Indo-Chicano societies, grounded in reverence for the Web of Life. What is a free society actually like? Here is what Gene Weltfish says about Pawnee society in the 1860's:

They were a well-disciplined people, maintaining public order under many trying circumstances. And yet they had none of the power mechanisms that we consider essential to a well-ordered life. No orders were ever issued. No

---

* From *Aztec Thought and Culture: A Study of the Ancient Nahuatl Mind,* by Miguel León-Portilla. Copyright 1963 by the University of Oklahoma Press. Used with permission.

assignments for work were ever made nor were overall plans discussed. There was no code or rules of conduct nor punishment for infraction. There were no commandments nor moralizing proverbs. The only instigator of action was the consenting person. . . . Whatever social forms existed were carried within the consciousness of the people, not by others who were in a position to make demands. As I talked to the old men and women I realized that this is what we wish for but do not have. . . .

Gradually I began to realize that democracy is a very personal thing which, like charity, begins at home. Basically it means not being coerced and having no need to coerce anyone else. The Pawnee learned this way of living in the earliest beginning of his life. In the detailed events of everyday living as a child, he began his development as a disciplined and free man or as a woman who felt her dignity and her independence to be inviolate.[6]

John Collier, Commissioner of Indian Affairs in the 1930's and 1940's, showed remarkable foresight when he discussed Native American societies as follows:

They had what the world has lost. They have it now. What the world has lost, the world must have again lest it die. Not many years are left to have or have not, to recapture the lost ingredient. . . . What, in our human world, is this power to live? It is the ancient, lost reverence and passion for human personality, joined with the ancient, lost reverence and passion for the earth and its web of life.

This indivisible reverence and passion is what the American Indian almost universally had; and representative groups of them have it still.

If our modern world should be able to recapture this power, the earth's natural resources and web of life would not be irrevocably wasted within the twentieth century, which is the prospect now.

True democracy, founded in the neighborhoods and reaching over the world, would become the realized heaven on earth. And living peace—not just an interlude between wars—would be born and would last through ages. . . .[7]

The great success of Native Americans in the "art of living" can be documented by the teacher in many ways. For example, the following description of Native culture along the Pacific Coast illustrates one approach to presenting Native life:

Native Californian civilization was of such a nature that at least five hundred autonomous republics could exist within the present boundaries of California in relative harmony and without imperialism. More significantly, in these republics the fundamental dignity and self-rule of each individual person was virtually universal. Can we imagine today numerous republics without armies, living largely at peace with each other, each without police or other formal instrument of societal coercion? Can we imagine societies bound together into leagues covering large areas, the links consisting primarily or solely in religion (ceremony-sharing) and kinship, with no formal "international" machinery or "peace-keeping" armies? Can we understand political systems where chiefs and leaders are powerless in a formal sense, depending upon the agreement of the people for all major enterprises? Can we imagine systems of decision making where all of the people are involved and where everyone has a right to be heard even if it means that meetings drag on and on until consensus is achieved?

There can be little question that Native Californians (and many other Native Americans) were profoundly successful society builders, for almost all of the individual republics were utopias from the perspective of much of classic political and social theory, and also from the viewpoint of modern Californians alienated by mass society, big government, crime and so on.

One might well argue that democracy reached its highest stage of development not in Greece (where, after all, most of the people were slaves or excluded from decision making) but in Native California. Of course, it is also true that Californian democracy was able to endure only because of certain religious and social conditions which might be regarded as disadvantages in some quarters.

The unfolding, creative process inherent in the Great Mystery takes the form of at least two levels of reality, a mystical level and an ordinary day-to-day world of sense perception. The mystical level is one typified by an absence of physical boundaries and an absence of linear space-time relationships. It is the realm, as it were, of ideal forms, a realm in which all creatures can and do participate both consciously and unconsciously. It is the realm where, by means of dreams and visions, Indians can enter and secure direct contact with the sources of "power" (ability and knowledge) and with the endless, cyclical creative processes of the universe.

The day-to-day level of sense perception is generally conceived of as a less significant, but real and necessary, part of the unfolding of the Creator. It is the stage, as it were, for the acting out or giving expression to the "power" (or potentiality) of the universe. For example, an Indian doctor acts out in this world the knowledge acquired by means of a vision-experience in the mystical realm. To put it another way, the "unconscious" of the psychologist does not exist in a separate area of the brain, but rather is a part of a larger reality connecting all creatures and life itself.[8]

Native Californians, and most other Indians, were, and are, earthy, hearty, and happy people (when among themselves) because their view of the universe avoided dualism. They did not create a gap between the "spiritual" and the "material" because, in their view, the "spiritual" and the "material" are but one process of unfolding and return. This avoidance of dualism is very important because it saved Indian societies from the kind of sickness and repression which has so often typified European groups (which tend to swing to extremes, either the extreme of "puritanism" or the extreme of "hedonism," or the extreme of monastic denial or capitalistic wealth-worship).

I have devoted so much space to emphasizing religious and social behavior because Native Californian civilization must be viewed as a 15,000-year effort to perfect the inter-human and human-creation relationships. In other words, the Native Californians were not machine creating people, not monument creating people, not great city creating people, but rather they were applied philosophers, seeking not in theory but in practice to act out in their lives the beauty and harmony of the Great Mystery.

A grasp of this perspective is essential, since Europeans have ordinarily judged cultures solely on the basis of the size of their public monuments, the extent of their military conquests, the amount of surplus wealth accumulated, the elaboration of the material basis of life, and, of course, the numbers of slaves or poor people being successfully exploited. The greater the degree of exploitation, the greater the amount of "hard goods," the higher the ranking of the culture in question. But Native Californian society must be measured by a different scale, even as Jesus of Nazareth and Julius Caesar must be rated on different bases.

In practice, Western Europeans have given lip-service to Jesus but real reverence to Caesar. And as a result, California Indians were, and are, looked down upon because they failed to carve out empires by means of bloody wars and failed to devote their energies to building huge stone and steel monuments to materialism.[9]

This latter concept is extremely significant. All too often teachers fall into the trap of judging people solely on the basis of the material remains left behind, or the size of their empires. For example, the teacher may glorify the British Empire and compare it with, say, a small Native community, to the latter's disadvantage. But it has to be borne in mind that the British Empire brought about the enslavement and death of thousands from the Caribbean to India so that rich Englishmen could spend idle days in the English countryside in "pleasant conversation" and fox hunts.

It is significant that Indian heroes usually fall into two categories: leaders in the defense of the homeland, or holy men (religious leaders) and often they were both. One finds among North American Native heroes no Alexanders the Great (conquerers), no John D. Rockefellers (seekers after wealth), no Rudolph Valentinos (romantic entertainment figures or actors), and no "robber barons," slave-owners, military adventurers, ambitious politicians, or fakers. Such Indian heroes as Crazy Horse, Chief Joseph, Pontiac, Tecumseh, Deganawidah, Kentpuash (Captain Jack), Geronimo, Po-pe, Handsome Lake, and Sitting Bull were men of high character, purity of motive, and self-sacrifice, with lifeways unmarred by the exploitation of others, by self-serving expediency, or by a lack of personal restraint.

The student can, in no way, acquire insight into the realities of Native American life without a thorough knowledge of values. It is the Europe-

an's values which lead him to behave the way he does and it is the Indian's values which provide the mainspring for Native culture.

It should also be a primary objective of any curriculum dealing with Indians to provide a direct understanding of the contemporary status of Native American people. Such a need demands that adequate attention be given to Indian history (from an Indian perspective) and to modern realities as they really are and not as white social scientists might see them. First, let us begin with the present scene and then work backwards.

There are about 100 million persons of Native American descent in the Americas. At least 30 million speak Native languages while an equal number are of predominantly Native race but speak Spanish, Portuguese, or English. Does a person cease to be an "Indian" because he learns to speak English or Spanish? Does a person cease to be an "Indian" because he has some degree of non-Indian ancestry? Does a person cease to be an "Indian" because his ancient "tribal" or local loyalty is replaced by a new "pan-Indian" or "national" identification?

These questions have not yet been answered. They will not be answered by white social scientists but by people of Native race as the latter acquire the power to control the categories of their own existence. In any event, it is clear that people of Native race will exercise a powerful role in the future of the Americas and it will not matter what white people call them!

In the United States there are several millions of persons who are of predominantly Native race, including almost all Chicanos, many Puerto Ricans, and some Guatemalans, Nicaraguans, and Panamanians. All of these people need to be recognized as being of Native race, in whole or in part.

Most contemporary Native Americans are very poor, economically speaking. The teacher must be aware of this poverty and, at the same time, be able to explain why Indians exist under adverse conditions. It must be openly acknowledged that Indians are poor because white people are rich, that the land, timber, and minerals which white people use to produce their wealth were virtually all taken by force or deception. It must be recognized that Indian reservations usually exist in marginal land, not originally of value from the perspective of white economic development.

The teacher must also be able to deal realistically and truthfully with the political status of Native Americans. Constitutionally speaking, Indian tribes (or nations) are legally autonomous self-governing territories of the United States. They are not a part of any state, although included within state boundaries. Legally, each tribal government possesses the right to completely determine its own internal affairs in a manner directly comparable to the Commonwealth of Puerto Rico.

Unfortunately, however, the United States government has chosen to ignore the Constitution and treaties, in so far as Indians are concerned. From the 1870's to the 1930's the Bureau of Indian Affairs (The United States' "colonial office") illegally seized control over the internal affairs of tribes and transformed each Indian homeland into a colony. Since the 1930's the so-called "reservations" continue to exhibit many colonial characteristics, although some tribes have been able to regain a certain amount of local independence. The teacher must recognize that reservations are, by and large, colonies in which political power is exercised by foreign "rulers" in Washington, D. C., and from which economic and labor resources are extracted with little return to the Indian people. In spite of these problems, though, Indian people do not wish to have their "reservations" abolished. Instead, they wish to be liberated from bureaucratic dominance in order to possess self-government in their own homelands. It is also necessary, of course, that additional land be returned to Indian tribes so that each group can possess a viable economy.

The teacher must also attempt to deal with the history of Indian people, insofar as possible, from the Indian viewpoint. Let me make a few major points to illustrate what I mean:

1. The unsubstantiated theories of white anthropologists need to be treated as such. For example, Native Americans are not "mongoloid" because, first, there is no such thing as a "mongoloid" and, second, because there is not a shred of evidence linking Indians exclusively with any single "race."

2. The "Bering Straits" migration theory needs to be treated with great skepticism, since there is absolutely no evidence (except logic) to support it. Indian people generally believe that they evolved or were created in the Americas. This viewpoint should be respected although it is acceptable to discuss the possibility of migration as an alternative explanation. The point is that there is no empirical evidence to support any particular migration theory.

3. Indians should be treated as the original Americans and the first 20,000 years of American history need to be discussed *prior to* any discussion of European, African, or Asian migrations to the Americas. Likewise, in the discussion of the pre-European period data derived from archaeology should be supplemented by Indian traditional literature (as found in *The Book of the Hopi, The Sacred Pipe, The Constitution of the Six Nations,* and other available paperback books).

4. The on-going evolution of Indian groups needs to be dealt with, from 1492 to the present. That is, one needs to deal with the *internal* history of Native tribes and not merely with European relations. For example, the development of the Iroquois confederation, the Cherokee Constitution of 1824, the Handsome Lake religion, the Comanche-Kiowa-Kiowa Apache-Cheyenne-Arapaho alliance system, the westward movements of the Otchipwe, Cree, Dakotas and others, the teachings of the Shawnee Prophet, the Kickapoo Prophet, and so on, need to be discussed as significant developments in the *heartland* of America at a time when Europeans are only marginal (i.e., along the Atlantic Coast).

5. The teacher needs to deal truthfully with European expansion. Native wars of liberation and independence need to be dealt with as such and not as acts of aggression carried out against "peaceful" (but invading) whites.

6. The teacher will want to try to use accurate names for the Indian groups in his or her region (such as Otchipwe in place of Chippewa). The correct names can usually be found in Hodge's *Handbook of Indians North of Mexico.*

7. Native heroes and resistance leaders of the post-1890 period (such as Carlos Montezuma and Yukioma) need to be dealt with—Indian resistance *did not* cease with the "last Indian war."

8. American history, from the Native perspective, is not merely a material "success story" (bigger and bigger, more and more, better and better), nor does it consist solely in the reverse (that whites have actually brought about the near-destruction of this land). History is not progressive, but cyclical. That is, the evils of the white man and some Indians and others is a repetition of previous eras wherein other people went astray and contributed to the destruction of a cycle. We are now in the fourth or fifth world from the Native perspective.

This world may be self-destroyed because of man's evil. More and more inventions, etc., may not lead to any great "utopia" in the future, but simply to the end of this epoch. Furthermore, what really matters is the spiritual struggle of all creatures, the struggle for perfect "character development," not a great invention.

White people, for example, may exalt over the development of a new type of rocket ship and regard a flight to the moon as an event worth recording in a history book. But from a wholly different perspective the decision of an "ordinary" man to give up a needed job whose demands run counter to his ethics is more significant because it is a "spiritual" act directly relevant to man's highest level of aspiration.

From the traditional Indian perspective, at least, the history of America should focus on man's spiritual development and not on his material "progress."

Finally, let me conclude by emphasizing that the teacher in the United States has a tremendous opportunity, the chance to teach about two of the most inspiring sequences of events we can think of. First is the 20,000-year struggle of the Indian people to develop the art of living in harmony with the Universe. Second, is the 500-year struggle of the Native American people to resist conquest and to remain true to their heritage.

"A man can be outwardly conquered, and if he opens his soul to the conqueror, he can be inwardly conquered as well. But if he keeps his soul, he can remain free although his body is in chains. *Conquered but still free,* that is the secret of Indian survival from Alaska to Patagonia!"[10] If you can help your students to comprehend that message you can be proud of your role as a teacher.

Suggested Teaching Strategies

by Elizabeth O. Pearson*

Main Idea

A. Spiritual beliefs of Native Americans provide the foundation for their way of life.

1. Ask students to list their feelings toward nature. Pictures of plants, animals and natural settings such as rivers, oceans and deserts can be shown to help them probe their feelings more carefully. The list should be set aside while students familiarize themselves with American art, literature and religion. Students can choose to study one particular tribe of Indians, or three or four students can study Indian groups in a particular region of the U.S.

   A careful assessment should then be made of Native American attitudes toward nature. For example:

   a. Is nature to be conquered?
   b. Is its beauty to remain untouched by human hands?
   c. Is nature meant to be feared?

   The list of students' attitudes toward nature should be discussed and compared with the feelings of Indians toward nature. Students should discuss reasons for differences in their attitude compared to that of Indian groups.

2. Find art and legends which portray the values of Indian groups. *Waterless Mountain* by Laura Adams Armer includes Indian poetry within the novel as does *Ishi—Last of His Tribe* by Theodore Kroeber. Other books include *North American Indian Mythology* by Cottie Burland, useful for its illustrations and tales. *Indians on Horseback* by Alice Marriott deals with customs of Plains Indians. *Winter Telling Stories for Children,* edited by Alice Marriott, includes tales of the Kiowa Indians.

   After determining some basic values of Native American culture, students should identify current social issues which relate to particular values. For example, the preservation of nature relates to the issue of forest and national park usage, and logging.

   Students might then want to explore all sides of a particular issue, determine alternative means of solving the problem and look at consequences. The underlying values in each alternative should be delineated.

---

* See page 117 for biographical sketch.

3. Ask students to list and group Indian artifacts such as masks, kachina dolls, baskets, jewelry, rugs and cooking utensils. Allow them to group items on their list any way they wish, but they should explain their categories. Then have students do research on the artifacts, determining the regional and tribal origins, usage and significance of each one. A visit to a nearby museum which has exhibits on Native Americans would be a useful part of the research as well as reading Indian legends.

On the completion of research, students should again look at the list of artifacts and their categories. Comparison with the results of their research should reveal their initial accuracies and misconceptions.

Main Idea

B. Relations between Native Americans and whites have been characterized by whites exploiting Native cultures.

1. Indians were placed on reservations to allow more room for white settlement. The quality of land was poor and Indians had no choice of location. Have students examine the rationale of the American government for setting aside reservation land for Indians and the feelings of Indians about that action at the time.

What were the alternatives for the American government and the Indians? Consequences for each alternative should be considered. Ask students, considering all the knowledge they have about the move to reservations, to make a decision themselves as to what they think should have been done.

2. Feeling history makes it more alive to students, allowing them to get out of their cultural setting and familiarize themselves with a setting different in time, place and life style. Suggest that students become familiar with a specific Indian tribe and manner of life during the mid-nineteenth century through films, pictures, stories and nonfiction accounts. Study their ways of obtaining food, clothing and shelter, the customs, religious beliefs and the relationship with white men. Then have students enact scenes they write concerning aspects of the life of the particular tribe.

Discuss what it means to stereotype so that students will be aware of the difference between portraying how the Indian actually lived and the white man's biased view of how the Indian lived.

3. A comparison of Indian treatment by whites in the nineteenth century and twentieth century can delineate the differences between the Indian's tactics and effectiveness against white encroachment in two different centuries. Two films are useful for this purpose. "Custer: The American Surge Westward," distributed by McGraw-Hill Text Films, focuses on the effect of white settlement on the Plains Indians and their treat-

ment on reservations. The film ends with Custer's defeat in the Battle of the Little Big Horn.

"You Are on Indian Land," distributed by McGraw-Hill, presents a confrontation between the Mohawks and the Cornwall, Ontario police as the Indians protest a toll bridge and road put through their land. Although it takes place in Canada, the incident represents a common happening in the United States with tactics the same as in the United States.

Following are appropriate questions for comparing nineteenth- and twentieth-century treatment of Indians:

a. How have legal means for Indians to protest and redress injustices changed in 100 years?

b. Compare the methods of protest which Indians used against whites before reservations were established with protest methods which they have used in the twentieth century when reservations were a way of life for most Indians.

c. How successful were Indian protests 100 years ago compared to the 1960's and 1970's?

Main Idea

C. The Native American is faced with a conflict in values between his culture and that of contemporary white America.

1. "Geronimo Jones" by Learning Corporation of America is a superb film showing the conflict a Papago boy is faced with because he lives between two cultures. Other films which have a similar theme focus on the urban Indian. "Minority Youth: Adam" by BFA Educational Media is narrated by Adam, an Indian youth who talks about the inroads living in the city make on the survival of Indian culture. "Eddie: American Indian Boy" is a filmstrip in a series entitled *Children of the Inner City* by SVE Educational Filmstrips. Eddie's school life, family and father's work are described, with a reference to the Indian Center as a place of familiarity within a city of strangeness. Another film dealing with cultural identity is an animated film entitled "Charley Squash Goes to Town" by Learning Corporation of America. It poses the question implicit in all the other films: Is it possible to find an alternative to remaining Indian and living the life of a white man in America?

A complete study of cultural conflicts through these films and any other aids teachers can find, such as fiction, nonfiction, representatives of the Indian community, can be followed by exploring carefully possible alternatives and consequences for the Native American in the seventies. It is not expected that students will decide upon a solution. However, an awareness of the problem and knowledge of the issues are important for students to know if they are to understand Native Americans in today's society.

2. Ask students if they are familiar with Native American groups in your state which represent the interests of Native Americans in the press, legislature and on legal issues. Research by students who are unfamiliar with these groups should uncover active groups in your state. Through newspapers and local periodicals, students will learn the activities of Indian groups and methods of publicizing their message. Students should also find out how groups are dealing with the cultural conflict which exists between Indians and whites.

3. Although cultural conflict is present in the lives of most Indians, some have managed to come to terms with their Indianness in a technological society. Benny Bearskin is a Native American living in Chicago and is deeply attached to his Indian heritage, but at the same time exists happily in the city. A narrative by him is printed in *Division Street: America* by Studs Terkel. The following excerpt gives a brief insight into Benny's life.

"I came to Chicago in 1947, after I had been married, and later on I sent for my wife and my one child and since that time we've lived here in the city. The most important reason was that I could at least feel confident [of] perhaps fifty paychecks a year here . . . and you can't always get that way. Even though it might be more pleasant to be back home, for instance, Nebraska.

". . . this is one feature most Indians have in common. They have a deep attachment for the land. This has been so for a long, long time. Many different tribes of Indians are now residing in Chicago, but most of them maintain ties with the people back home. Even in cases where the older members of their families have passed away, they still make a point to go home. Many of them make the trip twice a year to go back to the place where they were born and raised.'"

A complete reading of Bearskin's account of life in Chicago reveals how he has come to terms with city life and his feelings about being an Indian. Other accounts of this kind will give students some idea of how life in an urban society is possible for the Native American.

FOOTNOTES

[1] These *goals* are taken from a manuscript developed by the author.
[2] Black Elk, *The Sacred Pipe,* edited by John Epes Brown (Baltimore: Penguin, 1971), pp. 5-7. Used with permission.
[3] John Epes Brown, "The Spiritual Legacy of the American Indian," *Tomorrow,* Autumn, 1964, pp. 297-307.
[4] From *Warpath,* Vol. 1, No. 2, 1968, p. 3. Reprinted with permission.
[5] Carlos Castañeda, *The Teachings of Don Juan: A Yaqui Way of Knowledge.* Originally published by the University of California Press; excerpt reprinted by permission of the Regents of the University of California.
[6] Excerpted from *The Lost Universe* by Gene Weltfish. Basic Books, Inc., New York.
[7] John Collier, *Indians of the Americas* (New York: New American Library, 1947), pp. 4 ff.
[8] Jack D. Forbes, "The Native American Experience in California History," *Neither Separate Nor Equal, Race and Racism in California* (San Francisco: California Historical Society, 1971), pp. 14-22.
[9] *Ibid.*
[10] Forbes, "The Native American Experience in Calfornia History," p. 22.
[11] Terkel, Studs, *Division Street: America* (New York: Pantheon Books/A Division of Random House, Inc.) p. 105. Reprinted with permission.

BIBLIOGRAPHY

There are many *bad* books about Native Americans, usually written by non-Indians. On the other hand, there are quite a number of excellent sources available, many of which are in an inexpensive paperback form and are useful as high-school supplementary material. The following are especially recommended:

Black Elk, *The Sacred Pipe,* ed. by John Epes Brown (Baltimore: Penguin, 1971). Provides keen insight into the religion and values of the Oglala Lakota (Sioux) people.
Black Elk Speaks, ed. by John G. Niehardt (Lincoln: University of Nebraska Press, 1961). The life-story of Black Elk, shedding light on Indian history as well as religion.
Gene Weltfish, *The Lost Universe* (New York: Ballantine, 1971). An excellent portrayal of the culture of the Chahiksichahiks (Pawnee) people as of the 1860's. It is perhaps the best book available by an anthropologist of non-Indian background.
Frank Waters, *The Book of the Hopi* (New York: Ballantine, 1969). A good book, although it suffers from a trace of anti-Nabahoo (Navajo) bias and may not always reflect traditional Hopi beliefs accurately.
Frank Waters, *The Man Who Killed the Deer* (New York: Pocket Books, 1971). A fiction work but one which provides insight into traditional Taiinamu (Taos) life, as well as a focus upon modern-day cultural conflicts. This is not a "perfect" book but it is, nonetheless, useful.
Jack D. Forbes, *Native Americans of California and Nevada* (Healdsburg: Nativegraph Press, 1969). The text itself focuses primarily upon California and Nevada but the general picture of Native history revealed is applicable elsewhere. The last one-fourth of the book contains sections of value to all teachers, including an extensive bibliography.

Jack D. Forbes, ed., *The Indian in America's Past* (Englewood Cliffs: Prentice-Hall, 1965). An anthology portraying Native history and Native-white-Black relations through 1965.

Vine Deloria, Jr., *Custer Died for Your Sins* (New York: Macmillan, 1969). An excellent overall discussion of the contemporary problems of Native Americans.

Stan Steiner, *The New Indians* (New York: Harper & Row, 1968). A satisfactory exposition of contemporary movements among Indians, especially during the early 1960's. The book suffers from certain inaccuracies but it still remains useful.

William R. Jacobs, *Dispossessing the American Indian* (New York: Scribner's, 1972). A good analysis, from a sympathetic although non-Indian viewpoint, of the early relations between whites and Natives in North America (with some attention devoted to recent events and consequences).

Edmund Wilson, *Apologies to the Iroquois* (New York: Vintage, 1966 edition). A journalistic, informative, interesting account of the struggles of Indians in one area to achieve simple justice in the face of continuous white aggression. The book emphasizes the 1957-1959 period.

Vine Deloria, Jr., *We Talk, You Listen* (New York: Harper's, 1970). An excellent follow-up to *Custer Died for Your Sins* designed to apply Indian thinking to many facets of modern American life.

N. Scott Momaday, *House Made of Dawn* (New York: Harper & Row, 1966). A well-known and deserving novel depicting the Indian-white clash of cultures, with emphasis upon the problems of the "urban Indian."

Jerome Rothenberg, ed., *Shaking the Pumpkin: Traditional Poetry of the Indian North Americans* (New York: Doubleday, 1972). A large (almost 500-page) collection of Native American songs, chants, and written poetry. This volume is not only very interesting, but it provides "firsthand" insight into Native values and viewpoints.

Francesco Cordasco   Diego Castellanos

FRANCESCO CORDASCO is Professor of Education at Montclair State College. He received his B.A. degree from Columbia University and his M.A. and Ph.D. degrees from New York University. He has taught at Long Island University, New York University, University of Puerto Rico, City University of New York, and the University of London. Professor Cordasco has served as a consultant to numerous agencies and institutions, including the Newark Archdiocesan Board of Education, the Commonwealth of Puerto Rico, and the National Education Association.

His many articles dealing with the problems of educating ethnic minority groups have appeared in a wide variety of journals and in the Congressional Record. *His books include* Educational Sociology, Puerto Rican Children in Mainland Schools, Education in the Urban Community, Minorities in the American Cities, The School in the Social Order, The Social History of Poverty: The Urban Experience, *and most recently,* Puerto Ricans on the United States Mainland: A Bibliography of Reports, Texts, Critical Studies and Related Materials. *Dr. Cordasco received the Brotherhood Award of The National Conference of Christians and Jews in 1967 (New Jersey Region).*

DIEGO CASTELLANOS is a candidate for a graduate degree at Montclair State College in the Spanish-Speaking Teacher Corps funded under the Education Professions Development Act and, with Dr. Cordasco, co-authored Puerto Ricans on the United States Mainland: A Bibliography of Reports, Texts, Critical Studies and Related Materials (1972).

FRANCESCO CORDASCO,
WITH DIEGO CASTELLANOS

10

Teaching the Puerto Rican Experience

Jesús Martínez is about to enter school. He is a fine looking five-year-old. He has perfect eyesight, normal hearing, and good strong teeth. He speaks very well, is in excellent health, and of above-average intelligence. Hence, *he has no learning disabilities.* Yet, this young American cannot be educated in most school districts of the states. In fact, most educators here cannot *begin* to teach him.[1]

His father, José Martinez, migrated to the United States mainland 20 years ago at the age of six. At a time when he was ready to learn to read and write his mother tongue, José was instead suddenly thrust into an exclusively English-speaking environment where the only tool he possessed for oral communication was completely useless to him. When he went to school it was as if the teacher were broadcasting in AM but José was equipped to receive her only in FM. He remembers it this way: "My teacher and I could not communicate with each other because each spoke a different language and neither one spoke the language of the other. This made *me* stupid, or retarded, or at least disadvantaged." Since teachers cannot be expected to "work miracles" on kids who are disadvantaged, José fell victim to the self-fulfilling prophecy, "He won't make it." They agreed, however, to allow him to "sit there" because the law required that he be in school.

For the next two years José "vegetated" in classes he did not understand—praying that the teacher would not call on him. The fact is the teacher rarely called on him and seldom collected his papers on the grounds that she could not expect of José what she demanded of the "more fortunate" children. Reasonable as this notion appears to be, it served only to cause the child's self-concept to deteriorate.

Another Puerto Rican boy in the classroom who spoke English was asked to teach José English and help him in the process of adjustment. They were not permitted, however, to speak Spanish to each other because it would "confuse José and prolong the period of transition"— also because it annoyed the hell out of other people who did not understand what they were saying. The other boy, then, could not translate academic subject matter for José. English was the one and only priority. In other words, he would have to "break the code" before getting the message. By the time he began to understand English, he was so far behind academically that he had to work twice as hard to keep from sinking. "It was," recalls José, "like swimming with lead bracelets." He was appropriately labeled "handicapped" by his teacher. Labels used by his schoolmates were not so kind. In fact, each time he would attempt to use his English, some of the other children would ridicule him for his imperfect grasp of the language. The teacher thought this was all right because it forced José to check his mistakes and provided him an incentive to learn proper English. Each day he went to school was as though he went to battle. The situation became unbearable when, as a result of a test administered in English, José was found to be *academically* retarded and was put in a class for the *mentally* retarded.

He retreated into a sort of psychological isolation and began to hate not only school, but the society he saw reflected by the school. Frustrated and discouraged, he began to find reasons for staying home from school and, as soon as permitted, dropped out (a human reaction to an inhuman situation). José, who refers to himself as a school "push-out," never really learned English well. He has a great deal of difficulty reading it and cannot write it. He speaks Spanish fluently but never learned how to *read and write* his mother tongue. He is a functional illiterate in two languages!

When (and if) he is working, it is usually at the lowest paying job. He is the first to be laid off, remains unemployed longest, and is least able to adapt to changing occupational requirements.[2] As José reflects—without smiling—upon his boyhood ordeal, his concerns turn to his young son who is about to embark on his own educational experience. He knows the educational process has undergone a drastic overhaul in the past few years. He wonders if the system is now able—or willing—to deal with his son and vice versa. He knows—too well—that a Puerto Rican child in the States who at the beginning of school is unable to acquire literacy in English in competition with his English-speaking classmates and who is not permitted to acquire it in his own language makes a poor beginning that he may never be able to overcome.

His one ray of hope stems from the fact that new dimensions have been added to the concept of accountability in education. In terms of behavioral objectives, for example, there is a growing emphasis on individual performance rather than class achievement. And in a philosophical sense, the burden of responsibility for success or failure in the learning process has shifted from the students to the educators.

This means school systems can no longer explain away children as unteachable because "they are deprived"—regardless of their cultural, linguistic and/or socio-economic characteristics.[3] Sociological adjectives have been used in the past to alibi non-education. Modern educators are striking at the long-held debilitating syndrome that the school can educate only those whose mold fits the curriculum. They are saying, if that is the extent of the school's capacity, then truly the school is a "disadvantaged" institution.[4]

• They admit that many children who have been traditionally tagged "deprived" have often proven to be no more deprived than the deprived budgets, deprived imaginations or—in some cases—deprived consciences of the school district brandishing the label.

• They admit that many children called *retarded* have simply been victims of antiquated school systems using obsolete methods of instruction for the sake of "maintaining tradition."

• They admit that many have suffered the effects of the ethnocentric philosophies and curricula of schools that offer only "assimilate or perish" alternatives for minorities and then employ scapegoating rationalizations for subsequent minority failures and dropouts.

• They admit that the system has historically brainwashed newcomers into believing that their language, culture, and system of values were inferior because they were different; that they believed these people had to be de-educated so they could be molded into our brand of citizenship; and that any group that resisted acculturation was thought to be uncivilized, un-American, and potentially subversive.

• They admit that non-English-speaking children usually have no other handicap than that imposed upon them by a school which tries to teach them in a language they don't understand.

In other words, a Puerto Rican child who has lived his first five or six years in a Spanish-language environment is ready to learn to read and write in Spanish but not yet in English. After all, they don't expect the Anglo child to begin his reading in material that is outside his listening-speaking vocabulary, so why expect it of another child? Especially when Anglo children profit from carefully prepared reading-readiness programs not available to non-English-speaking children.

The task of the beginning reader should not be compounded by expecting him to read a foreign language before he can read his own.

His initial task should be limited to one of converting the printed word into its spoken form which he already recognizes. (Incidentally, because of the excellence of the Spanish writing system, there are no "reading problems"—as we have here—among children in Puerto Rico.)[5] Many administrators and teachers in our schools try their best—in English—to make Puerto Rican children feel comfortable and welcome. But thousands of these youngsters have been cheated, damaged, or both by well-intentioned but ill-informed educational policies which have made of their language and culture an ugly disadvantage in their lives and have thought it more important to teach them English than to educate them. What we seem at times to be incredibly dense about is that it is just as normal to speak something other than English. Billions of people all over the earth do, including millions in the United States and thousands in our school systems. It is a striking contradiction that we spend millions of dollars to encourage students to learn a foreign language, yet virtually no part of school budgets goes to maintain and further develop the native language competence which already exists in children who speak these same languages as a result of their own family background. On the contrary, we go to all sorts of trouble to *eradicate* the child's language and substitute the school's *before* we begin to teach him. This is more than a contradiction; it is absurd!

A growing number of educators are now saying it may make more sense to change the school's language instead of the child's. This is an oversimplification, but the basic argument behind this thesis is that children learn when taught in their native language—especially in the early stages of their schooling.

While learning to read and write his mother tongue, the child needs careful training in learning, understanding, and speaking English as a Second Language (ESL) through an aural-oral approach before learning to read and write it. (If he has learned to decode his native tongue in such a manner that the skills can be transferred to the reading of English, then he has made a double accomplishment.)[6] Meanwhile, his concept development, his acquisition of information and experience—in sum, his total education—would not have to wait until he masters English because the entire curriculum would be taught in his native language while a gradual transition is being made to English. This approach, known as "bilingual education," permits making a clear distinction between *education* and *language;* i.e., between the *content* of education and the vehicle through which it is acquired.

The term "bilingual" seems to carry its meaning clearly within it. And yet a discussion involving the word soon reveals the strikingly different concepts that people have of it. If a child speaks *only* Spanish, he is not bilingual. And if the school offers him a course for English language

skills, without the use of his native tongue, that is not bilingual education. Bilingual education is instruction in two *languages.* It is the use of
both English and the child's mother tongue as media of instruction of
the school's curriculum. Academic subjects are taught in the child's
dominant language until he becomes functional in the second language.[7]

The "second language" concept is one of chronological primacy.
English must be second because the child has already learned the first
one. It has nothing to do with the inevitable fact of English being the
national language in the United States. English is neither native nor
indigenous, but was one of the group of languages brought here by the
colonial powers. There's no logical reason why everyone has to function
only in English. Even this is often misinterpreted by many educators.
English is not being taught as a *second* language if the process is
attempting to *supplant* the child's first (already-acquired) vernacular.
Furthermore, the techniques used in ESL are not identical to those used
in teaching English as a Native Language or English as a Foreign
Language. ESL is a precise discipline requiring a specific approach.

English, most people agree, should be taught by native English speakers who *need not necessarily be bilingual.* The rest of the curriculum
should be taught by native speakers of Spanish, who also *need not be
bilingual,* but who are able to relate to the cultural background of the
students. The rationale behind this is that children learn more by imita-
tion and analogy than by prescription. This is particularly applicable to
the learning of pronunciation and of cultural values. Authenticity—in
speech and in cultural representation—is of prime importance; and this
authenticity cannot be faked or acquired overnight. Consequently, a
team teaching approach is usually necessary for a good bilingual program.[8]

There is no bible on methodology for bilingual education. One common approach is to group the children with language difficulties and
begin educating them in their "home language," introducing ESL after
they have adjusted to the initial school experience. This program can be
implemented in an ungraded situation if the number of children does
not warrant a full-scale program. If the program cannot be extended to
all non-English speakers, the effort should be concentrated on the primary grades. But if a district's greatest needs prove to be in the upper
grades, the children's home language should be used to teach them those
subjects considered to be the areas of highest achievement in the children's culture (such as their history) and courses that may be expected
to be of particular occupational utility to the children.

Besides the pedagogical soundness of teaching young children basic
subjects in their own tongue, bilingual education is proposed as a more
humane and enriched school experience for Puerto Rican children. Its

"The content of the curriculum and the teaching strategies used should be tailored to the unique learning and incentive/motivational styles of the children of the particular district."

strengths are psychological as well as linguistic. A Puerto Rican teacher in the classroom does more than speak Spanish. She creates a familiar climate which lessens the child's anxieties and frees him to concentrate on his main job of learning. She also provides a means toward the development of a harmonious and positive self-image.

It would be well for those who are designing bilingual programs to keep in mind that the instructional use of the Spanish language in the classroom is not sufficient in itself to improve the education of these children and that a new curriculum must be devised with *cultural* as well as *language* requirements. A truly effective program of bilingual education should encompass bicultural education as well. It should include systematic curricular coverage of the history and heritage of Puerto Rico. In fact, such inclusions often are as important for the student's effective development as the use of the Spanish language is for developing his cognitive skills, or as the learning of English as a second language is for his socio-economic survival.[9]

The content of the curriculum and the teaching strategies used should be tailored to the unique learning and incentive/motivational styles of the children of the particular district. Irrelevant textbooks and materials should not be used. For example, social studies units in the Northeast should include materials on Puerto Rico and Cuba instead of Mexico or Spain.

As the students move toward a greater degree of independence in the second language, the curriculum naturally begins to include a gradually increasing quantity of reading and writing in the alternate language until it reaches parity with Spanish. At that point (usually around the third year) Spanish can be slowly phased out as the medium of instruction, and all subjects can be taught in English. Then the Puerto Rican students can be mixed in classrooms with other English-speaking children and Spanish may be taught as a *second* language to *any* student who wants it. Theoretically, classes where the composition is one half Puerto Rican have the perfect ingredients to create a fully integrated bilingual situation in which Puerto Rican pupils can learn English while native English-speaking volunteers can learn Spanish. After all, the native population should be afforded the same advantage (of speaking two languages). At the beginning of each school year, diagnostic tests should be used to determine the relative strength of the children's two languages to make it possible to record the factor of language balance each year. Provisions should then be made for increasing the instructional use of both languages for both groups in the same classroom. The resulting interaction between the two languages and cultures could indeed be the first step toward the desirable and attainable goal of a bilingual society.

Bilingual education is not a novelty. Many types of bilingual curricula are found throughout the world. Among the nations that have accepted this educational practice are Belgium, Canada, Finland, France, Mexico, Paraguay, Peru, Russia, South Africa, and Switzerland. Yet, the American school system, with students from various and different cultures, has virtually ignored the potentiality of bilingual education.

The Congress of the United States recognized this when it enacted the Bilingual Education Act—Title VII of the Elementary and Secondary Education Act (ESEA)—which represents a legal, moral, and financial (albeit tardy and weak) commitment to the promotion of cultural diversity and linguistic pluralism.[10]

The main priorities of Title VII at its enactment were:

(1) to provide equal educational opportunities to non-English-speaking children;
(2) to strengthen the education and self-concept of bilingual pupils;
(3) to promote bilingualism among all students.

The Act is designed to meet the special educational needs of children 3 to 18 years of age with limited English-speaking ability and who come from environments where the dominant language is other than English—particularly low-income families. The concern is for children to develop greater competence in English, to become more proficient in the use of two languages, and to profit from increased educational opportunity. It has been demonstrated that:

(1) Children in bilingual education programs progress better in school, with minimal grade retentions, and reach grade-level achievement in all subject areas.
(2) Non-English-speaking children in bilingual education programs become more proficient both in English and their mother tongue.
(3) Children in bilingual education programs develop a sure understanding and respect for their mother tongue and the culture associated with it. This understanding and respect lead to a more positive self-image and better social and personal adjustment.

Grants under Title VII are available for exemplary pilot or demonstration projects in bilingual *and bicultural* education in a wide variety of settings.[11] These projects should demonstrate how the education program can be improved by the use of bilingual education. Title VII funds may be used also for providing preservice and inservice training to teachers, supervisors, counselors, aides and other auxiliary education personnel, and for establishing and maintaining programs. The money may also be used for research, development and dissemination of instructional materials, acquiring necessary materials and equipment, making optimum use of educational and cultural resources in the area, and for improving *cooperation* between the *home* and the *school.*

These last two points cannot be overemphasized. It is unlikely that quality education can be brought to any community until its members participate in the decision-making process that will shape the future of their children's education. Parent participation is particularly indispensable in bilingual programs, for in most Puerto Rican communities parents have considerable knowledge of language and heritage.

Parents should be remunerated to serve as language and history consultants. Curriculum should be developed in such a way that parents can teach portions of it to their children at home. There should be special classes for parents to acquaint them with what their children are doing and how they can positively affect the youngsters' progress. The Puerto Rican parent will support the goals and values of the school when the school begins to recognize the worth of his culture and realize that he can make unique contributions to the educational process—not only in curriculum development but also in other school activities— including *policy decisions.*

Inherent in the educational structure is, and will continue to be, decision making at the top. Inherent in social change is citizens' participation in decision making. Too often, the attitude of the decision-makers has been that of one municipal official who recently said, "We know

how to solve your problems better than you do." There is every reason to believe that this statement is incorrect, and that participation by people who are close to the problems will help to design better programs which are more in touch with reality. It is a good idea for public schools to cooperate with Puerto Rican organizations which have thus far worked unaided and unrecognized to maintain two-language competence in their children.[12]

One detriment to bilingual education in the past has been the lack of Spanish-speaking personnel in schools—especially in the classroom. Excessive—often unrealistic—credential requirements, combined with discriminatory practices, account for the crying shortage. Administrators have attempted to remedy the situation in two ways—neither of which has been totally successful.

In some cases, readily available surpluses of Cuban educators have been certified through special programs. The programs, however, have experienced some "hang-ups." One is the unwillingness of school districts to employ its graduates—for various reasons. Essentially, most superintendents feel that although the historical, cultural and linguistic characteristics of Puerto Ricans and Cubans are very similar, Cuban teachers might not relate properly to Puerto Rican students in the areas of social orientation, national identity, and political attitudes.

Caught in the dilemma of either having Spanish-speaking Cubans teach their children or having English-speaking Americans, the Puerto Rican leadership has accepted the former. While it is known that Cubans as a group tend to be prejudiced against Puerto Ricans, their prejudice takes the form of disdain rather than hostility. The strong militant elements in Puerto Rican communities have undertaken the task of sensitizing these teachers.[13] Another effort by superintendents to alleviate the bilingual teacher shortage has been to recruit teachers directly from Puerto Rico. This, too, has been met with mixed emotions by the Puerto Rican communities. Their feeling is that islanders are not equipped to solve the problems that abound here because life here is different from life on the island. Anglo-American educators who have gone to Puerto Rico for fresh insights into the problem of teaching Puerto Rican children are amazed to find out that the problem doesn't exist in Puerto Rico. Communities should first develop the resources available here before importing outside help—in spite of the clamor for academic credentials.

It is tragic the way districts are failing to take advantage of human resources available through the community. With a little bit of pragmatic logic, bilingual paraprofessionals could be readily employed as teacher aides, truant officers and school-home liaisons. These aides could follow-up children who begin to display the results of culture conflicts, of home overcrowding, of malnutrition—or any other difficulty. In addition, family counseling should be instituted to improve the home environment of the students.

A core set of bilingual counselors should be hired to serve the needs of students and to act as ombudsmen or liaison between the school district and the community. At least one bilingual or bicultural staff person should be available at all times to meet with parents. In addition to hiring bicultural and bilingual teachers and other key people, schools should require inservice training programs on Puerto Rican culture, which would strengthen the total school staff effectiveness. Administrators of schools where half the student population is Puerto Rican should be bilingual educators, either native speakers of Spanish who also have a good command of English or native speakers of English who have a good command of Spanish plus a sympathetic understanding of the culture of the consumers of their institutions' precious commodity. Else, they should be required to take a course or attend an institute dealing with the Puerto Rican cultural heritage and contemporary social movement.

Educators must always bear in mind that the attitude displayed by school personnel can make or break good relations with the community. Frequently, teachers betray an ill-disguised contempt for the schools and neighborhoods in which they work. (The same applies to the other extremely important people: the school secretary, the nurse, social worker, counselor, the curriculum coordinators, the assistant principals, *and* the superintendent.) In addition to being well-trained in academic subjects, successful "barrio" teachers must possess these effective skills:

(1) they must be "attitudinally adjusted" to working with bilingual, bicultural students from economically deprived environments
(2) they must be aware of the bilingual student's built-in language resources as a valuable asset in advancing his education and contributing to the public welfare
(3) they most possess an effective familiarization with the Spanish language
(4) they must have deep knowledge of the characteristics of economically deprived people and also of the cultural traits of the Puerto Rican population, and be able to distinguish between the differences in the cultural strata
(5) they must be dedicated to establishing a sound school-community relations program
(6) they must project to their students an expectation level that will raise their visions for school success and that will cause high achievement efforts

A renewed sense of moral responsibility must be instilled in guidance counselors. Counselors must endeavor to be more than glorified clerks, score keepers or statisticians. Guidance sessions should also include parents. Higher education is now possible for the poor; but sometimes parents have to be sold on the idea. We don't think counselors, in general, are keeping up with the times. It is obvious that those who need counseling the most are getting it the least. The absence of necessary academic services is not only contrary to common sense, but the hardships it imposes on certain children may be in direct violation of the law. A case in point is Title VI of the Civil Rights Act of 1964, promulgated to prevent discrimination resulting from English language deficiencies in the operation of any federally assisted program.

Title VI compliance reviews conducted in school districts with more than 5 percent Spanish-surnamed student enrollment by the HEW Office for Civil Rights have revealed a number of common practices which have the effect of denying equality of educational opportunity to Spanish-speaking pupils. Rules under the Code of Federal Regulations declare essentially that:

(1) where inability to speak and understand English excludes Spanish-speaking children from effective participation in the educational program offered by a school district, the district must take affirmative steps to open its instructional program to these students
(2) school districts must not assign Spanish-speaking students to classes for the mentally retarded on the basis of criteria which basically measure or evaluate English language skills
(3) any ability grouping or tracking system employed by the school to deal with the special language skill needs of Spanish-speaking children must not operate as a permanent track or educational dead end
(4) school districts have the responsibility to adequately notify Spanish-speaking parents of school activities which are called to the attention of other parents—even if such notices have to be provided in Spanish

Perhaps more fundamental and basic than these recommendations of Title VI is the spirit and attitude in which they are carried out. The motive for implementation ideally should not be out of a sense of guilt for past injustices to the Puerto Ricans, for political reasons, or forced legislation. Structures with pity, expediency, or fear as foundations are not as enduring or as admirable as those built on humanism, trust, and justice.[14]

Puerto Ricans represent both a responsibility and a potential educational resource. Just how educational agencies meet this responsibility

and exploit this resource depends on the attitude and conscience of the communities. Some ethnic groups, whatever their true feelings, make little display of interest in maintaining their mother tongue; the Puerto Ricans are clamoring for this right. The question of whether or not to establish a program of bilingual schooling should be faced by the board and the superintendent without waiting for the community to take the initiative and most certainly before they are forced to do so by public pressure.

The social and political imperatives are strong. Puerto Ricans are no longer the patient, "romantic," non-violent figures of the past. They are no longer mute while the social worker, the priest, or the politician transmits his version of Puerto Rican life to the middle-class world, a version which was more myth than fact. They are beginning to speak for themselves, perhaps not as objectively but with a lot more accuracy than well-meaning outsiders. Those who had changed their names from Juan to John and from José to Joseph are changing it back to Juan and back to José. There is a new-born pride in belonging to a bicultural society; and this awareness is reflected in the increasing demands for bilingual, bicultural education.[15]

The bilingual concept should extend from the cradle to the grave. It should involve early childhood, vocational, secondary, continuing and adult education—as well as higher education.

Professors of Spanish should be replaced (as they retire or leave) with Puerto Rican educators. In fact, more Puerto Rican personnel should be employed at all levels. Colleges can—and should—provide services to the community other than higher education. Some colleges are beginning to find ways and means to bring the community to their campuses. Puerto Ricans must stop thinking of college campuses as hallowed ground not to be trespassed. Colleges should include Puerto Rican ethnic study programs in their minority history curriculum. Many are only offering courses in Black history, which is but an essential first step in this society. Forums should include lectures by Puerto Rican speakers.

The Puerto Rican "bridge" generation, whose progress was dwarfed by various reasons already mentioned here, never reached the threshold of higher education. The first generation of children born of Puerto Rican parents and reared in the mainland United States is just beginning to get its feet in the doors of the institutions of higher learning.

All sorts of gimmicks have been used to keep Puerto Rican children out of colleges and universities.

Consider, for example, the foreign language requirement for college admission. Simple logic tells us this requirement can be met easily by a Puerto Rican. Not so. Schools don't give students *credit* for a language unless they learn it in the classroom (even if it happens to be one's mother tongue). Eligibility to study a "foreign" language is based on one's *reading* scores in English. A poor reader of English doesn't qualify to take another language. No language credit means no college admission.

Inequities in the methods of testing bicultural children must be eliminated. Puerto Rican children still tend to complete the phrase "Bread and ..." with coffee instead of *butter*. And they are still not sure whether "it is raining or it is sunny" when they see a drawing of a person carrying an umbrella. Testing has always been a serious educational roadblock for Puerto Rican students. The failure of psychometric instruments to measure Puerto Rican children validly is recognized as a principal reason for the over-representation of that ethnic group in special education, as well as in other low tracks. Tests designed to measure English comprehension and middle-class cultural values cannot possibly measure cognitive growth, communication skills, and social and emotional adjustment of non-English-speaking children who come from underprivileged families. Poverty is not measured by the IQ tests. The hunger quotient is not registered. Nor is the psychological effect of poor clothing, disease, illness, and discrimination computed in the surveys of the lack of motivation, educational achievement, and rates of dropout.

Puerto Rican students have the worst dropout rate of all students— even worse than that of Blacks. Some statistics show that if the dropout rate of English-speaking Black students is twice as bad as that of white students, the rate of Puerto Rican dropout is *two and a half* times as bad as that of English-speaking whites.

Is bilingual education a long-range solution to the dropout syndrome? Hopefully, yes. That's one of its objectives. The bilingual approach is not a panacea, but it is the most promising technique available today. If successful, it could mark the beginning of a new era of educational opportunity for the Spanish-speaking of this country. This opportunity will, of course, be converted to economic—and eventually to political—power for this minority.

The Bilingual Education Act on balance is a relatively radical piece of legislation, a more potent means of affecting social change than most congressmen would like to have around. So they have surrounded the measure with more sound than substance.[16] There has been an appalling discrepancy between Title VII funds *authorization* and *appropriation*. The amounts actually allotted do not even approach the level of funding required to adequately meet the needs in this area, not only for operational program support but also to provide such necessary components of a successful bilingual education program as specialized training for teachers and teacher aides and the development and dissemination of bilingual instructional materials and special testing instruments. It will be left to the lobbyists that every large city school system maintains in the capital to convince Congress over the next few years to close the gap between the rhetoric and the reality.

Administrators interested in bilingual programs should bear in mind that Title VII is not the only source of monies available for bilingual education. Many districts have operated bilingual programs through Titles I and III of ESEA and with Model Cities monies. Then, again, there is really no reason why school districts have to wait for federal funding or legislation before they start fulfilling their reponsibility to their communities—to all members of their communities.

Possibly, the most direct evidence of lack of concern for this failure is the unwillingness of school boards to use local funds to deal with these problems. Consider a district in which 2% of the children have audiological deficiencies while 15% have language problems arising from a different cultural background. The district will hire therapists and aides for the 2%, yet provide little or nothing for the 15%. Responsibility for the inequities, though, does not lie only with the teacher because this is not a pedagogical problem, but a question of educational policy. Districts in which Puerto Rican students comprise one fourth, one third, or one half of their total school population often do not see fit to spend an equivalent proportion of their budget to meet the needs of those students. The same thing can be said of representation on the local boards of education—especially when members are appointed by the municipal authorities. It would seem apt, although admittedly a radical notion, that in a school district where the ethnic composition has changed from predominately Anglo-Saxon to Puerto Rican the content and style of education—as well as administrative and staffing patterns—in the schools would change accordingly. But radical notions—if they are to be responsible—require thinking through and school systems in the cities draw their particular character from tradition closer to clubhouse politics (which in political circles, in many places, was thought to be dead). This one doesn't change the system, just the names by which the system knows itself.

It is not always educators' altruism that is coming to the fore, however. Often, it is the controlling political groups who see that societal peace is threatened and demand whatever school action is evident. This political reality prompted recently a prominent Puerto Rican civic leader to make the following observation:

> For the past quarter of a century Puerto Rican students in the States have been *conditioned* for the role of third-class citizens they will play in the bigoted, prejudiced society in which we live.

The statement might not be entirely objective, and it may or may not be accurate in every sense, but the message is very clear.

The role of the school is seen as a reflection of the mores of society. Educators' perceptions, beliefs, and expectations are manifest in the structure and procedure of the school. The school sorts children into the types necessary to fill the recurring status vacancies within society, and Puerto Ricans are taught subordinate roles. While teachers show preference for Anglos and regularly choose them for school leadership roles, Puerto Rican children are tracked into redundancy and, when they protest with non-performance, are despised as reprobates. While bigotry and prejudice have no place in any part of our country, the practice is especially contemptible in American schools, for it is these very institutions that, with "forked tongue," *teach* the story of democracy and equal opportunity and then *act out* patterns of individual and wholesale discrimination.

So by "conditioning" the aforementioned spokesman meant that our children are programmed to fail by culturally-biased school systems which subtly infer the children are inferior because they are different. A notion that is false. Both common sense and some highly sophisticated social science investigations thoroughly document the fact that learning capacity has nothing to do with where one is born. These children's lives are scarred with failures, not because they are Puerto Rican, but because they are so badly educated and so poor. For it is lack of education with its attendant poverty that has helped keep Puerto Ricans in the impossible situation they are in today.

The children are losing all hopes of learning or succeeding; the schools are losing all hopes of teaching; and the nation is losing another opportunity, perhaps its last, to put flesh on the American dream. Education offers the single best path out of poverty for the vast majority

"*Puerto Ricans realize that their culture is in danger of passing into oblivion unless the home values, the traditions, the customs, and the language are retained.*"

of this country's poor, but educators are playing a losing game as long as they persist in assuming that:

(1) the home culture is the cause of school failure
(2) the school is satisfactory as it is
(3) a principal function of the school is to Americanize foreign peoples by eliminating their language and cultural orientation

Peddlers of that philosophy must be made aware that the traditional "Americanization" approaches in education turn Puerto Ricans off. Those who are proud to be U.S. citizens resent the connotation that that approach carries. Those who resent U.S. citizenship, reject the approach altogether. Puerto Ricans will cynically, and sometimes not so quietly, describe such educational programs in poetic profanities.

This is a subtle but important point. "Citizenship" indoctrination has created a state of ambivalence within the Puerto Rican child. At school he is told in essence: "Speak English: be American." At home in the barrios, the appeal is different: "Don't forget whence you come; don't speak English around here!" This dilemma has often resulted in his being a cultural schizophrenic in an effort to please both home and school. As for the Puerto Rican who does become anglicized, he is often lost to his community and culture. He has added to the brain drain out of the barrio.

Puerto Ricans realize that their culture is in danger of passing into oblivion unless the home values, the traditions, the customs, and the language are retained. They are desperately trying to keep what they have, and to regain that which they have lost through the acculturation of the schools. Their spokesmen advance the model of a pluralistic, egalitarian society in which ethnic minorities maintain and develop their own cultural heritage. This does not imply that Puerto Rican children will never become identified with Anglo values and life styles; it merely states that they should not have to do it at the expense of their identity with their ethnic group. They should be given the opportunity to select the best from both cultures and have life-style options open to them. This is cultural democracy in action!

Suggested Teaching Strategies

by Elizabeth O. Pearson*

Main Idea

A. Life in an urban neighborhood produces barriers which tend to limit inter-action of those living in the neighborhood.

1. Charlotte L. Mayerson's *Two Blocks Apart* (New York: Holt, Rinehart & Winston, 1965), a story of Juan Gonzales and Peter Quinn who live in close proximity in a New York neighborhood but have never met, is a fascinating tale of life in a city. The book could be read to the class by the teacher at junior high levels, or one or a group of students may wish to read it. Discussion questions could focus around the reasons for the lack of contact between two persons who live in such close physical proximity. For example:

   a. What are the life styles of Juan and Peter?
   b. What qualities in Juan's life do you like? in Peter's?
   c. What characteristics of Juan's life do you think Peter would like? What in Peter's life do you think Juan would like?
   d. What difficulties does Juan have because he is a Puerto Rican? How does he deal with these difficulties?
   e. Why do Juan and Peter have their own territories in their neighbor-hoods?

2. So that students can understand more clearly the concept of territorial-ity, have them plot, on a map of the general neighborhood around the school, the way to school, the route to the home of a good friend, and the way to a store that they visit frequently. Ask them if there are any stores that are closer to their home than the one they visit, or if there is a route they could take to school which would be shorter. Then ask them why they don't take the shorter route or buy from the store nearer their home. Perhaps a busy arterial street is a boundary or a large apartment complex or a railroad track keeps them from taking a different route. Psychological barriers could also exist, such as unfamiliarity with an-other area or street. Compare their territorial boundaries to the ones which Juan and Peter recognized.

3. Another case study of territoriality is seen in *Spanish Harlem* (New York: Harper & Row, 1965) by Patricia Cayo Sexton. Her description of Puerto Ricans, Blacks and Italians in East Harlem illustrates how different

---

* See page 117 for biographical sketch.

racial and ethnic groups co-exist and interact in an urban setting. A teacher might be interested in presenting this case study to the class using an overhead transparency of a map of the neighborhood showing the living area of each group. Territorial borders such as railroad tracks, housing projects and a hill are evident in this neighborhood. The author also provides a description of the culture of the Puerto Ricans which can help students understand how a migrant group (remembering that Puerto Ricans are American citizens) has adapted to the mainland and at the same time maintained some of the customs of the island and its life-styles.

Main Idea

B. Because many Puerto Ricans are newcomers to the United States mainland, cultural conflicts will occur between parents and children, and between Puerto Ricans and those persons already living in the neighborhood.

 1. To help students understand how neighborhoods are affected by new members and how Puerto Ricans are affected by living on the mainland in urban areas, view the film "Ask Miguel" by Learning Corporation of America. Then pose the following questions to students: What are the consequences for Puerto Rican individuals and families living in a large city such as New York in terms of:

    a. what kind of housing is available.
    b. what jobs will be available.
    c. how well they can use English while maintaining the ability to speak Spanish.
    d. how schools will prepare Spanish-speaking students.

    It is generally known that persons feel threatened when their way of life is impinged upon. For example, ask students why:

    a. apartment dwellers might panic when a Puerto Rican family moves in.
    b. older residents feel their jobs threatened by the newcomers.
    c. older residents feel threatened when newcomers have a different language.
    d. schools don't attempt to work with Puerto Rican children in the context of their own culture and language instead of expecting them immediately to be able to function in the classroom.

    Cultural conflict will occur when any new group moves into an established residential area. Puerto Ricans are newcomers to the mainland and are undergoing similar difficulties that other groups have encountered. "The Adjustment of Puerto Ricans to New York City" by Joseph Fitzpatrick in *Minorities in a Changing World* (New York: Alfred A.

Knopf, 1967), edited by Milton L. Barron, is a useful reference for teachers to explain why older residents feel anxiety over the arrival of newcomers, in this case, Puerto Ricans.

2. Cultural conflict is based on a difference in values. After students have done the previous activity, ask them to determine the values of the two groups, Puerto Ricans new to the mainland and established residents. Students might be asked to state the values they think are exemplified by the two groups. They may suggest security and cultural pride as two values. After the list is made, ask students to apply them to the appropriate group. Security might be applied to both groups while cultural pride could relate to the Puerto Rican group. A chart such as the following might be useful.

Values	Puerto Ricans	Established Residents
Security	X	X
Cultural Pride	X	
Stability		X

3. Student awareness of cultural conflict can be increased by making students more aware of their own feelings. The teacher can ask questions to which students should respond privately. Questions such as the following should help students probe their own feelings without having to publicly state them.

   a. How do you react when you hear someone speaking a foreign language?
   b. How do you feel when a new student from a different cultural background is assigned to your classroom?
   c. Are you aware of the presence of persons with a racial background different from yours? What do you think about when you recognize this awareness?
   d. How do you feel when you are visiting someone with customs and traditions different from yours?

   These responses should be filed in a place where others will have no access to them. They may be taken out two or three months later so that students may note if their feelings have changed.

Main Idea

C. Life in Puerto Rico provides a contrast with life on the mainland.

1. So that students may become more aware of characteristics of life in Puerto Rico and compare and contrast them with, for example, life in New York City, ask students to look at a map of the Western Hemisphere

to determine the location of Puerto Rico. They also should compare the land size of Puerto Rico with New York City and the population of each place. Comparisons can also be made of climate and major industries. They might look for personal accounts of life in Puerto Rico from books in the library and persons who could speak to the class about life in Puerto Rico.

After this data is obtained, one group of students could write a narrative about life in Puerto Rico and another group about life in New York City. Photographs and student illustrations should accompany the narratives.

2. Reasons for Puerto Rican migration to the mainland are made clearer when students are familiar with the history of Puerto Rico. A book such as *Puerto Rico: A Profile* by Kal Wagenheim (New York: Praeger, 1970) is an informative history for junior high and high school students. Of particular value to the high school student is Francesco Cordasco and Eugene Bucchioni, *The Puerto Rican Experience* (Totowa, New Jersey: Littlefield and Adams, 1972), which is a paperback collection of readings. After students familiarize themselves with the history of Puerto Rico, they could focus on the following questions in a panel discussion.

   a. What are some comparisons and contrasts between the kind of governance which has characterized Puerto Rico and the U. S.?
   b. How has Puerto Rico broken away from its Spanish ties?
   c. How has its relationship with the U. S. affected its development?
   d. What are the present economic conditions in Puerto Rico?

FOOTNOTES

¹ The composite student portrait derives from F. Cordasco and E. Bucchioni, *The Puerto Rican Community and Its Children on the Mainland: A Sourcebook for Teachers, Social Workers and other Professionals* (New York: Scarecrow Press, 2nd edition, 1972); and from Richard J. Margolis, *The Losers: A Report on Puerto Ricans and the Public Schools* (New York: Aspira, 1968).

² For the economic realities of employment, housing, and general participation by Puerto Ricans on the mainland, see Joseph P. Fitzpatrick, *Puerto Rican Americans* (Englewood Cliffs, N.J.: Prentice-Hall, 1971).

³ See F. Cordasco, "Poor Children and Schools," in W. W. Brickman and S. Lehrer, eds., *Education and the Many Faces of the Disadvantaged* (New York: John Wiley, 1972), which is a critique-review of the extensive literature on the subject.

⁴ See, generally, M. Fantini and G. Weinstein, *The Disadvantaged* (New York: Harper & Row, 1968); and F. Cordasco, "Educational Pelagianism: The School and the Poor," *Teachers College Record*, vol. 69 (April 1968), pp. 705-709.

⁵ See Mary Finocchiaro, *Teaching English as a Second Language*, Rev. ed. (New York: Harper & Row, 1969).

⁶ Finocchiaro, *op. cit.*, discusses the concept, *passim*.

⁷ For "bilingualism" and its varied connotations, see F. Cordasco, "The Challenge of the Non-English Speaking Child in the American School," *School & Soceity* (March 30, 1968), pp 198-201.

⁸ See Vera P. John and Vivian M. Horner, *Early Childhood Bilingual Education* (New York: Modern Language Association, 1971).

⁹ For commentary on this important concept, see Manuel Maldonado Denis, *Puerto Rico: Una Interpretación Histórico-Social* (Mexico City: Editores Siglo XXI, 1969).

¹⁰ For Title VII, see F. Cordasco, "The Bilingual Education Act," *Phi Delta Kappan* (October 1969), and *Idem*, Footnote #7.

¹¹ See, for grants under Title VII, "Bilingualism," *The Center Forum*, vol. 4 (September 1969), the entire issue of which is devoted to analysis of funded programs.

¹² For community participation, see Harry M. Levin, ed., *Community Control of Schools* (Washington: The Brookings Institution, 1970), which is much more than its title suggests; and *Reconnection for Learning: A Community School System for New York City* (New York: Praeger, 1969), which was the report to Mayor John Lindsay on the decentralization of the city's schools. The report's recommendations were not implemented, and the report is, at the present time, the most comprehensive study of urban schools and strategies for community participation. See also Leonard Covello, *Teacher in the Urban Community: A Half Century in City Schools* (New York: Littlefield & Adams, 1970).

¹³ For an expression of the Puerto Rican new militancy, see Juan A. Silén, *We, The Puerto Rican People: A Story of Oppression and Resistance* (New York: Monthly Review Press, 1971).

¹⁴ See, generally, Title VI, Civil Rights Act.

¹⁵ This was made eminently clear as early as 1968. See *Hemos Trabajado Bien: A Report on the First National Conference of Puerto Ricans, Mexican Americans and Educators on the Special Educational Needs of Puerto Rican Youth* (New York: Aspira, 1968).

¹⁶ See F. Cordasco, "Educational Enlightenment out of Texas: Toward Bilingualism," *Teachers College Record*, vol. 71 (May 1970), pp. 608-612.

BIBLIOGRAPHY

General Bibliographies

Cordasco, Francesco with Eugene Bucchioni and Diego Castellanos. *Puerto Ricans on the United States Mainland: A Bibliography of Reports, Texts, Critical Studies and Related Materials.* Totowa, New Jersey: Rowman & Littlefield, 1972. An annotated bibliography of 754 main entries dealing with bibliographical resources; the migration to the mainland; the island experience; conflict and acculturation on the mainland; education on the mainland; and social needs encompassing health, housing, employment, and other human needs.

Cordasco, Francesco and Leonard Covello. *Studies of Puerto Rican Children in American Schools: A Preliminary Bibliography.* New York: Department of Labor, Migration Division, Commonwealth of Puerto Rico, 1967. (Some 450 entries.) Also published in *Education Libraries Bulletin,* Institute of Education, University of London, #31 (Spring 1968), pp. 7-33; and in *Journal of Human Relations,* vol. 16 (1968), pp. 264-285.

Cordasco, Francesco. *The People of Puerto Rico: A Bibliography.* New York: Department of Labor, Migration Division, Commonwealth of Puerto Rico (1968). (Some 500 entries.)

Dossick, Jesse. *Doctoral Research on Puerto Rico and Puerto Ricans.* New York: New York University, School of Education, 1967. A classified list of 320 doctoral dissertations completed at American mainland universities.

General Studies

Burma, John H. *Spanish-Speaking Groups in the United States.* Duke University Press, 1954. Includes a sketch of "the Puerto Ricans in New York" (pp. 156-187). Burma assumes that there is a fundamental "unity of culture" among diverse groups because they speak the same language. In light of the widely differing historical backgrounds which have given rise to different cultures among Spanish-speaking groups, the assumption does not seem valid.

Chenault, Lawrence. *The Puerto Rican Migrant in New York City.* New York: Columbia University Press, 1938. Reissued with a New Foreword by F. Cordasco. New York: Russell & Russell, 1970. The one book that puts together data available on the early movements to New York City of Puerto Rican migrants. Includes a discussion of the various ways these movements affect the established community and the migrants.

Cordasco, F. and David Alloway. "Spanish-Speaking People in the United States: Some Research Constructs and Postulates," *International Migration Review,* vol. 4 (Spring 1970), pp. 76-79.

Fitzpatrick, Joseph P. *Puerto Rican Americans: The Meaning of Migration to the Mainland.* Englewood Cliffs, N. J.: Prentice-Hall, 1971. An overview and trenchant study with materials on the dynamics of migration: the problem of identity; the family; problem of color; religion; education; welfare. See *New York Times,* September 12, 1971, p. 96.

Glazer, Nathan and Daniel P. Moynihan. "The Puerto Ricans." In: *Beyond the Melting Pot: The Negroes, Puerto Ricans, Jews, Italians, and Irish of New York City,* by Nathan Glazer and Daniel Moynihan. Cambridge: M.I.T. and Harvard University Press, 2nd ed., 1970. Puerto Ricans in New York City are discussed in terms of who migrates to the United States; their relationship to the island of Puerto Rico; business, professional, labor opportunities, and average earnings in New York; and the effect of migration on the culture of the migrants.

Lewis, Oscar. *La Vida: A Puerto Rican Family in the Culture of Poverty—San Juan and New York.* New York: Random House, 1966. Begins with a long introduction which describes Lewis' methods, the setting, and the family involved in the study. A discussion of the theory of the "culture of poverty" is included. The rest of the book is the story of a Puerto Rican family, as told by the members of the nuclear family and some of their relatives and friends. See also Oscar Lewis. *A Study of Slum Culture: Backgrounds for La Vida.* New York: Random House, 1968. Provides the general background, data, and statistical frame of reference for *La Vida.*

Mills, C. Wright; Clarence Senior; and Rose Goldsen. *The Puerto Rican Journey: New York's Newest Migrant.* Harper, 1950. Reissued, New York: Russell & Russell, 1969. A carefully researched field study of the Puerto Rican population in two core areas of New York City. Although many of its statistics are now out-of-date, the book deals with basic concepts, such as the factors in "adaptation," cultural and language differences, and their influence on the progress and problems of the migrants.

Puerto Rican Community Development Project. Puerto Rican Forum (New York), 1964. This report highlights the problems—income, housing, education, family, etc.—that confront the Puerto Rican community in New York City, though not all of its population. Data are presented to support the thesis that Puerto Ricans generally are not well off and need to make much more rapid gains in a contemporary technical, urban society such as New York. Read from the point of view of its purpose, it is an illuminating study.

"(The) Puerto Rican Experience on the United States Mainland," *International Migration Review,* vol. II (Spring 1968). Entire issue devoted to a comprehensive account of the experience.

Sexton, Patricia. *Spanish Harlem: Anatomy of Poverty.* Harper & Row, 1965. Report by a sociologist who spent part of two years "getting acquainted" with East Harlem. Shows awareness that she is dealing with the pathologies of a minority of the area's population ("still, the majority of the people are self-supporting"). However, she does not gloss over the problems that confront many of the self-supporting, low-income urban dwellers. The book is informed by the important insight of the need for "the poor" to be involved in working out their destiny.

Education

Anderson, Virginia. "Teaching English to Puerto Rican Pupils," *High Points* (March 1964), pp. 51-54.

Bilingual Education: Hearings, U.S. Senate, Committee on Labor and Public Welfare. Special Sub-Committee on Bilingual Education, 90th Congress, 1st Session. Washington: U.S. Government Printing Office, Part I, May 1967; Part II, June 1967. On Title VII (Elementary and Secondary Education Act) which was enacted in 1968.

"Bilingualism," *The Center Forum,* vol. 4 (September 1969). Entire issue is given to analysis of Title VII (Elementary and Secondary Education Act) programs and related matters. Includes an important annotated bibliography.

Bucchioni, Eugene. *A Sociological Analysis of the Functioning of Elementary Education for Puerto Rican Children in the New York City Public Schools.* Unpublished doctoral dissertation, New School for Social Research, 1965.

Cordasco, Francesco. "The Puerto Rican Child in the American School." American Sociological Association *Abstract of Papers,* 61st Annual Meeting (1966), pp. 23-24.

Cordasco, Francesco. "Puerto Rican Pupils and American Education," *School & Society,* vol. 95 (February 18, 1967), pp. 116-119. Also, with some change, in *Journal of Negro Education* (Spring 1967); and *Kansas Journal of Sociology,* vol. 2 (Spring 1966), pp. 59-65.

Cordasco, Francesco. "The Challenge of the Non-English-Speaking Child in the American School," *School & Society,* vol. 96 (March 30, 1968), pp. 198-201. On the proposal for the enactment of the Bilingual Education Act (Title VII, Elementary and Secondary Education Act), with historical background.

Cordasco, Francesco. "Educational Pelagianism: The Schools and the Poor," *Teachers College Record,* vol. 69 (April 1968), pp. 705-709.

Cordasco, Francesco and Eugene Bucchioni. *The Puerto Rican Community of Newark, N.J.: An Educational Program for Its Children.* Newark: Board of Education, Summer 1970. A detailed report on the implementation of a program for Puerto Rican students.

Cordasco, Francesco and Eugene Bucchioni. *Education Programs for Puerto Rican Students.* (Jersey City Public Schools.) Evaluation and Recommendations. Jersey City: Board of Education, 1971.

Cordasco, F. and Eugene Bucchioni. *Newark Bilingual Education Program, 1970-1971.* Newark: Board of Education, 1971. Evaluation report of a massive program for Puerto Rican students.

Cordasco, Francesco and Eugene Bucchioni. *The Puerto Rican Community and Its Children on the Mainland: A Sourcebook for Teachers, Social Workers and other Professionals.* Metuchen, N.J.: Scarecrow Press, 2nd ed., 1972. "The original structuring of the text has been retained, and it is within this framework that new materials have been interpolated. New materials have been added to Part I (Aspects of Puerto Rican Culture) whose basic design is to afford a politico-cultural kaleidoscope of island life; to Part II (The Puerto Rican Family), bringing into clear focus the family's transition to mainland life; to Part III (The Puerto Rican Experience on the Mainland: Conflict and Acculturation), in bringing into sharp view the new politicization of the mainland experience; and in Part IV (The Puerto Rican Experience on the Mainland: Puerto Rican Children in North American Schools) in affording additional materials on bilingual education and in providing outlines for course content and staff-training. Appended to the bibliography are selected additional references." (Preface to the 2nd ed.)

Cordasco, Francesco and Eugene Bucchioni. "A Staff Institute for Teachers of Puerto Rican Students," *School & Society,* vol. 99 (Summer 1972).

Diaz, Manuel and Roland Cintrón. *School Integration and Quality Education.* New York: Puerto Rican Forum, 1964.

Hemos Trabajado Bien. A Report on the First National Conference of Puerto Ricans, Mexican-Americans and Educators on the Special Educational Needs of Puerto Rican Youth. New York: Aspira, 1968. Includes a series of recommendations.

John, Vera P. and Vivian M. Horner. *Early Childhood Bilingual Education.* New York: Modern Language Association, 1971. Invaluable. Includes a "Typology of Bilingual Education Models"; excellent documentation and bibliography.

Margolis, Richard J. *The Losers: A Report on Puerto Ricans and the Public Schools.* New York: Aspira, 1968. An important report on visits to a number of schools with description and evaluation of programs for Puerto Rican children.

(Puerto Rican Children) "Education of Puerto Rican Children in New York City," *The Journal of Educational Sociology,* vol. 28 (December 1954), pp. 145-192. An important collection of articles.

Morrison, J. Cayce, Director. *The Puerto Rican Study: 1953-57.* New York City Board of Education, 1958. Final report of the most complete study of the impact of Puerto Rican migration on the public schools of New York City, and how schools were affecting Puerto Rican children and their parents. Specialized studies were done within the framework of the large-scale study. These smaller studies focused on the "socio-cultural adjustment" of the children and their parents, and digests are presented in final report. About a third of the book deals with the special non-English-speaking program developed by the city school system. Description of some of the methods and materials developed is included. Reissued with an introductory essay by F. Cordasco (New York: Oriole Editions, 1972).

Part Three

TEACHING ABOUT WHITE ETHNIC GROUPS AND WOMEN'S RIGHTS

Parts One and Two of this book explore the problems of ethnic minority groups and suggest ways in which the classroom teacher can incorporate their cultures into the social studies curriculum. While Black, Red, Brown and Yellow peoples are victims of the most harsh kinds of dehumanization in America, other groups within our society also experience discrimination and cultural assaults. White ethnic groups and women often encounter problems in America which must be honestly dealt with by every teacher who is committed to making America an open society. We are defining an open society as one in which individuals from diverse ethnic, cultural and social class groups have equal opportunities to participate. Today, white ethnics and women are often denied opportunities because of the groups to which they belong. Part Three focuses on the problems of these groups and suggests ways in which information about them can and should be incorporated into the social studies program.

Recently, the concept of white ethnicity has evoked a great deal of concern and controversy. The popularity of Novak's *The Rise of the Unmeltable Ethnics* reflects this concern. Perhaps the most important question which has arisen for educators is "Should the concept be studied in the schools?" In the first chapter, Mark Krug provides a perceptive analysis of this and other important questions concerning white ethnics. He presents a strong argument for including a study of white ethnic groups in the social studies and discusses some issues and problems which should be investigated, including the melting pot theory

254

and the relationship between ethnic identification and political participation. He argues that the study of ethnicity and politics is one of the most promising yet neglected topics for students to pursue. While Krug believes that white ethnics should be studied, he warns that such study might have some negative consequences. The reader should note the conflicting perceptions presented by Sizemore in Part One and those discussed by Krug regarding the melting pot theory.

The roles and perceptions of women in America must be changed, argues Janice Law Trecker in the final chapter. She contends that the social studies teacher has a special responsibility to help shatter pervasive stereotypes about women, and suggests some promising ways in which this might be done. Trecker documents how women have been written out of American history, and offers some concrete and highly useful suggestions as to how they can be put into proper perspective. Trecker's arguments merit deep pondering. Sexism, like racism, is a debilitating and destructive social phenomenon that is deeply rooted in the American experience. It must be decisively and massively attacked by those with vision.

"White ethnic groups and women often encounter problems in America which must be honestly dealt with by every teacher. . . ."

 Mark M. Krug

MARK M. KRUG is Professor of Education in History and the Social Sciences at the University of Chicago. He graduated from Hebrew University in Jerusalem, and received his M.A. degree from Roosevelt University and his Ph.D. in history from the University of Chicago. Professor Krug was formerly a high school social studies teacher. His articles have appeared in a wide variety of journals, including the American Historical Review, Harvard Educational Review, School Review, *the* Journal of Negro History *and* Social Education. *He is the author of* Lyman Trumbull—Conservative Radical, Aneurin Bevan—Cautious Rebel, History and the Social Sciences: New Approaches to the Teaching of Social Studies, What Will Be Taught—The Next Decade *and* White Ethnic Groups: Unity in Diversity, *and coeditor of* The New Social Studies: Analysis of Theory and Materials.

MARK M. KRUG

11

Teaching the Experience of White Ethnic Groups

A respected newspaper columnist, Garry Wills, suggested in a recent column that talk about white ethnic politics is a horrendous hoax, perpetuated by crafty politicians on the unsuspecting American public.[1] He charged that ethnic politics, instead of promoting pluralistic variety, "flattens people out in racial stereotypes." He concluded that fundamentally, racism is the basis for the newly discovered consciousness among the white ethnic groups. "If you take away racial rivalry and envy, that is claims that blacks (or Poles) are genetically inferior, WASPs (or Irishmen or Jews) are genetically superior," Wills wrote, "what we get is one cultural influence interacting with a thousand others, with unpredictable results in each individual." Wills, and others who share his view, maintain that white Americans, with few exceptions, are so ethnically and culturally intermingled that ethnicity and ethnic voting blocs are largely figments of fertile imaginations.

On the other hand, spokesmen for various white ethnic minorities speak repeatedly about the "death" or "the failure of the American Melting Pot Theory." The British poet and essayist W. H. Auden, who, after many years of residence in New York, moved to Oxford, asked in a touching farewell to his adopted city: "Whoever invented the myth that America is a melting pot? It is nothing of the kind and, as a lover of diversity, I say thank God. The Poles, the Ukrainians, the Italians, the Jews, the Puerto Ricans, who are my neighbors, may not be the same as they would be in another country, but they keep their own characteristics."[2] Monsignor Geno Baroni, Director of the National Center for

257

Urban Ethnic Studies, who on another occasion stated that America is in the process of becoming a "multi-ethnic society," appealed in a recent speech to a conference of black and white ethnic leaders for "a new American dream—the urban ethnic pluralistic society." He predicted that "white, middle American ethnics will set the agenda for the nineteen-seventies."[3]

At the same conference which was intended to forge a united front of blacks, Puerto Ricans and white ethnics in order to get a bigger slice of the economic and political pie, the black civil rights leader Bayard Rustin declared that "there never was a melting pot. There never will be a melting pot. If there ever were, it would be such a tasteless soup that we would have to go and start all over."[4]

Murray Friedman of the American Jewish Committee, a prestigious Jewish communal organization, argued in an essay published in the book *Overcoming Middle-Class Rage*[5] that "America is going through a period of re-ethnication." Some voices have been raised questioning the wisdom of accentuating ethnic differences. Naomi Bliven, in a perceptive review of a book of another leading exponent of ethnicity, Andrew Greeley, wrote in the *New Yorker Magazine:* "He (Greeley) extols pluralism and diversity, but his system of multiple apartheid promises that Americans tucked into ethnic and racial Bantustans would encounter not diversity but homogeneity."[6]

What is one to make out of these sharply conflicting views? The first step would be to reject some of the obviously exaggerated assumptions of both sides—and then to sort out the many separate issues which have become entangled in the thicket of the debate on ethnicity. After this is done we must weigh soberly those problems which deserve serious consideration. The repeated statements of the leaders of the white ethnic minorities about the death or the failure of the melting pot idea can be dismissed as rather obvious maneuvers aimed at attention-getting at gatherings of the various ethnic groups. On the other hand, one can not quarrel with Bayard Rustin and other black spokesmen who speak with derision and contempt about the melting pot concept. For blacks, the melting pot theory is so much nonsense. They have not melted into the American society. The white dominant society not only has failed to make reasonable efforts to eradicate the barriers between the whites and the blacks after the abolition of slavery but on the contrary erected legal barriers to segregate the races. Until recently many states south and north of the Mason-Dixon line had laws which forbade interracial marriages. The relation of the blacks and to a large extent of the Spanish-Americans, the Chinese, and the Japanese to the concept of the American melting pot is *sui generis* and ought not to be lumped together with that of the white ethnic groups.

The black and the Chicano communities present a variety of unique problems which do not apply to the white ethnic minorities. These problems are the result of their history and the color of their skin. A Pole, if he wishes, can lose the special characteristics of his particular ethnic group and literally lose himself in the general dominant society, but a black, with the exception of those few who are extremely light-skinned, cannot do so. It makes little sense, therefore, to treat the concepts of ethnic identity and of the melting pot, or of cultural plural-ism as if they relate in the same way to white and non-white ethnics. There is room for debate as to the degree to which the melting pot has succeeded in the various white ethnic groups, but, as far as the blacks are concerned, the melting pot theory is irrelevant.

But in spite of the proclamations issued at regular intervals by the leaders of the white ethnic groups that "the melting pot myth is dead," the fact is that the American melting pot worked, on the whole, remark-ably well. It is estimated that the United States had absorbed between the years 1880 and 1920 over forty million immigrants mainly from Ireland, Scandinavia, Central and Eastern Europe. Millions of children and grandchildren of these former Poles, Irishmen, Germans, Italians, Swedes and others have indeed "melted" and consider themselves, and are considered by others, "just Americans." The descendants of the

American society of the decades preceding the period of large immigration and the descendants of the hundreds of thousands of the pioneers who have settled in the vast Western frontier areas have also, with few exceptions, shed any ties they had with their respective ethnic communities. Figures on the existing white ethnic groups are all rough estimates but even if we assume that there are today forty million ethnics, plus twenty million blacks and ten million Spanish-Americans, that still leaves over 130 million people in America who are quite indifferent to their ethnic origins.

In addition, there is an infinite variety of modes of identification, even among those who keep some ties to their respective ethnic groups. Andrew M. Greeley, the foremost expert on the Irish in America, has repeatedly asserted that the Irish can no longer be considered a separate ethnic group in America. Teddy Kennedy, Richard Daley and Mike Mansfield are "Irish" but that identification, as is true for millions of Irish-Americans, means little more than a few ethnic sentimental attachments. The variety of ways in which the five million American Jews identify with their ethnic group suggests how unwise it is to generalize about the effectiveness of the melting pot theory. Whatever can be said about the religious and cultural values that bind Jews into a recognizable ethnic group, they are *American* Jews and they little resemble the Jewish immigrants who came to this country around 1900.

In general, it can safely be postulated that Monsignor Baroni is mistaken in his assumption that America is on the way to becoming a "multi-ethnic society." The United States will not become a modern version of the Austro-Hungarian Empire. In an important sense, it is the general effectiveness of the melting pot theory which makes such a balkanization of America impossible. Soccer, in spite of all of the efforts of the ethnics, has not taken root in America and has not been a challenge to baseball and football. Spokesmen for the white ethnics seem to forget that outside of the large urban centers in the East and a few cities in California, the issue of ethnicity and ethnic separatism is non-existent and irrelevant. This includes most of the South, the Midwest (with the exception of Chicago and Milwaukee), and the Far West. The same is true even on the Eastern Seaboard. Of course, there are several million Poles, Dutch, Irish and Italians in Pennsylvania and in Massachusetts but the bulk of the population of these states has no separate ethnic identity.

America, in fact, owes a debt of gratitude to the inventors of the melting pot theory. How otherwise could a young nation like the United States have absorbed such a large and unprecedented influx of immigrants from so many countries, speaking so many languages, worshiping in so many different ways, and still survived as a united country? It was indeed the theory—or rather the social outlook—that resulted from the melting pot idea that greatly minimized the deep political, religious, and cultural cleavages among the various immigrant groups and virtually forced public opinion-makers to frown on too much emphasis on religious and ethnic separateness. The stress on American unity and the conscious attempt to ignore or to minimize the ethnic backgrounds of the children of the immigrants made it possible for thousands of able sons and daughters of the newcomers to rise rapidly to positions of prominence in business, government, education and the professions.

Greeley in *Why Can't They Be Like Us?*[7] and other writers on "new ethnicity" wrote with derision about the often crude attempts to "Americanize" the immigrants by forcing them to resemble as quickly as possible the dominant Anglo-Saxon society. There is no doubt that the process of socialization of the immigrants to the new American environment included a large dose of contempt and hostility for the ethnic sensibilities and values of the immigrants. Few of us now believe that Americans generally welcomed the successive waves of immigrants. This myth started in schools where children were taught to recite the lines from the poem of Emma Lazarus, which are inscribed on the Statue of Liberty:

> Give me your tired, your poor,
> Your huddled masses yearning to breathe free,
> The wretched refuse of your teeming shore.
> Send these, the homeless, tempest-tost to me,
> I lift my lamp beside the golden door!

These are beautiful words and fine sentiments, but they do not correspond to historical reality. In truth, Americans did not welcome the tired and the poor immigrants and were often terrified by the "wretched refuse" of Europe.

Leaders of industry wanted the immigrants as a much needed labor force, but a considerable portion of the population mistrusted, ridiculed and feared the immigrants. The descendants of the earlier immigrants feared that the huge numbers of immigrants would change the American way of life and more importantly bring into the country the intensity of their ancient feuds. Heeding the advice of George Washington, they wanted no involvement in the "mess of Europe." They cherished the ideal picture of the new American, so well painted by Jean de Crèvecoeur in his famous *Letters from an American Farmer,* published in 1782:

He is an American, who, leaving behind him all his ancient prejudices and manners, receives new ones from the new mode of life he has embraced . . .

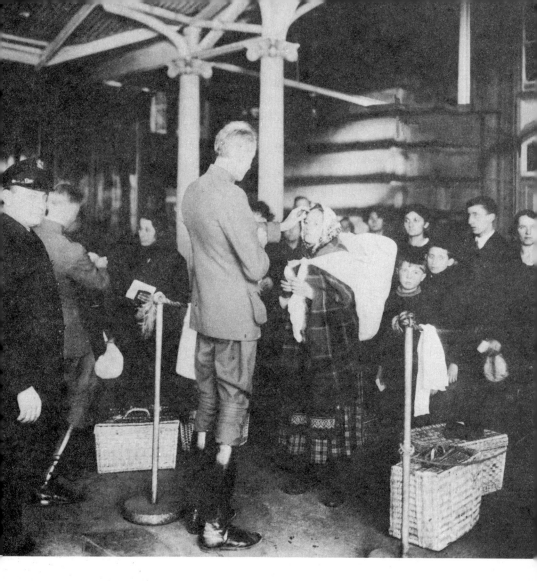

"In truth, Americans did not welcome the tired and the poor immigrants. . . ."

Unwanted and bewildered, the newcomers sought a measure of comfort and security by settling in the neighborhoods of their compatriots. In this manner, ethnic neighborhoods were established. But it would be wrong to disregard the fact that the overwhelming majority of the immigrants were eager to shed their ethnic identity and heritage and to blend as rapidly as possible into the dominant society and its values and mores.

Many leaders of white ethnics disparage the record of the public schools in relation to the children of various ethnic groups. It is true that some teachers showed little respect for the values held dearly by the children of the new immigrants. But on the other hand, the public schools did a magnificent job of molding and adjusting millions of immigrant children to their new role as citizens of the new country. Public schools were the basic workshops of American democracy. It is in schools that children of many racial, ethnic and religious origins learned, however painfully, to live together and to take advantage of the precious gifts of American freedom. Subsequently, the public schools made it possible for thousands of Jewish, Polish, Italian and German children to attain positions of prominence in all walks of life.

There seems to be a serious contradiction in the recent movement for re-ethnization. On one hand, the leaders of the white ethnic minorities speak about the need for solidarity between the blacks and white ethnics who have long been deprived of their political rights and many economic benefits, and on the other hand, the new ethnic consciousness has a significant racist origin. The Catholic National Center of Urban Affairs and the American Jewish Committee have sponsored in recent years a number of conferences bringing together blacks, Chicanos, Jews, Italian-Americans, Polish-Americans and other ethnic groups, in order to forge a common front and a common cause. In one such recent conference one speaker began his speech by asking: "Can we develop a political majority—whites, ethnics, browns, blacks to reorder the national priorities?"[8]

But it is also generally conceded, even by the spokesmen of the white ethnics, that the revival of ethnic solidarity stems in a large measure from the rivalry with, and the fear of, the blacks in the large urban centers. There is, in many cities, the making of a white ethnic-black confrontation which stems primarily from the residential pattern of the various ethnic blocs and from economic competition for the same jobs. Barbara Mikulski, a Polish-American leader and a member of the Baltimore City Council, stated on several occasions that the black-ethnic antagonism has its roots from their fight "for the same urban turf." Many Poles and Italians who do not have the money to buy homes in the suburbs feel threatened by the blacks who want to move into their neighborhoods. White ethnic leaders openly suggest that the Federal Government spends an inordinate amount of money and effort to help the blacks but does nothing for the so-called white Middle-Americans. Monsignor Baroni made an astonishingly frank statement on this point. He was quoted in *Newsweek Magazine* as having said: "The ethnics were taught that they would get their slice of the American dream in a matter of time if they only stayed quiet. But it didn't turn out that way. The ethnics felt that the blacks were getting what they needed but that the ethnics were paying for it. Now the ethnics are asking for their own slice."* It is difficult to see how Father Baroni can hope to build a solidarity front with blacks on this type of reasoning.

In Newark, where blacks comprise a majority of the population and where Italians are the largest white ethnic minority, the relations between these two major blocs are strained to the point of explosion. The black majority on the school board ordered the display of the black national flag in all the school rooms and Susan Barone, a teacher and a leader in the powerful Italian North Ward Organization, told a *New York Times* reporter, "Now we are beginning to insist on our share. For better or worse, the old ideal of the melting pot is dead around here. *The kids in school today don't want to be known as Americans but as Italians.*"[9]

The demands of blacks for a share of jobs on local and federal levels have spurred similar demands from Italians and Poles for jobs in city and state governments, and especially in big city school systems. The Irish and the Jews have not voiced these demands because their proportion in governmental positions and in the school system has been high, and any demand for racial ethnic quotas could seriously diminish their present proportion of jobs. There is no minimizing the growing fear and antagonism of Jews in New York, Chicago, Boston and other cities who are threatened with the loss of jobs as teachers and principals, jobs which they won in tough competitive examinations. On the other hand, blacks, and now Poles, Italians, and Chicanos are asking for a redress for a long history of job discrimination.

There is a dilemma in this issue, a dilemma which will grow as the white ethnic groups voice even more vigorously their demands for their share of jobs. The problem is not only a social one of equal treatment for all, but also a constitutional one. In all of the discussion of ethnic quotas a point which was well defined by Naomi Bliven seems to be overlooked. "But the main difficulty," she wrote, "in emphasizing, perpetuating, or even having respect for ethnic and racial differences within this country is simply that our state and federal constitutions, our public

---

Newsweek, April 3, 1972, p. 86. Copyright Newsweek, Inc. 1972, reprinted by permission.

"Human beings are not metal and do not melt. . . . Ethnicity remains an important
force in American society. . . ."

institutions, and the spirit of our laws have always been opposed to such divisions."[10]

Here is the grave dilemma. While quotas and the abandonment of rigid and equitable filling of jobs on the basis of qualifications alone ought to be avoided as iniquitous and self-defeating—some way must be found to redress the old pattern of job discrimination against blacks and members of some white ethnic minorities. The solution will be difficult. What will probably happen is that, in a typically pragmatic American way, federal and local jobs will be given more and more often to eminently qualified persons who happen to be black or are of Polish or Italian origin.

We have made the point that there is little evidence to suggest that the melting pot theory has been a total failure. But it is true that the melting pot concept did not work as well as its originator, the British-Jewish writer Israel Zangwill, thought that it would. Similarly, the predictions of some of America's sociologists, including Talcott Parsons and Louis Wirth, who were sure that ethnic differences would disappear in the third generation of immigrants, also proved to be incorrect. The reason is rather simple. Human beings are not metal and do not melt, at least not easily and not completely. Ethnicity remains an important force in American society, and while most children of immigrants have assimilated, millions of white ethnics were and are determined to preserve their identity and cultural heritage. In our free society, they must be allowed to do this.

America is not becoming a federation of ethnic groups and the reawakening of ethnic solidarity is limited both in scope and in area but ethnic politics are a reality in this country. The existence of ethnic voting blocs is not a hoax invented by some politicians as Garry Wills has suggested. On the contrary, in view of the generally close elections for the Presidency and for many seats in the House of Representatives and the Senate, the influence of ethnic voting can hardly be exaggerated, and it surely can no longer be ignored by political scientists and by secondary school and university teachers.

Why political scientists and civics textbooks have for so long overlooked the impact of ethnic politics is difficult to understand because the phenomenon is quite visible even to cursory examination. Everybody active in politics in Rhode Island knows that the two Senate seats for that state are likely to reflect the two largest voting blocs, WASPs and Italians. The state is now represented by Senators Claiborne Pell and John Pastore. Similarly New Mexico apparently has to have an "Anglo" Senator and a Chicano. Clinton Anderson and Joseph Montoya are the present Senators from New Mexico. There are Congressional districts in Minnesota that apparently only a Swede or a Norwegian can represent in Congress and similarly several districts in Northwest Chicago and South Milwaukee are always represented by men with names like Rostenkowski, Kluczynski or Zablocki. The same is true in many other Congressional districts in New York, Connecticut, New Jersey and other states.

The primary elections in Illinois in March, 1972 provide a classic demonstration of the existence and the influence of ethnic bloc voting in large urban centers. The primaries were deemed very important because an indicted States Attorney, Robert Hanrahan, who was dumped by Mayor Daley's Democratic machine, ran against Judge Raymond Berg, the candidate of the regular organization, and against Donald Moore, an independent liberal candidate. Hanrahan, who was indicted for an alleged conspiracy to suppress evidence in a raid on the headquarters of the Black Panthers, ran strictly as a "law and order" man. In the election campaign, Hanrahan was portrayed as the savior of the white community from black extremists.

An analysis of the voting results in the city wards showed that the Polish and Italian voters went solidly for Hanrahan and assured his sensational victory. The Irish vote was split, largely because of loyalty to Richard Daley and the efforts of his Irish lieutenants. Negro districts went for the regular candidate, Judge Berg, and the sizeable Jewish population voted overwhelmingly for the liberal independent candidate, Donald Moore. Moore carried eight wards in Chicago and, without exception, all these wards have a substantial Jewish population. The same Illinois Presidential primary gave a victory to Edmund Muskie because Chicago's Poles voted for him, hoping to have the first Polish-American in the White House.

Similarly, in the 1970 elections for New York State, Nelson Rockefeller was elected by defeating the Democratic candidate because, as an analysis of voting results disclosed, Rockefeller received the massive support of the usually Democratic Italian and Irish neighborhoods in Greater New York.

Yet, in spite of this clear evidence, American history and politics are generally taught as if ethnic politics did not exist. What is even worse, history and political science courses in colleges and secondary schools often ignore, distort or underplay the history of the immigration and story of the adjustment of millions of immigrants which, after all, is one of the key factors in the entire history of the United States.

One civics textbook in a section entitled "Your Political Interests" poses the question, "Why do many descendants of early immigrants support the Republican Party?" It answers: "Let's look a little closer at some of the questions. One concerned your ancestors. America has always been a land of immigrants. The people who voluntarily came during the 1600's, 1700's and 1800's were mainly from countries from northwestern Europe such as England and Germany. Most of these early immigrants became successful businessmen, craftsmen, and farmers. Their descendants continued to thrive in America. They disliked government interference in their lives. Today most back the Republican Party, which has traditionally sought less government interference in peoples' lives.

"Africans also came to America in this early period, but not as immigrants. Rather they were forcibly brought here as slaves. The Democratic Party has by and large won the allegiance of Afro-Americans.

"The more recent immigrants to America came from countries in southern and eastern Europe, such as Italy and Poland, or from countries south of us, such as Mexico and Cuba. Most have turned to the Democratic Party, which has welcomed the poor and foreign-born.

"Can you now see why many Catholics are Democratic? It is because the more recent immigrants came from Catholic countries such as Ireland, Italy, Mexico and Cuba."[11]

In a sense it is unfair to quote this simplistic, patronizing and confused account from this particular textbook. Most other textbooks give the subject of immigration and ethnic groups the same inadequate treatment. Some say nothing on the subject. The index of the cited civics textbook, and of almost all such texts, has no entry under the words Italians, Poles, Jews, and no reference to "ethnicity," "ethnic groups," "ethnically balanced slates," or "ethnic voting groups." The textbook does, however, give a reasonably adequate treatment to the status and problems of the black minority.

A deservedly popular textbook on government and civics[12] does not have an entry in its index under "Poles," "Italians," or "Jews," "ethnic groups," or "ethnic blocs," which simply means that the teachers and the students can and do study the operations of the American political system without once discussing the making of ethnically balanced state tickets in most of the big states of the Union, or the influence of the Polish vote in Chicago, the Jewish vote in New York or the Italian vote in Newark and Rhode Island. These students will never know, at least as long as they are in school, that as we have seen in many Congressional districts in the United States, only members of certain ethnic groups can and are usually elected to Congress. Even more importantly, they will learn nothing about the contributions of the major ethnic groups to the working of our political system.

Textbooks in political science used in colleges and universities are hardly any better when dealing with ethnic groups. A college student can easily graduate from a respectable college, with a major in political science, without ever encountering a serious discussion of ethnic politics in Chicago and without a professor suggesting that he study the voting patterns of Jews in New York or the Italian vote in Rhode Island. The most popular textbooks used in political science courses generally ignore the political role played by the white ethnic groups in America. The reason for this is quite simple. Political scientists and sociologists on the campuses of eminent universities where most of the research which eventually finds its way into textbooks is done do not consider ethnicity to be a respectable subject of study. In addition, few if any political science departments in top ranking universities have professors who have done much scholarly work on the white ethnic groups in America.

Politics, Parties, and Pressure Groups by V. O. Key, Jr., has been for years a basic text used in political science courses in colleges and universities throughout the country.[13] The book, since its publication in 1942, has appeared in several revised editions. The reputation of Key's book is well deserved, but one looks in vain for a reasonably extensive treatment on the ethnic groups and their influence on American politics. Key mentions "groups of particular national origin" in his extensive general discussion of the operation of lobbies and special pressure groups. He disposes of the entire question of ethnicity in one paragraph, in which he says that "the land abounds with Irish, German, Italian, Scandinavian and Polish societies. Such groups do some lobbying, but the volatility of their electoral preferences assures a respectful consideration of their sentiments by politicians even without a reminder from the lobby." Here again is the usual patronizing tone so prevalent in reference to the ethnic groups and ethnic feelings.

The long and excellent section on "Electoral Participation" in Key's textbook discusses the voting patterns of various economic groups, city and suburb dwellers, the question of black voting rights, but has nothing to say about the German voting bloc in Milwaukee, of the Catholic Irish voting bloc in Connecticut, or of the Polish group voting in Chicago. The index to Key's book includes no entries to any of the major ethnic groups, with the exception of Jews, who are briefly referred to as trying to influence United States' foreign policy toward Israel.

Government by the People, by James MacGregor Burns and Jack Walter Peltason, is also a widely used political science textbook on university campuses. It was originally published in 1952, and has been reprinted in many editions ever since. A separate chapter, missing in many other textbooks, deals with immigration history and the rights of aliens, and with laws on naturalization.

The section on "Political Behavior" deals with voting patterns and interest groups and with political parties. It is thorough, cogent and well written, but ignores the role of ethnic groups in the American political process. The authors list patterns of voting in America. They find that

there is "state voting," "sectional voting," "national voting," "split voting" and pattern of voting overtime.[14] The "ethnic pattern" of voting, which is so obvious to candidates for the Presidency, to governors and mayors, and to chairmen of both national political parties, has been completely overlooked. In a section entitled, "Why We Vote As We Do?" the authors list a fruit grower, a housewife, a stenographer, a young barber, a local surgeon, a factory worker, a housewife, an industrialist, an unemployed person, and a salesgirl—all of whom list their own particular special interest which caused them to vote either Democratic or Republican. Curiously, the authors did not include in this list a "Polish-American," a "Jewish-American," or an "Italian-American," who also often vote in state and national elections according to their respective ethnic considerations.

In the chapter on interest groups, Burns and Peltason have a section entitled "National, Racial and Religious Groups," which, with the "Nationality groups," "are another important factor in American politics."[15] The authors list the influence of the Irish in Boston, of the Germans and Scandinavians in north-central states, of the French-Canadians in New England, and of the Spanish in New Mexico. There is no discussion of the considerable influence on American politics by the other large ethnic groups, the Poles, the Jews and the Italians. Professors Burns and Peltason, after this sketchy and inadequate reference to the ethnic groups, assert that these nationality groups are a passing phenomenon on the American political scene. These nationality groups, the authors say, "may gradually lose political leverage as their members become increasingly absorbed into the mainstreams of American life."[16] This hope and prediction has been voiced by Anglo-Saxon scholars for many decades, but the ethnic groups seem to be blithely ignoring them.

The picture is dismal and needs correction, but the task of writing and teaching about white ethnic groups is a formidable one. Those who press for courses on white ethnic minorities cannot brush aside the difficulties and the dangers inherent in the introduction of ethnic studies into the school curricula.

We have already pointed out the existing anti-black feelings among considerable sections of the white ethnic groups. There is little doubt that racism played an important role in the massive voting for Hanrahan by Poles and Italians in Chicago. Similarly, there is little doubt that the Italians and the Irish turned against the Democratic Party in the New York 1970 gubernatorial elections, at least in part, because the Democrats ran Arthur Goldberg for Governor and Basil Paterson, a black man for Lieutenant Governor. Teaching about white ethnic groups and their grievances will have to be very skillful if it is to deal effectively with these touchy ethnic white-black relations.

Another factor complicating the problem of teaching about white ethnic minorities is the fact that there is a large measure of accumulated distrust and antagonism among some of these groups. These feelings of hostility are the direct result of the old feuds which were (and are) so prevalent and bitter in Europe. A teacher who wants to teach about the Serbs, their culture and history had better beware of saying anything that may be derogatory to the Croats who have been (and are) the bitter enemies of the Serbs in the Balkans and in the new Yugoslavia. If during a lesson on Polish history, a statement was to be made that the city of Wilno was a Polish city, it would result in bitter protests from Lithuanian priests and organizations who consider that city an ancient capital of Lithuania which was taken by force by the Poles. Any suggestion that there was anti-semitism in pre-war Poland may be loudly protested by Polish-American organizations. Woe to the teacher who would teach about Armenian history and culture and not condemn the Turks for their massacre of the Armenians in the 1920's. The task of teaching about the Italian-Americans presents a very difficult problem of how to deal with the question of organized crime, the Mafia, etc. The flap surrounding the filming of The Godfather and the protests of Italian-American organizations indicate the magnitude of the problem. Again, these difficulties are not insurmountable, but they must be faced and overcome by study and research.

It is not an easy task to summarize this complicated discussion of the problems connected with the teaching of the experience of white ethnic groups in America. First, let us reiterate our assumption that the United States' white population is basically a united nation of descendants of immigrants. Second, there are important pockets of white ethnic minorities which for a variety of reasons, and albeit in a variety of ways, wish to preserve their identity. It is also clear that there are ethnic voting blocs in this country which, because of the delicate balance of power between the two major political parties, play an important role in American politics.

Finally, it is suggested that the history of the culture and the political impact of the white ethnics has been ignored in the social studies and political science curricula and that this omission has to be corrected. The teaching of the experience of the white ethnic minorities presents, however, serious problems and pitfalls which will have to be carefully avoided. What is needed now is an intensive effort which may well be spearheaded by the National Council for the Social Studies to do scholarly research into the entire problem of white ethnic studies. This could probably best be done by a joint effort of school people and scholars working in the areas of ethnic history and cultures.

Suggested Teaching Strategies

by Elizabeth O. Pearson*

Main Idea

A. When cultures meet, they combine and adapt traditions and customs.

1. Ask students to list the customs of an ethnic group such as the Swedes, Germans, Irish, or Czechs which are honored in their native country. Arrange interviews with people who identify with that ethnic group now to find out what customs are still followed and how they are carried out. Students may choose to read a biography or fictional book about an immigrant from the country being discussed to determine customs.

2. Show the filmstrip on the Irish from the series entitled "Immigration: The Dream and the Reality" by Warren Schloat Productions. Focus on how immigrants from white ethnic groups have adapted to American culture. Adaptation in the slum is the subject of *How the Other Half Lives* by Jacob Riis, and *Giants in the Earth* by Rölvaag tells of the struggles of an immigrant farming family. Biographies and novels will be useful supplements to the filmstrip.
Use these guiding questions to focus on cultural adaptation:

   a. What problems did the immigrants encounter upon their arrival in the U. S.?
   b. In what ways did they try to solve their problems?
   c. Develop criteria to rate the success of adaptation.
   d. Determine their success from the criteria.

3. Ask students what their ethnic backgrounds are. Discuss their degree of awareness of that background. Ask if it is referred to at home, if any family customs stem from that ethnic background, and what they feel toward their ethnic heritage.

Main Idea

B. Ethnic groups still remain a powerful force in American politics.

1. Studying the makeup of presidential tickets is a guide to the power of ethnic groups in American life. Ask students to determine the ethnic origins, religion and section of the country from which each presidential and vice presidential candidate originated.

---

* See page 117 for biographical sketch.

damn
poverty...
vote to get rid of it!
vote for your representatives in your
ommunity corporation election
place:
date:
time:

From this data they should determine the effect that ethnic groups and region of the country have on the makeup of the presidential tickets. A close look at a recent vice presidential choice will be a means of determining how important a balanced ticket remains today.

2. Some towns are made up of predominantly one ethnic group. In these towns the leading political offices are held by members of that ethnic group. Student interest might be aroused if they researched the names and backgrounds of leading political leaders from their town in the past twenty years. The mayor, city council members and members of the board of education would most characteristically reflect the ethnic makeup of the town.

An in-depth study of one local campaign would indicate whether candidates directed special attention to certain ethnic groups. If the town is represented in the city council by persons from different parts of the city, a survey of population areas would indicate whether or not councilmen reflect the ethnic makeup of the areas they represent.

3. While it may be determined that ethnic groups tend to vote one way in an election, do they consistently vote one party? Or does a candidate with certain characteristics attract voters of a particular ethnic group regardless of party? A study of past elections may give some clues. For example, what happened when Barry Goldwater was the Republican Presidential candidate in 1964? Did ethnic groups who voted for Nixon in 1960 continue to vote Republican in 1964? Did John Kennedy draw more ethnic voters to his side in 1960 than did Lyndon Johnson in 1964?

A survey of voting statistics for these elections could provide answers and also give students some experience in understanding election statistics.

Main Idea

C. White ethnic groups have assimilated into American society successfully, but at the same time maintain identities of separateness.

1. What reminders of white ethnicity still exist in the U.S. of the 1970's? Obvious items come to mind such as the Italian protest over the film *The Godfather*, and novels about Jewish people such as *Herzog* by Saul Bellow. The nationally celebrated St. Patrick's Day belongs to the Irish, and the Swedes have their Swedish Clubs. Ask students to name other aspects of white ethnicity with which they are familiar. Then discuss how essential these characteristics are in maintaining ethnic diversity.

2. Some interesting materials are available which deal with diversity and unity among white ethnic groups. *Makers of America* is a ten-volume

documentary history of American ethnic groups put out by Encyclopedia Britannica Corporation and edited by Wayne Moquin. Students may choose to follow a particular ethnic group through American history using documents. Student interest could be aroused initially with the film *A Nation of Immigrants* from Films Incorporated.   A concluding question for all students to ponder is: Are white ethnic groups distinctive in name only?

3. The public's perception of ethnicity could be obtained through a student survey. Ask a small group of interested students to write a questionnaire which will focus upon the public's perception of the existence of white ethnic groups. A community person who is familiar with the technique of writing questionnaires would be a useful consultant for students.

   Students could either poll persons in their neighborhood or concentrate on family friends. More complete results will be obtained if students ask the questions and record answers rather than asking the interviewee to respond on his own. An interesting comparison could be made between student poll results and the findings expressed in the previous article.

FOOTNOTES

¹ Garry Wills, "Great White Ethnic Hoax in Politics," *Chicago Sun-Times,* January 25, 1972, p. 24.

² *New York Times,* March 18, 1972, p. 31. © 1972 by The New York Times Company. Reprinted by permission.

³ *New York Times,* March 19, 1972, p. 45. © 1972 by The New York Times Company. Reprinted by permission.

⁴ *Ibid.*

⁵ *Overcoming Middle-Class Rage,* Murray Friedman, editor. New York: Westminster Press, 1972, p. 31.

⁶ *New Yorker,* Nov. 20, 1971, p. 225.

⁷ Andrew Greeley, *Why Can't They Be Like Us?* New York: Institute of Human Relations Press, 1969.

⁸ *New York Times,* March 19, 1972. © 1972 by The New York Times Company. Reprinted by permission.

⁹ *New York Times,* April 18, 1971, p. 17. (italics mine) © 1971 by The New York Times Company. Reprinted by permission.

¹⁰ *New Yorker, op. cit.,* p. 225.

¹¹ Grant T. Ball and Lee J. Rosch, *Civics Study Lessons.* Chicago: Follett Educational Corporation, 1969, pp. 286-287.

¹² Robert P. Ludlum, Franklin Patterson, Eber N. Jeffery, and Allan Schick, *American Government—National, State and Local.* Boston: Houghton Mifflin Co., 1969.

¹³ V. O. Key, Jr., *Politics, Parties, and Pressure Groups.* New York: Thomas Y. Crowell Company, 1964.

¹⁴ James MacGregor Burns and Jack Walter Peltason, *Government By the People.* Englewood Cliffs, New Jersey: Prentice-Hall, 1965, pp. 244-246.

¹⁵ *Ibid.,* p. 297.

¹⁶ *Congressional Record,* Vol. 117, No. 3, 92nd Congress, p. 1012.

BIBLIOGRAPHY

Nathan Glazer and Daniel Patrick Moynihan, *Beyond the Melting Pot* (Cambridge, Massachusetts: MIT Press, 1970). A splendid pioneering survey of the white ethnic communities in New York.

Edward C. Banfield and James Q. Wilson, *City Politics* (Cambridge, Massachusetts: Harvard University Press, 1968). A study of city politics focusing on machine politics.

Peter Binzen, *Whitetown, U.S.A.* (New York: Random House, 1970). A survey of the problems and grievances of the white blue-collar residents in Philadelphia's Kensington section.

Andrew Greeley, *Why Can't They Be Like Us?* (New York: American Jewish Committee, Institute of Human Relations Press, 1969). An exploration of the white ethnics, their identity and confrontation with the blacks. Greeley is eloquent when he talks about the need of the white ethnics to find comfort in their group.

Michael Novak, *The Rise of the Unmeltable Ethnics* (New York: Macmillan, 1972). A rather one-sided but interesting attack on the WASP mentality and ethic.

Murray Friedman, editor, *Overcoming Middle-Class Rage* (Philadelphia, Pa.: Westminster Press, 1972). A helpful compilation of essays on white ethnics and the "new pluralism."

Janice Law Trecker

JANICE LAW TRECKER is a free-lance writer who lives in West Hartford, Connecticut. She received her B.A. degree from Syracuse University (Phi Beta Kappa), a teaching certificate from the University of Hartford, and an M.A. in English Literature from the University of Connecticut. Ms. Trecker was formerly a junior high school teacher. Since 1967, she has been a free-lance writer and weekly film reviewer for the West Hartford News. *Her articles have appeared in* Social Education, Saturday Review, *and* The American Scholar. *Ms. Trecker is currently working on a series on Connecticut history to be published by Pequot Press, and has completed a series of four filmstrips on women in American history. In 1971, she presented a paper on the militant suffragettes of the Women's Party at the Association for the Study of Connecticut History.*

JANICE LAW TRECKER

12

Teaching
the Role of Women
in American History

Social studies occupy a unique position in the American school curriculum. Social studies teachers are not only responsible for one major discipline, history, but they are also charged with developing students' capacities for citizenship, and for guiding them through governmental structures, current affairs and contemporary problems. The dual role of the social studies could make it an important force for analyzing and changing the status of female students and for affecting the role of women in the larger society.

There are three areas in the social studies which are in need of intelligent revision with respect to women: history, current problems and citizenship. Each of these areas is of vital interest to women, and it can be shown that the omission of women and of women's problems from these areas does great harm, not only to the self-image of female students, but to the competence and intellectual honesty of the educational enterprise.

Until very recently, it was fashionable to respond to questions about women in history by saying, "but women haven't done anything." Current research into women's history, however, shows that women have taken an active part in American history at all periods and that only cultural stereotypes and resistance to change have kept them from their rightful place in the nation's story. Unfortunately, few of our popular history textbooks have shown any awareness of new information about the contributions and position of women. Most books stick to the traditional model. Women receive a few paragraphs of extravagant

279

praise as essential to America, their high position in our culture is stressed, and a few are even mentioned. For the other 99 percent of the book, women are ignored. That this procedure is inaccurate, biased and out-of-date is only now gaining recognition.

What current texts seem to be telling students is that women are secondary beings, incompetent, unimportant, passive and contented with the status quo. The authors largely ignore major social developments initiated by women or those concerned with women's status. The whole story of the rights movement is lucky if it receives a page; the bitter struggle for birth control is ignored. Women's work in colonial and frontier America is displaced by eulogies to the frontiersman and the repeating revolver. Women thinkers are squeezed out by inane commentaries on lengths of women's skirts. America's female artists—actresses, writers, dancers, painters, sculptors, singers—take second place to descriptions of the Gibson Girl or the Flapper.

Can anything be done about women's history—aside from complaining loudly to the major textbook firms? Fortunately, the answer is yes. More and more material is being produced, especially designed for secondary students. Even now, the resourceful teacher should have few problems in finding a wealth of information and many points in the curriculum where consideration of women is not only possible, but necessary.

It is difficult to see, for example, how one can discuss the history of industrialization and the labor movement without major consideration of the position of women. Who operated the nation's first textile mills? Was not the fact that these eighteenth-century "manufactories" gave employment to women and children, who "would else be idle," the justification for industrial as opposed to agricultural development? Was it not the factories that gave employment to the immigrant women and offered native born farmers' daughters their first chance to be independent and to contribute cash to the family coffers? Were not women and children the most exploited workers, whether in sweatshop tenements or in barn-like factories? Was not their very exploitation a threat to the wage stability and organization of male workers? Did not women strike and organize and support male unions even under extreme hardship? And did not women, women workers and women organizers fight to end child labor abuses and the frightful conditions of the nation's factories? How then can women in labor be dismissed with a few lines when a wealth of documentary and secondary material is available in paperbacks, old newspapers and in any good library?

There are other topics equally worthy of investigation. Humanitarian reform is one of the few topics given coverage, but even here there is much more to be discussed. Elizabeth Massey's *Bonnet Brigades,* a

How can one "discuss the history of industrialization and the labor movement without major consideration of the position of women"? In 1860 eight hundred women employees demonstrated to support the shoemaker's strike in Lynn, Massachusetts.

volume in the Harvard Civil War Series, discusses the many contributions of women to the war efforts. She notes that women not only raised gigantic sums of money for uniforms, provisions and the war effort but they also took on nursing and what are now USO services. They developed diet kitchens for the sick, and after the war, aided alcoholic soldiers, worked with soldiers' families, searched for graves and assisted with pension claims. In fact, women developed and performed the services now provided by massive organizations like the Veterans Administration.

Women also worked in the urban ghettos pioneering in the establishment of visiting nurse services and the study of industrial medicine. They developed social work and provided a variety of services for the poor, the consumer and for children. Sometimes these services are mentioned, rarely are the reasons why women were attracted into these new fields discussed. The women of the late nineteenth century literally had to invent new professions to be of service, because their society had no place for them outside of home and children.

One of the greatest battles of the early twentieth century is inexplicably omitted—the crusade for birth control. How many students know that men and women were jailed for advocating birth control? That books were seized, that clinics were raided by the police? That desperate birth control workers went on hunger strikes to plead their case? That slum workers were confronted by women lined up for quack abortions and helplessly watched patients die from bungled operations, disease and childbearing? How many know about bitter religious opposition to birth control—or to other aspects of the women's rights movement? Yet, the material is on many library shelves.

The fight for birth control touches a number of themes unjustly neglected in American history. At least at the secondary level, textbook authors appear anxious to avoid discussion of sex prejudice, censorship, the connection between religious ideas and political pressures, and ideas of "decency" and sexuality. Is it tact, prudery or timidity which prevents discussion of clerical and religious conservatism, from the denunciations of early female suffragists and abolitionists by Protestant clergy to vitrolic criticisms of birth control by the Catholic hierarchy? In either case, a topic of importance, the relationships between church and state, is neglected along with the whole troubling question of American attitudes toward sexuality, especially toward female sexuality.

There are many other areas where women's history is neglected, as well; one is the early position of women. For example, nothing was more essential to the early colonies than a rapid increase in population. Yet, little is ever made of this fact. What about the high infant and maternal mortality rates in the early colonies? How large were families? What sorts of social control were exercised over women to insure early marriage and large families? Further, what did women do, inside and outside the home? Usually, it is assumed that women stayed home and did their house work, but this is inaccurate. Books like Julia Cherry Spruill's *Women and Work in the Southern Colonies* show that women, especially single women and widows, had considerable freedom. They were planters, traders and entrepreneurs in their own right; they wielded economic and, sometimes, even political power. Women in the early period were essential to the basic economic unit—the family—not only as mothers and wives, but as producers of goods and as workers. If this is true, it is not adequate to treat only the lives of the men of the frontier, the colonies or the American Revolution.

Women's education is another largely untouched subject. How many students know that women literally bought their way into schools? How many know the sacrifices women and girls made to open education to women, the weight of theory and social custom they breached or the problems they still face? Confronting women like Emma Willard, Catharine Beecher and the other early educators can we say, complacently, that Victorian women were passive and genteel?

No doubt the greatest obstacle to the serious treatment of women in American history is the pervasive notion that women are weak, silly creatures, who have been indulged by their society. The facts, however, are the best corrective to that notion. No one who has read the diaries, letters and records of the women of the Western migrations can believe the textbook picture of the noble, but sadly idealized and undefined, pioneer woman. No one who has read the story of the suffrage movement believes the assurances that "women were *given* the vote." No one who has read narratives of the Triangle Fire of 1911 will be satisfied with a sentence about women workers. No one who knows about Margaret Sanger, Isadora Duncan, and Alice Paul will believe that the Flapper was the most important female phenomenon of their time. There are many topics which need re-examination in American history. Students need to know about great women and events and about their society's attitude toward women. They need information about how a politically powerless group operated, what the lives of average women were like and how they related to males. Even the briefest acquaintance with the material available raises serious questions about the present manner of presenting our nation's story and about the casual loss of a heritage precious to both female, and male, students.

If the treatment of women in history continues to be inadequate, the same may be said for examinations of contemporary problems. History books which include information up through the terms of Presidents Kennedy and Johnson rarely suggest that discrimination against women was a continuing problem even after women won the vote. Frequently, discussions of the landmark Title 7 provision of the 1964 Civil Rights Act omit the fact that the new legislation was amended to cover women or that women, in fact, still needed legal help.

There are many other topics in current affairs which should include references to women and discussions of women's status. Problems such as poverty, race relations and population control are complicated by the inferior legal, economic, and social status of women. Other problems, often completely neglected, are directly concerned with women: sex discrimination, birth control, abortion and the persistence of cultural stereotypes of female inferiority. Students cannot be expected to deal intelligently with any of these issues without information about women and their place in society. As an example, it might be worthwhile to look at one major topic discussed in problems of democracy and current affairs courses: Poverty. Although poverty is one of our most pressing national problems, the general public remains surprisingly ignorant of the factors in poverty that are linked to sex. Statistics published in *A Matter of Simple Justice* (1970), the report of President Nixon's Task Force on the Status of Women, however, reveal very clearly the factor of sex discrimination in deciding who shall be poor.

The poor, by and large, are women and their children. Two-thirds of the adult poor are female, and although minority group families are much more likely to be poor than their white counterparts, the majority of the poor are still white. Women are poor, among other reasons, because they earn less money. Government census figures show that for full-time, year-round workers, average earnings for white males are $7,396; for black males, $4,777; for white females, $4,279; and for black females, $3,194. The impact of both sexual and racial discrimination is clearly shown.

There are other factors which also insure that the poor will be prominently a female population: discrimination in education; discrimination in the labor market and by labor organizations; the lack of day care facilities; and difficulty of access to family planning, contraceptives and abortion. Despite the overwhelming numbers of poor women, despite the fact that females are the poorest of the poor, federal monies for job training, for example, favor males, and the public continues to deny that sex prejudice could have any bearing on such problems as welfare, poverty and the urban crisis. Surely, the social studies have a responsibility to see that evidence of the true position of American women is made available to students.

If women are an invisible majority in discussions of poverty, they are an invisible minority in examinations of crime and delinquency. True, women represent only a tiny fraction of the criminal population. They

"Surely, the social studies have a responsibility to see that evidence of the true position of American women is made available to students."

are worthy of notice, however, because the criminal or delinquent woman represents a special and neglected problem. For one thing, most female criminals are apprehended for the so-called "victimless crimes," chiefly prostitution and addiction. Compared to male criminals they are a relatively harmless lot, yet their prison conditions are as harsh and often harsher than those of their male counterparts. Female delinquents offer an even sharper example of the way social attitudes influence what is considered criminal behavior. Many of the delinquent females confined in various reformatories are innocent of any crime; they are categorized as "persons in need of supervision." In some states young females may be arrested simply because they may be in "manifest danger of falling into vice," vice usually being interpreted as sexual activity. While protecting minors from adult exploitation is certainly important, treatment of female delinquents raises many questions about criminal justice, the efficacy of reform schools and the role that sex attitudes play in labeling females either delinquent or criminal.

Other problems would also benefit from additional information about women. If would be difficult to discuss censorship, for example, without reference to attitudes toward women and toward female sexuality. Attitudes toward women, ideals of female chastity and fears of miscegenation have long complicated American race relations. Yet, the part that attitudes toward women have played in race prejudice is rarely mentioned. Discussions of contemporary labor problems tend to neglect women, just as do historical studies of the labor movement. Today, women make up forty percent of the American work force, but they are utilized primarily as a pool of expendable labor in the lowest paid positions. In an economy where jobs are scarce, what information do future citizens need about working women? How will they be equipped to decide such difficult questions as who should get the available jobs? How will our national policies have to be changed if women continue to go to work in increasing numbers? These are questions that rightfully belong in any discussion of current affairs, women's status or labor relations.

The matter of women in the work force raises another major area of concern; namely, how may the nation best utilize its human resources? Various forms of discrimination have constantly deprived us of the benefits of large amounts of brainpower and talent. Our major untapped source of intellectual power today is female. Something of the loss can be appreciated when we learn that of the top ten percent of our high school students, twice as many girls as boys have no college plans. It has long been noted that female students avoid mathematics and science. Yet, recent research by the World Health Organization indicates that the differences between male and female talents in mathematics and science are so small as to be insignificant. Only forty percent of our undergraduates in college are female and the percentages drop off rapidly at higher academic levels. In the skilled trades, mechanical and technical work, the loss is almost complete; females with talent in these areas are simply lost to the nation. Considering the desperate need for skilled personnel, the waste of female talent is a major national problem. Perhaps it should be an area for study and analysis in the social studies.

There are many other areas, from legal theory to examination of American ideals, which necessarily involve women. One of the newest problems definitely does: ecology and population control. At first glance the special significance of the position of women does not seem crucial to ecology, but it most definitely is. Women are the great consumers in our culture and while the nation spends millions to clean rivers, air and landscape, American corporations spend billions to persuade Americans to buy the detergents that pollute, the convenience packaging that litters and the motors that gulp available power. Much of this advertising is directed basically at women and is designed to enforce old cultural

"Our major untapped source of intellectual power today is female."

stereotypes: woman's place is in the home; domestic prowess is the only area of competition for women; female attractiveness is a woman's highest possession. The relationships between cultural images of women, the media and ecological movements is a most provocative area—and one which rightly belongs to the social studies.

The problem of population limitation is even more directly related to women and to their place in our culture than is ecology and consumerism. For centuries, the dearest interests of women have been sacrificed by society for its own perpetuation. Unless women had lots of children the society died. Today, the reverse is more nearly true. Unless women have and want fewer children, we may all be starved off the earth. But are our culture, our education and our ideals changing to fit changed conditions? Unless our society is willing to allow women more satisfactions outside the home, and unless a woman's value and self-image can be recognized apart from her roles as wife, mother and sexual partner, we will face a social problem of titanic proportions with the majority of the population schooled for roles they cannot possibly be allowed to fulfill. When we realize that the average American woman has her last child before the age of thirty, we can see that there is already a limit to the extent that motherhood can be "woman's profession." Furthermore, since the average woman works for twenty-five years outside the home, she will be condemned to menial or low paying jobs unless she is encouraged to pursue career training and to aspire to a definite vocation.

Our rapidly changing social conditions make such topics as social conditioning and sex role socialization important for the social studies, as well as for psychology. There is no more basic factor in any culture than its ideals of what constitutes masculinity and femininity. It does not take much analysis to see the far-reaching social consequences of radical changes in the role and relative position of the sexes. It appears that these changes are underway, if not as a result of feminist movements, as a result of the drastic need to control population growth.

It becomes important, therefore, for students to understand the forces that shape concepts of femininity and masculinity not simply to understand themselves, but to understand the social and political structures of their society and to gauge the impact of movements designed to effect change in sex roles. There are a number of ways in which such material could be incorporated—through analysis of current ideas of masculinity and femininity, through theories of socialization and sex role stereotypes, and through cross-cultural and historical comparisons. Considering the importance of how societies look at sex role and at the differences between the sexes, it is rather surprising that courses presenting different attitudes and examining the consequences of different definitions of masculine and feminine are not popular and prevalent.

Examination of the persistence of cultural stereotypes leads us to problems of specific concern to women or to fifty-one percent of the national population. Of these concerns, one of the most complex and emotionally charged is abortion. While primarily a women's issue, abortion repeal or reform also raises basic questions about ethical beliefs, medical practice, and religious pressures in government. Given the pace of court tests on the legality of anti-abortion statutes, this matter of conscience and of human rights will no doubt be one of the matters that today's students must decide. It seems wrong for prudery or sensitivity to public pressures to keep pupils from an awareness of all facts and issues surrounding abortion and women's control over their own bodies.

Similar timidity is also evident in unwillingness to handle the problems and questions raised by sex education. While the social studies department is not charged with the teaching of programs in sex education, the issue of whether or not minors have a right to knowledge about the functioning of their own bodies very definitely does belong in current affairs or problems in democracy type courses. In this issue, as in historical treatments of birth control and the debates about abortion, we can see the same complex of issues: female sexuality and societal control, political and, especially, religious pressures on social structures and the effect of ethical standards on freedom of inquiry. In addition, sex education raises important questions about the validity of universal mandatory education, about parents' right to control their children's education and children's right to knowledge which may well be essential for their successful functioning in their society. It is perhaps unnecessary to notice that the resolution of this issue, as is the case with birth control and abortion, has potentially far greater effect on female than on male students.

Nor are issues related to biological sex the only matters that affect great numbers of American women. While civil rights and discrimination are chiefly presented as racial and ethnic matters, the fact remains that the largest group of persons facing discrimination today are the majority sex. There are indications that women are at last realizing the obstacles they face in law, education, employment and public policy. Students need facts about this pervasive discrimination, and there is certainly no dearth of information. Books like Leo Kanowitz's *Women and the Law* and testimony before the U. S. Senate and House committees on the proposed Equal Rights Amendment provide ample documentation of remaining legal abuses, as do the reports of the Presidents' Task Forces on women's status. The latter are eminently concise and readable documents, entirely suitable for classroom use.

Discrimination in education is also receiving ample documentation, and it would be hard to argue that secondary students do not have a right and need to know the extent of discrimination in education, the legal remedies now available to them and the gaps which still exist in civil rights legislation in this area. Yet, how many girls are aware that they can be, and most likely will be, required to have higher college board test scores than boys? How many have wondered why their state universities may have a female enrollment of only forty percent when the female population is larger than the male? How many girls are currently deprived of access to vocational and technical training either *de jure*, as was the case in some NYC schools until 1972, or *de facto*, as is often the case where biased recruiting policies or "unsuitable facilities" discourage female applicants? How many girls are denied equal opportunity in extracurricular activities for leadership and entertainment, especially in athletics? How many social studies courses take up these topics? It would be easy to get suitable course materials.

Discrimination in education is compounded for females by discrimination in employment. How many students who face prejudice because of race, ethnic origin or sex are given a clear understanding of what to do against discrimination? How many students know the legal and historical background of such prejudice? How many understand the agencies and mechanisms that are designed to help aggrieved parties? While the civil rights movement has helped to focus on remedies for discrimination because of color and race, there still exists a widespread feeling that sex discrimination is not serious or that sex discrimination is somehow "all right." The reasons for this attitude are worth analysis, as are the facts about employment discrimination and the ways individuals can fight to get jobs for which they are qualified.

It should be clear that while all students need information about discriminatory practices, the importance for females and minorities is practical as well as theoretical. Female students need to be able to fight discrimination. As the department charged with training students in the exercise of their citizenship, the social studies clearly seem to have special responsibilities to female students and other groups facing discrimination.

There is no way, after all, that individuals who are denied equal access to power structures, to government, to employment and to education can participate on an equal basis in society. Individuals who receive unequal legal treatment or whose interests are not given serious consideration in decisions of national policy cannot exercise their citizenship to its fullest. Further, the current practice of more or less letting girls discover prejudice for themselves, and finding out how to deal with it on their own, amounts to little more than the abnegation of responsibility for the majority of the school population.

What exactly should the schools, and the social studies, be providing female students in the way of a "survival kit"? First, a clear awareness that discrimination exists in education, law, business, industry and government. Reports such as the *President's Task Force on the Status of Women* and the recent HEW study on the position of women provide ample information for alerting young women to potential problems, before they are allowed to become discouraged or to think that failures and obstacles are simply their individual problem or incapacity.

Second, young women need to know about avenues of redress, as well as where present legal or legislative structures are inadequate. It would seem that one of the chief topics in responsible citizenship courses would be some indication of changes and new laws needed to allow all citizens equal opportunity and equal influence in government and in society.

Third, young women need to be encouraged to develop a positive self-image, through awareness of women of achievement, and of women's history, through role models to follow and through awareness of their own skills and talents. The force and prevalence of stereotypes of female inferiority make efforts to break through such conditioning of prime importance. It is no secret that large amounts of female talent are wasted through low aspirations and feelings of inferiority, and it is up to educators to see that the schools no longer contribute to that process.

Finally, young men and women need to be aware of the process and the power of social conditioning. They need to be aware of the forces that shape their lives if they are to make intelligent decisions about their futures.

If teachers and schools decide that such material is properly a part of the curriculum, how is it to be incorporated? Should information about women, discrimination and male-female relations be completely integrated into the overall curriculum or should separate women's studies courses on these topics be established? Probably the ideal situation would be for information about women to be properly represented in all areas of the curriculum. If the aspects of sex discrimination present in poverty were included in discussions of economics and social welfare, if women's history was incorporated in history texts, if other problems and questions concerning women and their problems were not universally omitted or slighted, there would be no need for special courses or units of study.

Unfortunately, such a utopian situation will probably be a long time coming. The teacher who is serious about improving female education is, therefore, faced with two possibilities—include such materials as can be incorporated into the regular program or set up a separate women's studies course which might be women's history, women in literature or a general program on women and ideas about femininity and feminism. Each alternate has certain advantages. Clearly, there is more than enough material to create women's studies courses. With over 400 courses in women's studies now offered on the college level there are many models to follow and ample bibliographic material, as well as a number of new teaching techniques to be explored. In addition to providing a more thorough treatment of the problems, women's studies courses may well provide the added bonus of increasing the awareness and the pride of secondary school women and, thus, be a valuable educational force in their own right.

On the other hand, incorporating material about women in standard courses may be a more feasible approach, especially when dealing with more conservative systems and administrators or with apathetic student groups. Such a procedure also has the potential of reaching more students and especially the students who might not be enthusiastic about taking a course devoted solely to women. Realistically, decisions about how best to include material about women may depend on such non-educational factors as scheduling, staff and administration attitudes, as well as student demands. Fortunately, both approaches may produce worthwhile results, and they are definitely not mutually exclusive. The presence of even several good women's studies courses should never be used as an acceptable excuse to omit women in other parts of the curriculum.

An informative and responsive curriculum is a major step toward improving women's education but it needs a sympathetic teaching staff to make it work. It is foolish to pretend that teachers, even the most sensitive, capable and concerned, have escaped the prejudices which our society holds about women. The stereotypes that limit female aspirations and opportunities also condition the ways in which teachers regard material about women and their responsibilities toward women and their education.

Teachers who are serious about revamping educational systems and content to insure improved schooling for women must also examine their own attitudes and assumptions. They must become alert to stereotypes and bias, not just in texts and materials, but also in the operation of their classrooms and in their relations with students. Awareness of bias, stereotyped assumptions and unfairness is always a painful revelation, but it is the first step toward improving the education of women and toward making our educational systems responsive to all the people.

No one has ever pretended that providing equal opportunity in education was going to be easy. If that goal has seemed increasingly difficult and complex, it is perhaps because we have increasingly become aware of assumptions and injustices that earlier generations took for granted. Awareness of the barriers to equal opportunity is the necessary preliminary to attainment of equal education. The design of educational systems and procedures that provide high quality education for all Americans and which strengthen the aspirations of each child is, without doubt, a noble endeavor. It is an endeavor in which social studies teachers have the opportunity to make a unique and lasting contribution.

Suggested Teaching Strategies

by Elizabeth O. Pearson*

Main Idea

A. The changing image and role of women in American society has been revealed through the communications media of the times.

　1. Television commericals are a powerful means of creating an image. Ask students to watch television for two hours during a weekday morning or afternoon. They should make a record of each commercial they see indicating the item advertised, the persons in the commercial (child, mother, father, single woman, etc.), and a characterization of women in each commercial. (Woman as housewife, career woman, woman interested in beauty aids.) Ask students to compare their data and make a general statement about the treatment of women in commercials.

　2. The same data can be collected from magazine advertisements. Divide the class into groups according to the content of the magazines. For example, one group could focus on women's magazines, another on men's magazines such as *Esquire* and *Playboy,* and another on news magazines such as *Newsweek, Time* and *Ebony*. An example of a data retrieval chart to organize the data follows.

WOMEN'S MAGAZINES

	Item Advertised	Persons in Advertisement	Characterization of Women
McCall's			
Seventeen			
Woman's Day			
Cosmopolitan			

　Ask students to develop generalizations about the treatment of women in advertisements in women's and men's magazines, and news magazines. Then have them compare treatments to see if they can generalize about the relationship between the image of women and all advertisements.

---

* See page 117 for biographical sketch.

3. To enlarge the view for younger students of the broadening opportunities for women in contemporary society along with achievements of women in America's past, ask students to name well-known women. List them on the board. Then ask students to group the names according to their own designations. They may develop categories such as women pioneers, scientists, women from the past and present, women who came upon their achievement after great hardships. Students may then be interested in reading about a woman with whom they are not familiar. Perusing an anthology may be an easy way for students to find a woman about whom they might be interested in reading at greater length. *Heroines of the Early West,* a Landmark book by Nancy Wilson Ross, *They Showed the Way: Forty American Negro Leaders* by Charlemae Hill Rollins, and *Famous American Pioneering Women* by Edna Yost are some useful introductory anthologies.

After students have done further reading, bring the class together and again have students list the women about whom they have read. Ask them to categorize the names according to when they lived. Fifty-year time periods would be sufficient. Then discuss whether or not opportunities for women have expanded since the early days of the United States.

Main Idea

B. The number of women working outside the home has tended to depend on the amount of time the woman has had to spend at home as wife and mother.

1. To focus on the changing role of a woman's work, ask students to find statistics on the number of married women, single women and mothers over the last 150 years. Statistics for every thirty years would provide sufficient intervals. They should also find the number of women who were working outside the home during that period. Ask them to look at the changes in statistics, taking into consideration the total population of women. They then can try to explain the changes in the context of the historical periods represented.

2. Present to students a statement by an advocate of women's rights, an unemployed female head of household and an unemployed male head of household recommending their priorities in hiring people for jobs.

Ask students to state the problem which is posed in the statements they have read. Divide the class into three groups:

a. Representing the advocate of women's rights.
b. Representing the unemployed female head of household.
c. Representing the unemployed male head of household.

Then ask these questions:

a. What does each person whose statement is represented think is most important about assigning job priorities?
b. How do their values differ?
c. What are some other values which each person could have chosen?
d. What would have been the consequences of each of their choices?
e. What choice would you have made if you were:

   (1) an advocate of women's rights?
   (2) an unemployed female head of household?
   (3) an unemployed male head of household?

f. How would you feel about your choice?

Teachers might wish to extend this study in values by opening up to more thorough study the subject of employment policies of private business and government. A survey of the unemployment rate indicating how many women and men are unemployed along with the largest groups of workers who are jobless could be included. The whole question of how jobs should be provided and on what priorities their assignment should be based could be a major thrust in the study of job opportunities.

3. Inventions which have taken over some of the work in the home have made it easier for women to work outside the home. Have students list all the inventions that have taken over duties which had to be done at home. Have them research the dates of these inventions. Ask them:

   a. What is the effect of each on a housewife's work?
   b. Is there a relationship between the number and quality of home conveniences and the percentage of women who work outside the home during different historical periods?

Main Idea

C. In American history, women have been subject to many kinds of discrimination.

1. To focus on job discrimination, ask a small group of students to gather statistics on the number of women employed as secretaries, public school teachers and administrators, college and university teachers, factory workers, lawyers and doctors in your state in 1925 and 1970. Have them compare with the number of men in each of these fields. Then ask:

   a. Which professions have a high concentration of women?
   b. What changes have occurred over a forty-five-year period in the employment of women?
   c. How do you explain the change or lack of change in employment of women?

2. Ask students to compare Want Ads in newspapers of the 1920's or 1930's with Want Ads in current newspapers. They should make a chart for each of the two newspapers compared, indicating what jobs were advertised for women only, for men only, and for both sexes. Have them explain any differences they find in terms of the historical setting of the earlier year compared to contemporary America. Ask another group to find out what state and federal laws say about discrimination in advertising for jobs and use this information to help explain the data.

3. Ask a student to read a history of the woman's suffrage movement such as *Woman Suffrage and Politics* by Carrie Chapman Catt and Nettie Rogers Shuler. Both of these women were very prominent in passing the amendment giving women the vote. The student can then give a report on the kinds of discrimination Catt and Shuler report that people in the suffrage movement encountered. An interesting comparison might be made if another student read a history of the woman suffrage movement written twenty or more years after the woman's vote was accomplished. One such book might be *Century of Struggle* by Eleanor Flexner.

   After a report to the class on the second book, a class discussion could be held focusing on the following questions:

   a. What portrayal of the opposition to woman suffrage did each book give?
   b. What expectations of the results of woman suffrage did each book focus upon?
   c. What events did the authors of both books view as the most important in achieving the passage of the suffrage amendment?
   d. If there were differences, why?
   e. What differences in the content of each book and the interpretation of that content resulted from the backgrounds of the authors?

BIBLIOGRAPHY

Bird, Caroline. *Born Female* (New York: Pocket Books, 1969). Concise and readable, *Born Female* is particularly good on women in the business world.

Flexner, Eleanor. *A Century of Struggle* (New York: Atheneum, 1968). A well-written, scholarly account of the rights movement with much valuable information on women's education, women in industry and the early status of women.

Freidan, Betty. *The Feminine Mystique* (New York: Dell, 1963). Still provocative, *The Feminine Mystique* has historical, as well as intellectual, interest as a force behind the current women's movement.

Kanowitz, Leo. *Women and the Law* (Albuquerque, N.M.: University of New Mexico, 1969). This scholarly study covers almost every phase of the legal status of women.

K.N.O.W. Press. A reprint house which provides articles, manifestoes and research studies pertinent to the new feminism, K.N.O.W. (P.O. Box 10197, Pittsburgh, Pa. 15232) is an excellent source of classroom material, reasonably priced.

Kraditor, Alleen, ed. *Up from the Pedestal* (Chicago: Quadrangle, 1970). A fine collection of source documents, feminist and anti-feminist, from the nineteenth and twentieth centuries' women's rights struggle.

Lerna, Gerda. *The Woman in American History* (Menlo Park, Calif.: Addison-Wesley, 1971). Designed for secondary school students, *The Woman in American History* gives brief accounts of almost every topic in American women's history.

Massey, Mary Elizabeth. *Bonnet Brigades* (New York: Knopf, 1966). A serious, but readable account of women in the Civil War, including the sanitary commission, home-front activities and actual battlefield participation.

Morgan, Robin, ed. *Sisterhood Is Powerful* (New York: Vintage, 1970). One of a number of readily available collections on the contemporary women's liberation movement.

O'Neill, William. *Everyone Was Brave* (Chicago: Quadrangle, 1969). O'Neill's study of American feminism includes portraits of women reformers and suffragettes, and material on groups like the National Consumers' League, as well as on the suffrage struggle.

Scott, Anne Firor, ed. *The American Woman: Who Was She?* (Englewood Cliffs, N.J.: Spectrum, 1971). Documents on the history of women in labor, education, reform movements and the suffrage struggle.

Spruill, Julia Cherry. *Women's Life and Work in Southern Colonies* (Chapel Hill, N.C.: University of North Carolina Press, 1938). Spruill's massive study covers social attitudes, legal status, contributions and work of Southern colonial women.

Trecker, Janice Law, "Women in U.S. History High School Textbooks," *Social Education* (March, 1971). This critique of current history texts includes many suggestions for women, events and ideas that ought to be included on the secondary level.

U.S. Government Printing Office. *American Women, The Report of the Commission* (1963). In addition to the overall report on the status of women, reports of committees and consultations on education, civil and political status, special problems of black women, etc., are available.

_____. *American Women, 1963-68.* This is the 1968 report of the Citizen's Advisory Council on the Status of Women.

_____. *A Matter of Simple Justice, 1970.* The report of the President's Task Force on Women's Rights and Responsibilities is a concise, hard-hitting document with practical suggestions for improving the status of women.

_____. *1969 Handbook on Women Workers.* Women's Bureau Bulletin 294. The handbooks of the Labor Department's Women's Bureau are a mine of information on women as workers and also on their legal, educational and civil status.

Photographs

PART ONE: p. xviii, Seattle Public Schools, Washington. CHAPTER 1: p. 11, Public Health Service, National Archives; p. 16, Seattle Public Schools, Washington; p. 18, Washington State Office of Public Instruction, Olympia; p. 22, (*Richard Bellak*) Office of Economic Opportunity. CHAPTER 2: p. 29, (*Linda Bartlett*) and p. 37, (*Roland L. Freeman*) and p. 46, (*Joan Larson*), Office of Economic Opportunity; p. 45, Xerox Education Publications. CHAPTER 3: p. 54, p. 57 (*Jan W. Faul*) and p. 59 and p. 66, (*Paul Conklin*), Office of Economic Opportunity; p. 63, War Relocation Authority, National Archives. CHAPTER 4: p. 79, Michigan Migrant Education Program, Title 1; p. 86, Seattle Public Schools, Washington; p. 89, published through cooperation of Allyn and Bacon; p. 99, (*Arthur Tress*), Office of Economic Opportunity. CHAPTER 5: p. 107, Housing and Urban Development; p. 110, Seattle Public Schools, Washington; p. 112, (*Larry Rana*), U.S. Department of Agriculture. PART TWO: p. 114 (*Bud DeWald*), *Arizona Days and Ways*. CHAPTER 6: pp. 121, 137, 139, 143, War Relocation Authority, National Archives; p. 127, Public Health Service, National Archives; p. 133, Washington State Office of Public Instruction, Olympia. CHAPTER 7: p. 150, Field Educational Publications, Inc.; p. 155, Toledo Public Schools, Ohio; p. 168, (*Carl Purcell*), National Education Association; p. 173, (*Jan W. Faul*) Office of Economic Opportunity. CHAPTER 8: p. 187, Washington State Office of Public Instruction, Olympia; pp. 189, 191, 195, U. S. Department of Agriculture. CHAPTER 9: p. 203, (*Paul Conklin*) and p. 204, (*Pete Liddell*), Office of Economic Opportunity; p. 208, Washington State Office of Public Instruction, Olympia; p. 216, Bureau of Indian Affairs. CHAPTER 10: p. 229, (*Michael D. Sullivan*) and pp. 236, 240, (*Jan W. Faul*) and p. 244, (*Day Walters*), Office of Economic Opportunity; p. 233, (*Nancy Rudolph*), Housing and Urban Development. PART THREE: p. 255, *Dan Stainer*. CHAPTER 11: p. 259, Washington State Office of Public Instruction, Olympia; p. 262, Public Health Service, National Archives; p. 265, (*Day Walters*) and p. 270, (*Morton R. Engelberg*) and p. 274, (*Jan W. Faul*), Office of Economic Opportunity. CHAPTER 12: p. 281, *Frank Leslie's Illustrated Newspaper;* pp. 285, 292, Washington State Office of Public Instruction, Olympia; p. 287, Office of Economic Opportunity.

COVER DESIGN by *Bill Caldwell*
BOOK DESIGN AND PRODUCTION by *Willadene Price*

NCSS Yearbooks

Forty-Second Yearbook (1972) *Teaching About Life in the City,* Richard Wisniewski, ed. $5.50 (490-15272); cloth $7.00 (490-15274).

Forty-First Yearbook (1971) *Values Education: Rationale, Strategies, and Procedures,* Lawrence E. Metcalf, ed. $5.00 (490-15268); cloth $6.50 (490-15270).

Fortieth Yearbook (1970) *Focus on Geography: Key Concepts and Teaching Strategies,* Phillip Bacon, ed. $5.50 (490-15264); cloth $7.00 (490-15266).

Thirty-Ninth Yearbook (1969) *Social Studies Curriculum Development: Prospects and Problems,* Dorothy McClure Fraser, ed. $4.50 (490-15240); cloth $5.50 (490-15242).

Thirty-Eighth Yearbook (1968) *International Dimensions in the Social Studies,* James M. Becker and Howard D. Mehlinger, co-editors. $4.50 (490-15212); cloth $5.50 (490-15214).

Thirty-Seventh Yearbook (1967) *Effective Thinking in the Social Studies,* Jean Fair and Fannie R. Shaftel, co-editors. $4.00 (490-15188); cloth $5.00 (490-15190).

Thirty-Sixth Yearbook (1966) *Political Science in the Social Studies,* Robert E. Cleary and Donald H. Riddle, co-editors. $4.00 (490-15162); cloth $5.00 (490-15160).

Thirty-Fifth Yearbook (1965) *Evaluation in Social Studies,* Harry D. Berg, ed. $4.00 (490-15128); cloth $5.00 (490-15126).

Thirty-Fourth Yearbook (1964) *New Perspectives in World History,* Shirley H. Engle, ed. $5.00 (490-15108); cloth $6.00 (490-15106).

Thirty-Third Yearbook (1963) *Skill Development in Social Studies,* Helen McCracken Carpenter, ed. $4.00 (490-15064); cloth $5.00 (490-15062).

Thirty-Second Yearbook (1962) *Social Studies in Elementary Schools,* John U. Michaelis, ed. $4.00 (490-15000); cloth $5.00 (490-14996).

Thirty-First Yearbook (1961) *Interpreting and Teaching American History,* William H. Cartwright and Richard L. Watson, Jr., co-editors. $4.00 (490-15838); cloth $5.00 (490-14840).

NATIONAL COUNCIL FOR THE SOCIAL STUDIES

1201 Sixteenth Street, N.W., Washington, D.C. 20036